# PRAISE FOR
## CHIEF CUSTOMER OFFICER

"Jeanne Bliss is a force to be reckoned with when you tell her you want to focus on your customers. With her great energy and uniquely strong background, she was able to help us accelerate our performance, which translated to revenue growth and profitability. Here, she lays all of it down on paper so that you can have the benefit of those years, that passion and that know-how. Learn from Jeanne how to navigate through the corporate structure and the key things senior leaders and executives must know to make customer profitability the priority in their organization."
—Chandler Barton, retired president and CEO, Coldwell Banker Corporation

"*Chief Customer Officer* blows past theory and gets right to the practical matter of how to bring a company together on behalf of customers. Bliss tells how to overcome the impasse of silos and varying agendas in realistic ways with approaches that can be practiced today. She's lived inside the corporate structure and imparts sage advice on how to best navigate through it to get results."
—Edward Benack, senior vice president of the customer experience and service, Monster Worldwide, *http://www.monster.com*

"Jeanne Bliss's pithy, down-to-earth style, and realistic solutions come straight out of her unparalleled background inside corporations as the 'chief' for driving customer focus and profitability. Anyone trying to clear a path across the organization for customer accountability would be wise to read this book cover to cover and complete the thought-provoking exercises."
—Joe Wheeler, author, *Managing the Customer Experience*

"Save yourself years of trial and error! Just pick up this book, enjoy the read (because you will), and do what it says. And get your leadership to read *Chief Customer Officer* too. Jeanne will tell them what you want them to hear but may be afraid to say in the frank, no-punches-pulled way that she does it here. Jeanne Bliss has been out there herding cats across the silos and with leadership. She's done everything you're thinking of doing to get the action moving, and then some. *Chief Customer Officer* is an MBA on driving customer profits—Jeanne Bliss style!"
—Cyndie Beckwith, vice president, customer experience, California State Automobile Association

"All the tools, technology, and training to drive customer profitability won't get you where you need to go if you don't first address the corporation, its agenda, and how to drive this work across the constituencies. *Chief Customer Officer* debunks how to get this done. It gives realistic perspective and real-world techniques for instilling the motivation, the metrics, and the mechanics required to make traction inside the corporate machine."
—Bill Price, former first global vice president
of customer service, Amazon.com; president, Driva Solutions;
and cofounder, LimeBridge Global Alliance

"*Chief Customer Officer* gives a realistic view of what this work of driving customer focus and profitability is really all about. Jeanne Bliss has been there, she's one of us. And she gives the tools, support, and real-world advice that we need to move this work ahead in our own organizations."
—Matt Woody, vice president, customer support services,
Fidelity Investments

"Jeanne Bliss has gotten down the rigor of what really happens in the daily quest to bring customer focus into an organization. She gives clarity to what we are living, but never seem to have the time to think through and strategize our way out of. These are: bringing the different factions of the organization together for a common customer purpose, setting aside the individual silo priorities, and creating metrics that rally and unify disparate parts of the organization. Finally, the best thing Bliss does is offer ideas, answers, and tools so you're left with hope that you can get this work done and a game plan for how to do it."
—Pat Barry, chief operating officer and chief financial officer,
Bluefly, Inc., *www.bluefly.com*

"Jeanne Bliss's take on how to drive customer profitability management into our organizations is clear and actionable. She gets right to the heart of what makes this work challenging, and provides realistic approaches, tools, and her personal stories of how she persevered her way through the work. *Chief Customer Officer* is a reference which I'll reach for again and again as I drive this work inside my own organization."
—Mike Webber, manager, customer support program & project office,
Bombardier Business Aircraft

# CHIEF CUSTOMER OFFICER

## Getting Past Lip Service to Passionate Action

Jeanne Bliss

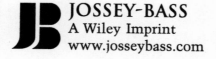

JOSSEY-BASS
A Wiley Imprint
www.josseybass.com

Published by Jossey-Bass
A Wiley Imprint
989 Market Street, San Francisco, CA 94103-1741   www.josseybass.com

Jossey-Bass books and products are available through most bookstores. To contact Jossey-Bass directly
call our Customer Care Department within the U.S. at 800-956-7739, outside the U.S. at 317-572-3986,
or fax 317-572-4002.

Jossey-Bass also publishes its books in a variety of electronic formats. Some content that appears in
print may not be available in electronic books.

**Library of Congress Cataloging-in-Publication Data**

Bliss, Jeanne.
    Chief customer officer : getting past lip service to passionate action / Jeanne Bliss.
       p. cm.
    ISBN-13: 978-0-7879-8094-8
    ISBN-10: 0-7879-8094-3
  1.  Customer relations—Management.   2.  Industrial management.   I.  Title.
    HF5415.5.B565 2006
    658.8'12—dc22                                                              2006000891

Printed in the United States of America
FIRST EDITION
*HB Printing*   10 9 8 7 6 5 4 3 2

# Contents

# INTRODUCTION

Here's the deal about this book. It's about reality. How to get the customer thing (you know, the public proclamation to focus on customers, followed by mass confusion on what to do) done beyond the lip service, T-shirts, coffee mugs, and big kickoffs. It's about how to push the customer rock up the hill by turning the focus on the obvious: customer profits. It's about how to figure out how big that hill is. And it's about how to keep that rock from falling on your head . . . as little as possible. It's about figuring out if you've got the leadership guts to take this effort on, and it's about navigating the corporate machine to figure out how and where to best leverage this effort from. And, yes, this book is also about knowing when to pick up your marbles and go home. So enough with the hand waving and chanting that this year *really* is about the customer! Enough with the crazy task forces, the meetings before the meetings, the meetings after the meetings, and the actual silly meetings that accomplish little more than pushing peas around on our plate. Let's get something done.

There's a lot of talk going on now about having a "chief" to own the customer effort. Sounds great, right? Well . . . maybe. Don't put your money down until you know what you're buying, how this role can fit in your organization and how hard you have to work to make it a success. This is expensive real estate in terms of commitment, time, people, and changing how people work. It will send some into a state of happy delirium and will annoy others. You need to know exactly what it will do to whom and why before you pull the trigger. Does this chief give everyone the ability to wipe their hands of doing the customer thing? Does this chief person make it easier for the CEO to make a public commitment to the customer? And just what are they "chief" of? Surely to lead the customer thing, don't they need to own the operations where the customer issues are created and resolved? Not necessarily. Who does this person report to? Is this an evangelist or a doer?

You'll get answers to all of these questions in this book. You'll examine your organization and determine if this is the right fit for you. Most important, this book will prod you into understanding what has stalled your efforts in the past. What are the deeply rooted things in the way your organization is wired that has gotten in the way, and what considerations are required before you step yet again into the customer commitment arena.

For twenty-five years, I've had the fifty-ton weight of "Just go fix it" strapped to my back regarding the customer thing. I've worked with enlightened leaders where we've been in lockstep every step of the way. Having had the good fortune to begin my customer zealotry career at Lands' End, reporting to founder Gary Comer, I received the foundation to know when that path was right. But I've spent way too much time pounding on doors to get into meetings and onto the agenda and to have a seat in the room where the big decisions are made. These experiences gave me a living laboratory to figure out how to navigate in less friendly waters. My instincts for knowing which kind of water I'm in has become quite sharpened, as have the different approaches required to get the job done. Over the years, these survive-and-thrive tactics have amassed into a playbook, which I have assembled into this tome you have in your hands.

It's my goal to give you as many ways as possible to fight the gravity of that rock. Along the way, you'll also need to become a bit of a Tom Sawyer, getting people to come paint your fence. And I pass along how to do this too, because the real joy in this work comes when it's not your own anymore but instead becomes the work of the organization. I hope you find real value in these methods behind the madness, passion, guts, and process to get a company to wrap itself around its customers. Keep pushing on that rock! Through this book, I've got my hand at the small of your back prodding you on.

## READER ROADMAP

*Chief Customer Officer* is written so you can discover the reality of the effect your organization is having on customer relationships and profitability and then do something about it. The process includes understanding what drives the organization, how you work together, and how readily you can come together to solve the tough customer issues. And, finally, what are your metrics and leadership accountability? Do they line up to mean anything significant about managing customer relationships? The answer to your situation may be naming a chief customer officer—or it may not. This book will help you discover what the right answer is for your organization. Traversing it will lead you through four categories of information and decision making:

- **Why do customer efforts crash and burn?** What is your company's power core? Where is the organization predisposed to perform? How is it directing company priorities, the development of competencies, and the areas where people seek to excel? How do your collective company actions have an impact on customer relationships and profitability? How are the silos working together? Do silo conflicts and disconnects end up in the customers' lap? You'll find answers to these questions in Chapters One, Two, and Three.
- **Are you wrestling with customer leadership?** What role does leadership have in driving the customer agenda? Are they leading it, hindering it, or on the sidelines? Are your metrics a bowl of spaghetti? Do they line up to drive strategic customer management? Or are they the usual conflicting silo-based metrics used to manage the discipline? Are people held accountable by leaders for clear and actionable customer performance factors? Explore your company's customer leadership in Chapters Four through Six.
- **What are you actually doing to match the commitment to the customer to the actions of the organization?** What is the series of actions you should be taking to drive the focus? How many of them are you doing now? Is there a difference between the actions that leaders say the company is taking versus what the organization believes is happening? Take the Reality Check Audit in Chapter Seven to find out the answers to these questions for your organization.
- **Is a chief customer officer the solution?** Do you need a chief customer officer (CCO) to advance the action? As the CEO or corporate leader, do you know what you're buying when you put someone in this organization chart box? Are you willing to put skin in the game for the job to have optimum impact? What is the CCO job description, how can it be structured, and where should it report

in the organization? What will be its sphere of influence? What are companies who already have chief customer officers doing? Turn to Chapters Eight through Eleven.

## WHAT THIS BOOK WILL DO FOR YOU

**Executives and CEOs:** Use this book as a platform to evaluate your organization and your personal role in driving the customer agenda. You may be wondering why you just can't get traction on customer management and customer profitability even though you've named it as a corporate priority. Through this book's evaluations and outline of the issues, you can understand why the impasse exists. There is information here to assist you in determining if the answer is a single position or a whole host of conditions, attitudes, and actions that must change in your organization. Hiring or appointing a chief customer officer will require a personal commitment by you. This book will outline what you need to be ready and willing to step up to doing before you put a name on that organization chart.

**To the new and existing chief of the customer effort:** This is your comprehensive handbook packed with ideas on how to get this vital work accomplished. The tools, approaches, stories, and empathy contained in it will arm you with a place to start and a methodology for how to proceed in the first month, the first year, and those that go beyond when things really start to take hold. You'll get ideas for how to manage across the silos, where to weave in accountability, and how to engage the commitment of top leaders in the journey. Most important, it will provide ideas on how to break the work into segments so you can advance the organization down a specific path of improvement.

**Senior leadership and functional leaders:** You may be trying to crack the nut on how to deliver a comprehensive customer experience. You may be at the point where it's obvious that all of the factions you're trying to bring together to get that project done have different agendas. Or perhaps you're the service vice president with vast amounts of customer information that could drive the company forward, but people just aren't lining up to participate. You may have joined forces with another functional vice president to get the company to make some tough cross-company changes required to manage customer relationships. In your passion, you may have found yourself the de facto leader for this gnarly companywide effort. This book takes and translates the issues you're experiencing but may not have had time to articulate. It offers tools to move the logjams you're experiencing and tactics for how to proceed with your particular brand of challenge.

*January 2006*                                                           Jeanne Bliss
*Redmond, Washington*

*To my husband, Bill. He knows why.*

# CHIEF CUSTOMER OFFICER

# PART ONE

# WHY CUSTOMER EFFORTS CRASH AND BURN

# CHAPTER ONE

# MACHINE OF MEDIOCRITY
## Corporate Machine on Autopilot

For whatever hallucination-induced state I've been living in for the past twenty-five years, my entire career has been dedicated to driving the customer agenda inside highly respected corporate machines. The most important skill required for the job: pushing back on the answer "no." *"No, we can't change that policy. It makes too much money." "No, customers don't need us to resolve their problem on the first call." "No, no, no. There is no reason that we should talk to customers to understand why they left!"*

In the best of times, this work has enlightened companies to cultivate change in how they work to deliver experiences to customers. This is when we customer crusaders rejoice . . . as we recede into the background and the ideas blend into how the company begins to think and act. But then there is the state we usually live in. Like the guy at the circus spinning plates on those sticks, we get one change going and move on to the next, only to notice that the first is wobbling erratically and about to crash.

Why does it take such a push to wrap the focus of a company around the customer as the source of their revenue? I'm no shrinking violet, and I can tell you that for every battle I've won, I've lost just as many. The big question is, Why has it been a battle? Why have I even had a job? Largely reporting to company presidents, my charge has been to advance the customer commitment and drive action to achieve customer profitability. In a nutshell, I've been paid to be as annoying as the sound of fingernails on a chalk-board—to get the attention of decision makers (and frequently the president who hired me) so they consider the customers' perspective and the revenue impact of their business decisions.

For all the beating of breasts about the customer as king, we still haven't gotten very far. Why? In my experience, it's been because of the corporate machine and how we citizens of the machine have been programmed to achieve our success and reward.

The corporation has become a machine of mediocrity to its customers. Over the years, the organizational model has been cast as pushing widgets out the door. What goes out is defined by the traditional silos created to drive competency vertically: marketing, sales, shipping, and operations. Those in charge of building the competencies are motivated to create performance standards within their span of control. And those of us working inside the silos have learned that success can be achieved most easily through compartmentalizing our work and staying singularly focused on our mission. These separate standards inhibit executive leadership's ability to comprehend and manage their company's total situation with customers, as they are served up only a slice of how the company performs by silo. This frequently accounts for the random, reactive, and less-than-strategic responses I've seen presidents call for time and time again regarding customers. When squeaky-wheel issues are fixed per executive mandate, these efforts are heralded greatly, while pressing and strategic customer issues lie in wait as the corporate machine scurries to fix the one random issue that landed on the president's desk.

## SQUEAKY WHEEL WHIPLASH: SPINNING THE HEADS OF THE PHONE PERSONNEL

A highly regarded financial services company with a strong marketing department convinced leadership that they could get a lot more sales with every inbound customer service call. The solution: get the telephone personnel to up-sell and cross-sell customers when they call requesting help. Payout to the phone personnel was calibrated according to how many customers were convinced to take the offers and buy the value of the add-ons. Simultaneously a new effort was rolled out within customer service to improve the phone personnel's ability to build customer rapport and increase brand value in the customers' eyes. An elaborate system of surveys was created to measure customers' attachment to the brand. These results linked down to the phone rep so they could be held accountable for the results.

In order to win the payout for the up-sell and cross-sell promotion, the phone personnel had to stay within a talk-time boundary. At the same time, the new behavior to build customer rapport prompted longer conversations. Talk times naturally stretched over those previously tracked. There was payout for up-selling and cross-selling (read: "We care about this so we pay for it"). But there was no payout associated with achieving a customer-rapport phone call (whiplash! "We care about this too but don't pay for it"). So here's how those calls went. With one eye on the timer clocking minutes and prompting them to end the call, they'd try to build rapport. Then with talk-time dwindling, they'd rapid-fire offers to up-sell and cross-sell.

The result was uncomfortable customers, disappointing additional sales, and frustrated phone personnel. What caused these are classic. A single silver bullet was shot through the air to get more cash out of customers. It was fired from the marketing silo, which did not have the benefit of knowing what else was going on. That disconnect made a tangle of things for both customers and the reps trying to serve them. While the phone personnel wanted to build rapport, they also wanted to make their payout. The mixed messages about what was important drove them to go where the money was, compromising the results of both efforts.

## THE BIG "AHA!"

The corporation does not live in rapport with its customers because the customer doesn't experience a company through its silos. The customer experiences a company horizontally, *across* the silos. The typical silo structure bumps the customer disjointedly along to deliver the outcome of its experience. It's only when the silos clang and clash into one another that the total experience comes together. And the customer becomes the grand guinea pig, experiencing each variation of an organization's ability, or inability, to work together.

This outcome is the brands' defaulted customer experience, and it's what it becomes known for in the marketplace. Companies don't plan their brand experience; they leave it to chance. They leave the determinants customers use to decide if they'll return—their impression of the company, brand values, differentiation, and how they are treated—to *chance*. And they hope it will be all right.

But it isn't. Across the world, after all these years of supposed focus on the customer, up to two-thirds of all customers leave due to poor customer service (Tepe, 2003). This means that the breakdowns in the execution of our basic interactions with customers make them exasperated enough to walk. And customers are doing a lot more walking these days. That bit of information Frederick Reichheld (1996) delivered about the typical U.S. corporation losing half its customers every five years had us all aghast. That was just the beginning of customers' growing willingness to depart for the competition. Between 32 and 94 percent of all customers right now are thinking of walking away from the companies that currently serve them (Haughton, 2005). But it appears we have gotten somehow numbed by that dismal performance because we haven't done much to make those numbers change. What we have now is a frenzied awareness of a problem that often leads to an even more frenzied approach to a "solution."

CEOs asked by the Conference Board in 2005 to rank the challenges that keep them up at night (Barrington and Tortorici, 2005) put customer loyalty and retention third overall in the United States, just behind steady top-line growth and consistent execution of strategy by top management. Those three things are linked, yet another big aha! A company challenged to consistently execute across leadership divisions is also likely to experience challenges delivering a cohesive customer experience. This will have an impact on their ability to keep and develop profitable customers. The worldwide Conference Board results for this study expose yet another telling fact. Across the world, CEO respondents from companies classified as "more successful" (those that earned the highest average return on assets) more frequently listed customer loyalty and retention as a chief concern over CEOs of "less successful" companies.

The bottom line is this. The organizations we've built, the ways we've compensated and motivated people, and the accountability we've demanded have created a neat and ordered world for *us* to run our businesses. But for the most part, we've let down our customers. It's as if we're all working with one hand tied behind our backs. To see what I mean, answer these questions: Do you have to lobby other silos to work collaboratively so you can get the best outcome for customers? How much time do you spend lobbying versus actually working together? How many of the completed ideas look vaguely like the one you started with? And (the kicker), how many of them end up delivering something better for customers? I've spent much of my time inside the corporate machine lobbying; it sometimes amazes me when things get accomplished. I can't tell you the number of three-hump camels I've been involved in building:

### A Three-Hump Camel Story

We're in a conference room—a whole mess of us. In attendance are sales, service, and marketing and operations people. We're all there at the behest of our chief executive to establish a loyalty plan for a segment of customers. One executive "sponsor" was in the room. And that's all we needed for the show to begin. The ideas started flying. "We could give points!" "What about a birthday club?" "Let's offer discounts." The fact of the matter was that a bunch of information we had gathered indicated why we weren't keeping these customers: we had increased prices on services, reduced our availability, and were slower in responding to requests and resolving issues. My team had tabulated and followed the trends on these issues for a few months, so we knew what was up. And the latest customer feedback validated that information. When we presented these data to the group, it was pretty much seen as a wet blanket on those initial ideas. There was a pause. Then the three humps began to build. What we ended up with was an outbound phone call made by a telemarketer to offer the customer a discount on his or her next purchase. At the end of the call, a question was asked if there was anything the customer wanted to discuss about the company.

This was not exactly the rethinking of the service processes our team was primed to push for. The bone thrown our way was that question at the close of the call. In the end, this turned out to be a mediocre effort. It just had too many agendas. What we did was build a three-hump camel. *And* we spoiled many customers' dinners with our pointless telemarketing phone call.

# THE POWER CORE

Who approves the camel's design and the function of the camel can usually be traced to the power core of the organization. Most companies have a predominant power core. Frequently it is the strongest skill set in the company or the most comfortable to senior executives. Because executives know the power core best, people gravitate to perform in that area. Success in the power core competencies are assuredly met with acknowledgment and reward. The power core can be the most influential in directing the silos and is one of the biggest determinants of how success, metrics, recognition, and company growth are defined inside the corporate machine.

The complexity and scale of work required to drive customer profitability and loyalty into the business model is greatly affected by the strength of the power core and its distance from the customer.

When I left Lands' End and moved on to other companies, I had many watershed moments. Understanding the power core and its impact on the customer has repeatedly proven itself to be a crucial first step in assessing how to proceed. Why? Because understanding the company power core zeroes in on the corporate machine's motivation and ability to drive movement toward customer relationships and customer profitability.

At Lands' End, the power core was the customer (Figure 1.1). Almost everything we built was created from the customer perspective out. Performance metrics and recognition were grounded in how we delivered on the promise and guarantee made to customers. I can say unabashedly that it was highly rewarding personally and professionally to be in this type of environment. It spoiled me for the other experiences that were to come as I kept searching to replicate the Lands' End experience. However, it gave me the strong tools and abilities I needed to weave the customer perspective into companies where the power core resided elsewhere.

I got a loud wake-up call when I moved to the automotive industry and observed that the power core was not the customer but the sales and marketing of the product. During my time in the industry, the economy was shrinking, and the automotive product market was shifting and on the cusp of understanding customer value and retention. At that time, automakers relied heavily on what historically had brought them success: conquest sales, heavy

FIGURE 1.1. When the Power Core Is the Customer:
The Case at Lands' End

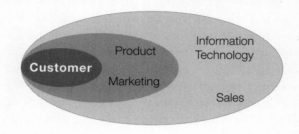

marketing, events, and incentives. Sales and marketing was the power core. Even a meeting presentation was called a "pitch." And I needed to understand how people processed and prioritized pitches in order to even make it onto a meeting agenda. If I wanted to talk about loyalty, it needed to be about a certain vehicle, not overall brand loyalty. To get attention, it was best to first provide sales numbers, followed by the customer retention and repurchase information. The lessons from that experience continue to ring true: know the source, methods of operating, and priorities of those with their fingers on the power button.

Understanding the power core source and its impact is key to framing how to proceed with the customer work. Whenever I work with companies now, early on I assess where the company power core resides and measure its impact in driving the corporate agenda. This yields an immediate understanding of the complexity and scale of the job required to integrate the customer experience and customer profitability into the business model. Chapter Two provides thorough information on the power core concept and a process for you to diagnose and understand your company power core and its impact on customers. As strong as the power core is, it can put up blinders to the other corporate competencies required to drive customer profitability and deliver a powerful customer experience. Chapter Two also identifies the potential customer profitability hot spots and potholes a company may encounter for each power core and offers a diagnostic tool for identifying the scale and complexity of work ahead.

# DUELING SILOS

As the mechanics of running the business take over, the corporate machine goes on autopilot and begins to lose sight of its customer. The machine moves further away from the strategic relevance of customers in business decisions. And then the customer gradually sinks out of sight. This is usually not purposeful, but it occurs repeatedly. In a company's quest to meet the numbers, strategy is bypassed for short-term hits, and the grueling work of figuring out how to deliver what's most desirable to customers is short-cut or avoided. To get me off their backs, I've even seen executives pick a date, create a push to drum up action, and commit their leaders to pledge to push them through. And that's when we tend to muck things up even more as a proliferation of tactics and messages gets cooked up that randomizes both the customer and the company.

You can recognize dueling silo agendas at work when short-term revenue requirements compromise long-term revenue efforts. It's when lack of clarity on what's really important to differentiate the company for the customer is not understood the same way by everyone who needs to know. And it's when there is an imbalance between the culture to drive revenue and the understanding and purpose of including customer investment to meet those goals. In their rush to push the customer thing forward on the corporate agenda (for what could be more blasphemous than not committing to the customer?), many organizations fail to address the metrics, the motivation, and the mechanics of just how to move the machine to improve with regard to their customers.

## DUELING SILOS AT WORK: FUNKY TASK FORCES

Think about the number of task forces you've been involved in around customers. Did anyone have a clue, beyond the first few meetings, on how you were going to get the wild things done that the brainstorming had birthed, where you were going to get the funding from, and who was going to lead the effort? How many of these have you been involved in during the course of your career? And WHY do executives keep calling for these things?

See if this sounds familiar to you: Alarm! Alarm! "Our customer satisfaction scores just came in. . . . We [expletive] at our scores. Let's get some people together to see what we can do about this." Everyone here means well. No doubt, the room is filled with your brain trust on the subject: the technical wizards, the customer service people, the marketers, and all of the others until you've got a room busting at the seams. There is great talk, great enthusiasm, and agreement to have another meeting. Everyone goes back to their corners of the business. Many, many more meetings and time and debating and finger-pointing later, little has changed. And the beat goes on. Here are three reasons why: (1) the customer thing is still considered something layered on to the existing work, (2) there's no one clearly in charge or able to take charge of knitting the pieces together, and (3) there are dueling silos. Unless you've been working in a non-Dilbert world somewhere, you'll know what this means.

### Hope in a Case Study: Even Harrah's and Royal Bank of Canada Had Funky Task Forces

Harrah's is the gaming and hospitality company admired by many because of its ability to target and develop its customer base and customer profitability. Senior vice president of business development Rich Mirman described Harrah's version of the funky task force as the "huddle after the huddle." This is the same as what we've all experienced in the halls before or after meetings where people make a decision in groupthink about how much they "believe" what is being advocated and how much they're thinking about lining up behind it. Heads nod in unison in the meeting, but as even Harrah's experienced at the beginning of its journey, you've always got some cat herding to do. For Harrah's, the individual casino properties would do the nod to a companywide approach being pitched and then would go back and decide if it applied to their market. They would dissent in private. Said Mirman, "All of a sudden you're spending 25% of your time trying to get people to run the play" (Gulati and Oldroyd, 2005, p. 10).

The same rang true at Royal Bank of Canada's credit card division. Product folks agreed in principle to the customer-focused approaches but dissented by continuing to do their own thing in marketing. When the metrics proved that current customers were more open and likely than noncustomers to become credit card customers, the tide began to turn.

## DUELING SILOS AT WORK: ANNUAL OPPORTUNITY MISSED

Annual planning is a missed opportunity for driving customer profitability inside the corporate machine. The silos usually pick their projects and plan their budgets independent of one another. Short-term tactics with outcomes easily attributable to individual departments (for purposes of "clean" compensation and metrics) comprise annual plans and financial commitments. These often come at the exclusion of messier companywide efforts that could resolve customer issues and subsequently yield more significant long-term revenue.

Frequently all the money invested in the big satisfaction survey can't even be applied, since the results are out of sync with the planning cycle. Some of the companies I have worked with did the hand wave to "customer satisfaction" when the annual survey results came in. Then, based on the culture, there was some rushing around to change some things, especially if we had egg on our faces from the results. The customer surveys typically come out of the annual planning cycle, so defining what's needed is usually out of whack in planning investments. This is hardly a continuous improvement effort with progressive metrics to drive an increase in customer experiences, customer profitability, and customer loyalty. There is typically no baseline for each of those three dimensions or goal line. Yet this is how most companies continue to approach the customer thing. Without common accountability targets, actions will continue to be planned tactically, based on the individual annual plans of the silos. Companies need to have an ongoing roadmap to define where they want to make progress in customer profitability, customer loyalty, and customer experience delivery. For example, they need to take a strategic look at how much prospecting for new customers or business needs to be done every year to replace the revenue lost in the previous year. They need to have annual goals for the movement of customers from one level of purchase behavior to another. Without these customer-centered goals, the company continues to focus only on business outcomes; wheel spinning continues, and companies continue to stand still regarding customers without knowing exactly why.

# MOTIVATION, METRICS, AND MECHANICS

Three areas are most accountable for creating the chasm between the corporate machine and the customer: motivation, metrics, and mechanics. When they don't factor in the needs of customers, they advance the corporate machine's lackluster performance, driving the advance of mediocrity and the decline in customer profitability. But when they are strategically executed to manage customer relationships and profitability, they can reverse the course of brand and customer erosion. Most important, they enable the corporate machine to work from a unified platform with customer profitability and company revenues as the unifying force. All three of these—metrics, motivation, and mechanics—are interdependent, just as the silos should be. And all of them have to be worked on. I've never seen a company (not even those whose power core is the customer) avoid sinking into at least one of these quicksand ingredients that form the muck of our dysfunctional relationship with customers.

Because of how we have been conditioned to act inside the corporate machine, the frenzy of activity that occurs throughout the company doesn't necessarily aggregate to mean anything to customers. Lack of clarity on what's really important to differentiate the company for the customer is not crystallized. It's certainly not understood the same way by everyone who needs to know. And the customer sinks deeper and deeper into the quicksand. Chapter Three provides more information on the obvious and unspoken impacts of the natural dueling that occurs between silos. There you'll also find diagnostic tools to determine how deeply each of these is being ignored or executed inside your corporate machine, as well as how to prioritize the execution of the elements based on needs and the reality of executing them in the short and long terms. That chapter also offers field-tested tools and approaches to try to keep those plates spinning in some semblance of order for the customer.

Let's now revisit those "no" comments from the beginning of this chapter to see some more customer quicksand at work.

- *"No, we can't change that policy. It makes too much money. Customers are ready for it."* This was a debate about how to ease in a contract change that would commit customers to a longer term of commitment than they were used to. A strong argument was made to earn the right of customers to want to commit longer by first understanding and resolving issues and fully training the field force in how to roll out the new policy. There was huge push back because the revenue upside had already been calculated and people wanted to see the additional revenue rolling in now. The initial source of the push back was finance. They had run the numbers on a cost basis to quantify the benefit of the policy change. The president was convinced of the revenue boost to the balance sheet and did not want to wait. Since this affected the sales force, the sales vice president was a powerful advocate for moving forward sooner rather than later. The result was high customer frustration and backlash for the decision. A massive and expensive process was put into place to try to rectify the situation. The company is still trying to make up for the customer ill will generated from the decision based on an internal quest to drive speedy revenue for the corporate balance sheet.

- *"No, customers don't need us to resolve their problem on the first call."* This push back came from the call center leader. He was evaluated and compensated based on his cost management ability so was in favor of a system that first triaged customers into buckets and then put them in a callback queue, or a holding pattern. This put customers into voice mail hell as they bounced through a system trying to classify them and get them to the right party, usually requiring a call back. It has been proven that the longer customers with a problem wait, the more they stew about it and the bigger the problem looms in their minds. The "fix" must then include not only resolving the initial problem but also resolving the miserable experience of trying to get the problem solved. This is exactly what happened here. Any costs saved on reduced calls through the triage process were more than spent with the additional salvos that had to be applied to overcome the bad experience it caused. (*Triage* is a term that drives me crazy. If customers weren't feeling sick at the beginning of the call, they got that way after they'd been triaged.)

- *"No, no, no. There is no reason to talk to customers to understand why they left!"* This scenario played out in the financial services industry where service agents had convinced the sales leadership that price, not service agent performance, was pushing customers away.

Outbound calls to find out the reasons were considered costly and not necessary. A great appeal was made, suggesting that if we could speak with these customers, perhaps not only could we find out why they had left, we could also potentially solve the problem and convince them to return. Finally, the funding was approved to make the calls to a sample of customers who had left. Customers who didn't renew their service agreement were asked why they had left. The result: 75 percent said that service agent quality was largely factored into the reason for their split. Armed with this information, the company secured funding to add more call center personnel who were especially trained to speak with customers who expressed issues with the company and who had left. Thirty percent of the lost accounts contacted reestablished contracts because (1) someone noticed they had left and contacted them (hint: know who's leaving you and ask them why) and (2) they had the issue that had caused them to depart resolved.

## CONCLUSION

The bottom line is that the organizational behavior we've all become proficient at has forced us into the narrow role of pushing our individual widgets out the door. What goes out is defined based on the silos we're in; marketing, sales, shipping, operations. It is true that the intent of the silo structure is to build strong competencies vertically. But it cuts the customer out. What they receive is frequently compromised to meet the agenda of the corporate machine.

And we all wonder why we haven't made more progress on the customer front.

It is these so-called soft elements that have become our quicksand. Examples of leadership balancing a culture of revenue and customer investment are extremely rare. In our quest to push the customer thing forward on the corporate agenda, we have failed to address the metrics, the motivation, and the mechanics of how to move the machine in concert to deliver meaningful customer experiences.

# CHAPTER TWO

# THE POWER CORE

This work is as much about knowing what motivates people as it is about getting the job done. That's where the power core comes in. Most companies have a predominant power core. Frequently it is the strongest skill set in the company or the most comfortable to senior executives. Because executives know the power core best, people gravitate to perform in that area. Understanding the strength and pull of the power core will help to uncover the hot spots and potholes for driving a customer profitability culture. It will frame the scope of work required to influence change. It will provide clarity on the approach to take in creating partnerships with leaders and in motivating people within the organization through the change process. And it will help to zero in on your company's motivation and ability to drive movement toward customer profitability.

People who lead customer improvement efforts frequently begin without understanding the impact of the power core's pull for driving the agenda. They don't think this through and begin work on customer issues in earnest, but it inevitably hits the brick wall of the power core. People want to do the right thing; they want to work on the customer stuff. But the pull of the priorities of the power core will always course-correct them in the next meeting with their boss. I've seen brave souls pull together enthusiastic task forces to fix the customer thing. The first order of business is to bring people together to figure out how to get an issue fixed. So far, smooth sailing; a funky task force has begun. But when it gets more serious with accountability, metrics, and a reporting schedule assigned to the task, the backlash begins: "We don't report to you." "There's no time for this." "This won't leave time to make sales." On and on it goes inside corporate machines around the world. This is because the power core hasn't been asked to the dance.

For example, I really had to scratch my head on how to approach driving the customer agenda with some technology-based companies. The greatest challenge was that I just hadn't gotten close enough to the power core to understand the best way to make early inroads. The process stuff—improving broken operational issues, improving the service experiences, and so forth—is where efforts typically gain momentum and establish a track for success within many other industries. But with these particular organizations, the product emerged as the power force that the world revolved around. It was about the software. I learned that lesson well. The customer work gained momentum when the efforts put a laser focus on using customer feedback to improve the product.

## The Elephant in the Room

The power core is an unusually strong yet often unspoken force. Never underestimate the power of its pull. Because executives make decisions through the filter of the power core, people want to perform there: they will be driven to perform where the enthusiasm is the highest, the understanding is the easiest, and the rewards are the greatest. As a soldier inside the corporate machine, which would you choose? Would you focus on something people talk about in high-level terms but has no day-to-day accountability or compensation tied to it (the customer thing)? Or would you excel at your quarterly sales goals that you receive urgent e-mail messages on, receive quarterly incentives for achieving, and for which stack ranking lists are posted comparing you to your peers?

The end game is to incorporate the drive for managing customer relationships and profitability into the power core. Because these goals and actions remain elusive, they're simply not called for with the same level of gusto. In many cases, they're not called for at all. Especially where there's success at pumping out sales, saturating the marketplace and growth, or the product demands continued updates and captive customer loyalty, it is difficult to take the time out to do what people consider the slow work of process: connecting the efforts across the organization and even counting the number and value of customers who go in and out your doors. The customer stuff always seems to be something to layer on top of the "real work" rather than being part of the work itself. It's often seen as the competition.

# SIX COMMON POWER CORES

There are six common power cores that determine how things go inside the corporate machine. You'll likely find one of them to be the dominant factor in decision making and direction in your company. You may also see another in a supporting second place of strength. Here are the six power cores that I've found to have the greatest impact on driving customer profitability inside the corporate machine. (You'll find them summarized in Table 2.1.)

## WHEN THE POWER CORE IS THE PRODUCT

The product *is* the company to the marketplace. Product development groups get the most resources and the most play, and they have the most power. Just look at the organization chart. Metrics are about new products, size of products, getting products out, speed of product development, and competitive progress of products in relation to competitors.

## WHEN THE POWER CORE IS MARKETING

The marketing department defines the tenor and tone of the relationship with customers. Customer relationships may be collapsed to marketing campaigns and tactics. Brand at the advertising messaging level is emphasized, but the implications for how to tie that to the experience can fall short. I've literally seen companies take their strategic direction from their advertising agency. While focus and vision can be very strong here, I've seen two pitfalls that sometimes occur when marketing is the power core. First, all eyes look up to the president or chief marketer for calling the shots because he or she is so strong on the vision that people stop trusting their instincts in exchange for predicting how the chief marketer wants it done. In addition, marketing strength doesn't necessarily beget the patience or skills to translate the vision into an operating plan that's executable.

## TABLE 2.1: The Six Predominant Power Cores

| Product Power Core | Marketing Power Core | Sales Power Core |
|---|---|---|
| Product development is the focus. The product is the company in the marketplace and in the boardroom. Metrics are about new products, size of products, getting products out of, and speed of product development and competitive progress of products in relation to competitors. | Marketing defines the tenor and tone of the relationship with customers. Customer relationship may be collapsed to marketing campaigns and tactics. Brand at the advertising messaging level is emphasized, but the implications for how to tie that to the experience can fall short. | Motivation is toward making the numbers, and performance is measured in short-term sales goals and targets. Sales targets are the strongest and most tracked corporate metrics. Frequently the organization hasn't worked together to ensure that the after-the-sale experience delivers on the promise of the sale. |

| Vertical Business Power Core | Information Technology (IT) Power Core | Customer Power Core |
|---|---|---|
| A business discipline is the specialty and forms the core of power. For example, the business focuses strongly on its proficiency in the discipline of insurance. The metrics revolve on the execution of an industry, frequently "as it's always been done." Processes can be inward focused rather than customer delivery focused. | As the bulk of spending related to IT projects far exceeds other financial requirements, IT has been given power in determining the priorities of the organization—not just in computer resources, but by having a large voice in representing, selecting, and enabling IT-dependent projects across the organization. | Company decisions emanate from understanding what will drive greatest value to customers in the short and long terms. Driving profitable customers aligns marketing, sales, product development, service, IT, and operations investment. They connect to enable optimum product and sales execution to ensure optimum customer value is delivered. |

## WHEN THE POWER CORE IS SALES

The quest for the sale pulls the weight in the company. In these organizations, people are motivated to make the numbers. Performance is frequently measured in short-term sales goals and targets. Sales targets are the strongest and most tracked corporate metrics. "Speed" sales are rewarded, even if they don't necessarily result in long-term customer profitability. Frequently the organization hasn't worked together to ensure that the after-sale experience delivers on the promise of the sale.

## WHEN THE POWER CORE IS A VERTICAL BUSINESS

This power core is based on a particular competency related to an industry or function. The term *vertical power core* is used because deliverables to customers are akin to a vertical line of business highly focused on one particular area. Banking is an industry where many businesses grew strong through the detailed execution of the functions of the account, the loan, and identifying the risk. In these types of deep competency businesses, there's a risk for customers to become anonymous. The process becomes the description for what the person is working on: "Big loan opportunity coming in at noon today." The financial services revolution, for example, has been in large part the realization and incorporation of the human process into the execution process. We've all experienced the strong vertical disposition of the medical industry: doctors still define their work by procedure rather than customer name ( "I've got an appendectomy at eight, then tonsils at three"). This makes sense given the ways medical practitioners have been classically trained: livers, hearts, the circulatory system, and so on. Bedside Manner 101 usually didn't show up on the medical school curriculum. And so where a vertical business is the power core, it is frequently because the foundation of the business and its growth are based on the execution of that function.

The insurance industry is yet another vertical power core business. Most insurance companies have classically run their businesses to be proficient in the disciplines of actuarial calculations, policy development, claims execution, and other traditional areas of the insurance business. However, shifting consumer needs and demands, new market entrants such as Progressive, and the heralded practices of USAA have prompted that industry to have a collective "aha!" moment. The race is on as they are trying to wrap a customer experience around the delivery of that policy.

## WHEN THE POWER CORE IS INFORMATION TECHNOLOGY

The technology tail wags the dog of the corporation. What I've come to call the "CRM (customer relationship management) hallucination" has created a strange forcing function where information technology (IT) becomes the power core in many organizations. Because the bulk of spending related to IT projects far exceeds other financial requirements, IT has been given an inordinate amount of power in determining the priorities of the organization—and not just in computer resources. It also has a loud voice in representing, selecting, and enabling IT-dependent projects across the organization. Typically these spending requests come through annual planning and lack a strategic plan relative to overall advancement for improving customer profitability or the customer experience. In its quest to serve the company, IT too has fallen into the well-intentioned trap of allocating resources by silo. This compromises what should be a strategic IT strategy into a bunch of silo-driven pieces that may not cumulatively have the most potent impact.

How many of you have been the recipient of some CRM engine that can do a million things? Yet when they are thrown over the wall to the field or to the customer service people, they're just not used. Why? Because IT got busy building the CRM systems that everyone said they wanted and needed right away (they were a *very* popular silver bullet). IT began the building process and quickly moved ahead of many business owners' ability to define the purpose of the system, what they wanted the data to do, and what company actions needed to kick in as a result of knowing the data. So IT was forced to make decisions and define the business rules! Not that they didn't want help. It's just that our brains weren't wrapping themselves around the new CRM world as quickly as their fingers were writing the code. It was rare when the processes requiring humans to drive actions from the data (such as calling customers, sending out targeted communications, resolving issues) were thought through. There was often negligible input from the field or the service folks who were the intended users (some called themselves victims) of this stuff. That time period from 1998 through 2003 (according to the budgets I was involved in) inadvertently placed IT dead center as a very strong power core in many businesses across the globe.

## WHEN THE POWER CORE IS THE CUSTOMER

Passion for customers prevails. Leaders are close to the customer, and it is often that leaders' passion that built the business. Employees feel that the handoff of that passion from founder through the ranks of the company is an inheritance that is theirs to pass on and nurture. Company decisions emanate from understanding what will drive greatest value to customers in the short and long terms. The company's long-term desire is to deliver a differentiated customer experience to drive the greatest amount of profitable customers. This is still rare, surprisingly, after all these years of effort. Corporate machines with the customer as their power core are, not surprisingly, the companies known in the marketplace to be best for customers. These companies began with the customer at their core. In a company with a customer power core, customer needs drive the overall plan for what's developed and delivered.

## OTHER POSSIBLE POWER CORES

It's likely that the power core in your company may not be one of the six most common identified; for example, operations may emerge as your organization's predominant skill set for running the business. You are a well-oiled machine driven by the mechanics of execution. This is sometimes seen in the hospitality business or distribution businesses. Your power core may be finance. The point is to identify your power core and use that understanding to frame the scale of the work to integrate customer leadership and customer profitability management. The six that I identified are simply the predominant ones. Regardless of what your power core is, it will have an impact on how you strategically address the work.

*Hope in a Case Study: International Health Insurance Put Customers into the Vertical Power Core*

Denmark's International Health Insurance (IHI) is an insurance provider for expatriates and corporations with a large presence overseas. In 2000, CEO Per Bay Jorgensen led the company to rethink its purpose. The new direction was to participate in the "lifetime health and personal safety" support of their clients. This focused on increasing wellness and illness prevention, which was more fiscally sound for their corporate clients and yielded better health management for patients. With this shift, IHI went from executing the vertical insurance competencies of policies and claims to creating a partnership with customers in the management of their overall health and wellness. Helping corporate clients with preventive solutions resonated well. It created a connection that more traditional insurance relationships had not fostered before and carved out an increased market space for IHI. By showing how wellness management helps companies prevent employee health problems and their expense 70 percent of the time, IHI became an ally and partner for client businesses. It learned to predict the needs and timing of clients and was therefore able to prepare and deliver relevant solutions that customers and corporate clients rewarded them for. International Health Insurance achieved a 20 percent annual growth rate while other insurers were suffering from a soft market (Vandermerwe, 2004).

## DON'T TRY TO CHANGE THE POWER CORE: DANCE WITH IT

I have learned that optimizing the strength of the power core and the differentiating value it brings to customers is the solution. The company has got to sign on to weave the customer perspective and experience into the operation of the power core. Changing the power core is not the answer. It's this: *know what the power core is.* Know who drives the power core, and know how to make a compelling partnership with the power core to integrate customer profitability efforts into the day-to-day activities that now define success for the business. That's where you get real traction.

### MEA CULPA

Make no mistake: do not try to morph the company power core into the customer power core. I spent more than my fair share of time in my business youth in a zealot-induced frenzy trying to do just that. A lot of energy was used up pushing that rock up that hill, where it rolled back to crush me repeatedly. Already fearful of shrinking from my five-foot, zero-inch stature, I did myself a real injustice in this particular valiant but misguided crusade. As the rocks repeatedly fell on my head, I was absolutely knocked down a peg or two. Moral of this story: Dance with the power core!

The power core makes a much better dancing partner than sparring partner any day of the week. The first ten years of customer crusading I spent with passion as the major ingredient. This works in a company already predisposed to customers as the core of business. But it's not the ticket for long-term sustainable change. Balancing that passion with pragmatism, partnering with key people, and developing the homing device for sniffing out the base of organizational power let me make much greater inroads over the years.

## POWER CORE STRENGTH AND DISTANCE FROM THE CUSTOMER

A set of competencies exists in organizations that have learned to develop and deliver customer experiences across the silos. These customer focus competencies shown in Table 2.2 form a chain of actions required to manage the handoffs of the customer experience across the enterprise. They need to become second nature to organizations wanting to become proficient at managing customer relationships and customer profitability.

Each power core naturally develops certain skills and pays less attention to others, so the power core will have an impact on the ease with which these cross-company customer competencies can be developed and integrated. How swiftly an organization can integrate them correlates to how closely aligned they are to the reinforced power core skills. The distance between where you are now and when you get to wiring in customer focus competencies will depend on how natural this work is to those who drive the power core. The power core of your company will likely make some of these competencies easier to develop than others. Some will seem nearly impossible; it may be that the inclination to work this way just doesn't exist naturally. That's why it's critical to figure out how strong the power core is in possessing or advocating the customer focus skills sets. You need to know how interested they are in coming to the customer party:

**TABLE 2.2. Customer Focus Competencies**

| Products, sales, services based on customer needs | Integrated customer experience | Metrics drive reliability in key interactions | Recognition based on actionable operational metrics | Clarity in handoffs and integration between silos | Customer feedback drives ongoing development |
|---|---|---|---|---|---|

- Where do you drop the ball repeatedly with customers?
- Where are you vulnerable because of your focus on other things?
- Which competencies are considered "optional" or up to the individual zealots to nurture and push in the organization?

# AN EXAMINATION OF EACH POWER CORE

An examination of each power core will connect the dots for you between what your company power core is and the ease or difficulty you experience in driving customer focus. It will illuminate why, based on the core of power in your organization, you are able to accelerate some things and hit roadblocks on others when it comes to customers. Putting you through these paces is meant to give you that Aha! moment, so that you can frame the scale of your effort and craft a realistic plan for your organization.

## WHEN PRODUCT IS THE POWER CORE

If your strength in the marketplace stems from the products you sell, you are striking a chord with customers on the tangible side of the experience equation. Table 2.3 identifies the typical areas of strength and vulnerability for companies with a product power core.

### Areas of Strength

Product strength in the marketplace means that you are doing well at understanding your competition and are strong about determining where to focus. Sustaining that position of strength is dependent on staying relevant. You're likely a well-oiled machine on making continuous product improvement. There are clear operational metrics that you are used to tracking and delivering on, which is the good news. The flip side of that coin is that they may or may not have anything to do with customers. I'm giving you the benefit of the doubt here that you are also a strong "listening" company, using customer feedback to constantly tweak and improve the products you create. That means that you should have your finger on the pulse of customer needs.

**TABLE 2.3. Product Power Core Strengths and Vulnerabilities**

| | Products, sales, services based on customer needs | Integrated customer experience | Metrics drive reliability in key interactions | Recognition based on action-able operational metrics | Clarity in handoffs and integration between silos | Customer feedback drives ongoing development |
|---|---|---|---|---|---|---|
| Strength | Products, sales, services based on customer needs | Integrated customer experience | Metrics drive reliability in key interactions | Recognition based on action-able operational metrics | Clarity in handoffs and integration between silos | Customer feedback drives ongoing development |
| Vulnerability | Products, sales, services based on customer needs | Integrated customer experience | Metrics drive reliability in key interactions | Recognition based on action-able operational metrics | Clarity in handoffs and integration between silos | Customer feedback drives ongoing development |

*Note:* Typical areas of strength and customer vulnerability are shaded.

## Customer Vulnerability and Hot Spots

In a product power core company, the vulnerability comes from the soft side of the experience equation. This is not the development of the tangible product. You've got that down. The hot spot is the experience wrapped around getting the product into customers' hands and serving them after the purchase. There's a real risk for a product power core company to deliver a defaulted customer experience, which happens when people don't plan the handoffs and the experience is random, dependent on the path the customer cuts across the organization. The handoffs between departments are tricky, and it's easy to see how the customer experience can fall between the cracks.

Getting your field up to speed on the knowledge and understanding for how they support the product can be a challenge. It's just not second nature. You may also find it tough to do the process work for setting up and maintaining service and service levels that are customer focused. So metrics around those competencies are probably spotty at best and vary wildly dependent on the leader of the particular operating areas.

### Case Study: When a Product-Centered Power Core Loses Sight of Customers

When the product is the focus, a company can get an "if we will build it, they will come" mentality. Think about the Polaroid camera, for instance. Powerfully strong in the marketplace because of its cutting-edge technology for a time, Polaroid Corporation thrived in an era where success came from immensely powerful product development silos that pushed their ideas out into the marketplace. Eventually they lost touch with their customers. Digital cameras and photography burst into the marketplace as a better way to get "instant" pictures. Customers were offered a total and expanded solution that met their desire to have immediate access to their photographic images. The Polaroid solution paled in comparison. As history showed, not reacting quickly enough to changing customer desires and increased market competition pushed Polaroid to a weaker place of relevance in the market and with customers (Ready, 2004b).

## A Kickstart for Integrating the Customer into the Product Power Core

In a product-driven organization, start wiring in customer focus with the product development process (Table 2.4). This will make sense to the organization. You can build competencies here that can translate over to the softer sides of the organization. But you will be doing it at that point after having had some early successes. This is the key: you must prove that you can make some things happen to get people to want to do more. The people leading the customer focus charge need to understand the product development process and decision-making mind-set. Zero in on the method being used to garner customer feedback for identifying issues and making improvements. Then make a clear and strong metric system for tracking and marking performance in this area.

For example, at Microsoft, the product development teams established customer-focused product improvements when a technology solution was created that let customers send on-the-spot messages when their software malfunctioned (Figure 2.1). Called "Windows Error Reporting," this piece of software created real-time tracking and tallying of software malfunctions sent from customers directly to Microsoft at the time when they occurred. This immediate tracking put the customer experience with the software right in front of Microsoft programmers. It had an actionable impact because it was still in the first language of the organization: software. It worked because it provided swift and relevant data. And it worked because the product teams took ownership of the process.

### TABLE 2.4.  Product Power Core Kickstart

1. Focus on product development.

2. Establish a customer feedback system.

3. Create initial performance standards.

4. Institute tracking and reporting.

5. Introduce guerrilla metrics.

### FIGURE 2.1. Windows Error Reporting Solution

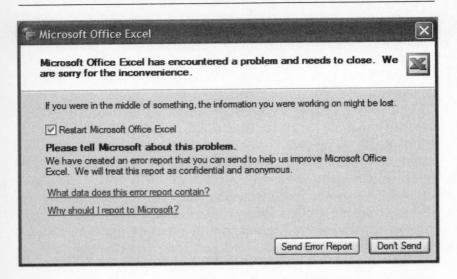

*Source:* Microsoft product screen shot reprinted with permission from Microsoft Corporation.

You need to introduce the customer language into the product development language, so next move on to bringing the "guerrilla metrics" into play. "Guerrilla metrics" is a set of five initial metrics I suggest you use to get the customer action moving inside your organization. (See Chapter Five for all the details.) The company needs a strong senior advocate to move this work forward in a product-oriented environment, so before you go further here; get the absolute agreement for doing this customer-centered work. One thing that works for me is to have a person from the product operating area be part of my team in the development of the tactics moving forward. The most important thing is sharing the reins of the customer leadership agenda with the product area. Forging a partnership with them and acknowledging the power they wield in driving the customer to the company is critical. Keep working on the approach. Don't develop solutions on your own and then try to get them to sanction it or bless it. That won't work.

## WHEN MARKETING IS THE POWER CORE

"Customer" is the language of marketers, so there is an inherent understanding of the need to connect the experience and create a comprehensive brand. Table 2.5 identifies the typical areas of strength and vulnerabilities for companies with marketing as their power core.

### Areas of Strength

Strong marketers create a solid platform to define the overall experience so the company has a sort of beacon to follow in executing its operating plans. If the marketing group is far along using campaigns and tactics, the data can be in good shape for examining and understanding what is meaningful to customers. Like the product power core, marketing groups have a clear set of metrics related to their discipline that they use for tracking, such as churn, campaign results, and direct marketing sales lift. This understanding will be of good use as the work is moved to progress from the internal metrics about the company business to the metrics about the customers' response about how they're treated by the company.

### Customer Vulnerability and Hot Spots

When marketing is the power core, it's a bit of a wild card. Some marketing functions own the customer experience. In this case, they have taken on the comprehensive efforts companywide. They are working to connect the operating areas for delivery of the contact points, and they are connecting the messaging and data. That's an enlightened environment, however. More traditionally, when the power core is marketing, the focus on the customer relationship is about marketing campaigns and tactics. Brand at the advertising messaging level is emphasized, but direction to the operating areas for how to deliver the brand experience can fall short. The biggest part of the work here is not in convincing the marketing power core of the importance of the work but in gaining its acceptance of its scope and expansive responsibilities. This work requires additional skill sets beyond marketing campaigns, data management, and communication plans. It requires process work, change management, and new leadership approaches. It requires

**TABLE 2.5. Marketing Power Core Strengths and Vulnerabilities**

| | Product, sales, service based on customer needs | Integrated customer experience | Metrics drive reliability in key interactions | Recognition based on actionable operational metrics | Clarity in handoffs and integration between silos | Customer feedback drives ongoing development |
|---|---|---|---|---|---|---|
| Strength | | | | | | |
| Vulnerability | Product, sales, service based on customer needs | Integrated customer experience | Metrics drive reliability in key interactions | Recognition based on actionable operational metrics | Clarity in handoffs and integration between silos | Customer feedback drives ongoing development |

*Note:* Typical areas of strength and customer vulnerability are shaded.

the development of different motivation and reward programs and a whole new approach to accountability.

*Feet on the Street: Research Report on Aligning the Marketing Role with CEO Priorities*

A study completed by the Association of National Advertisers (ANA) and Booz Allen Hamilton in 2004 identified a potential chasm between the priorities of CEOs and what central marketing organizations (CMOs) are focusing on. The baseline for CEO priorities in this study was the Conference Board 2004 CEO top challenges, where it named top-line growth, speed and flexibility and adaptability to change, and customer loyalty and retention as the top three priorities. The ANA/Booz Allen Hamilton study found that marketers focused on more tactical issues such as maintaining branding guidelines, sharing best practices, and counseling divisions. Driving the CEO's agenda and driving innovation were only prioritized by only 37 and 35 percent of marketers surveyed, respectively. These results have a connection to the work of driving customer profitability and relationships in that in many companies, the CEO looks to marketing to lead the customer effort. This adds to the growing importance for the CMO to align with the priorities of the CEO and take on a more strategic role across the organization. Table 2.5 identifies the strengths and vulnerabilities of a marketing power core. Table 2.6 shows how marketing departments can kickstart their efforts to lead the strategic drive for customer relationships and profitability.

### TABLE 2.6.  Marketing Power Core Kickstart

1. Gain agreement for scope of work.

2. Create process and change management competencies.

3. Define the customer experience and identify priority contacts.

4. Track and improve priority contact performance.

5. Introduce guerrilla metrics.

## A KICKSTART FOR INTEGRATING THE CUSTOMER INTO THE MARKETING POWER CORE

The goal here is not in convincing the marketing folks to believe in the customer; they already have that religion. The goal is gaining consensus with marketing to expand the scope of the work to include the process work and the integration across the silos. This can be an easy conversation to gain agreement on the need for establishing an overall customer experience (who among us has *not* had the 360-degree customer view hallucination?). But converting that conversation to realistic commitment and action is the challenge. Where will the resources come from to expand from traditional marketing work to process change and operations-oriented change? Next is the large-scale challenge of redefining the customer metrics. Customer loyalty performance is defined in many companies as loyalty programs driven by marketing campaigns. You've got to get past this limited definition and establish a set of metrics with relevance to understanding the outcomes of how you are treating your customers. And marketing needs to move past its traditional boundaries and look to the rest of the company to understand and define customer issues and priorities.

### Hope in a Case Study: How Marketing Crossed Continental's Divide with Customers

Continental Airlines' analytics group continuously understand what the customer issues are by tapping into the forty-nine thousand frontline folks who have contact with customers daily. Here is a great example of how marketing has taken supreme advantage of feedback to drive targeted actions. And in doing so, it has emerged as a key player in bringing the company silos together on behalf of the customer. Continental has formalized how it does this into a "think tank" experience across the organization.

Marketing "ambassadors" bring in flight directors, managers, flight attendants, and all other frontline personnel to provide their take on what is happening in the customer experience. There is a never-ending supply of relevant, actionable ideas that come forth and inspire the marketers to translate them to customer relationship improvement tactics. For example, there is a keen sensitivity to mollifying a customer whose flight was delayed. Thus began a series of ideas for how to soothe the travelers experiencing this frustrating situation.

After several test tries with different marketing vehicles, Continental now knows that sending out a letter of apology from the CEO has a great and genuine impact on customers. It has validated proof that this letter helps to keep customers flying with Continental. By listening to the "high touch" input from the frontline personnel, translating it to action, and then applying "high tech" analytics to determine the return on investment, marketing has connected the organization in the effort. It's hard to know if the marketing department would have ever gotten that information delivered to them about weary travels in the impassioned format that they received it during one of those think tank sessions. Survey feedback might have brought it up, but it was the pleas of the frontline that made it a priority.

The moral of the story is this. Marketing has the tools and the know-how to drive a powerful customer crusade. At Continental, it leads that crusade with the help of many others through all parts of the organization. And in doing so, customer focus becomes self-propagating as more and more people give ideas and think about the customer in preparation for their time in the "think tank" (Gulati and Oldroyd, 2005).

Marketing should emerge as the leader in bringing together all parts of the organization to do this work. Start with the definition of the customer experience. This will immediately put marketing in the role of including all parts of the organization to work through the execution implications—and well beyond the traditional marketing role. Take a breather then (a couple of weeks usually works) so the real scale of the work to do the customer thing sinks in. During this time, discuss the guerrilla metrics to strategize how the shift to the customer should take place for metrics and accountability. This will lead to the need to review the current ways that customers are measured and managed. Again, this is a comfortable space for marketing to live in. As stated previously, the biggest thing will be to determine (1) if they have the appetite to expand their role and (2) if they have the resources to make it happen.

## WHEN SALES IS THE POWER CORE

When sales is the power core, the sales force is a well-oiled machine that knows how to target and close customers. Table 2.7 identifies the typical areas of strength and vulnerabilities for companies with sales as their power core.

**TABLE 2.7. Sales Power Core Strengths and Vulnerabilities**

| | | | | | |
|---|---|---|---|---|---|
| Strength | Products, sales, services based on customer needs | Integrated customer experience | Metrics drive reliability in key interactions | Recognition based on action-able operational metrics | Clarity in handoffs and integration between silos | Customer feedback drives ongoing development |
| Vulnerability | Products, sales, services based on customer needs | Integrated customer experience | Metrics drive reliability in key interactions | Recognition based on action-able operational metrics | Clarity in handoffs and integration between silos | Customer feedback drives ongoing development |

*Note:* Typical areas of strength and customer vulnerability are shaded.

## Areas of Strength

Your sales organization has a perfected ability to position your product with differentiation that causes people to want to have it. You are tearing up the market. Through all channels, the prize is getting new customers in the door. New customers respond to your offers. You have a way of positioning your product in just the right way to close that sale. Metrics are a strong behavioral management tool that people know how to work within. They clearly understand them and know the consequences for meeting or not meeting the metrics. Great sales organizations have perfected the way to get customer feedback efficiently into the pipeline and know how to turn it into actionable steps.

## Customer Vulnerability and Hot Spots

The connectivity between the sale and the overall customer experience can be your Achilles' heel. What is the process to ensure that customers receive the information they need for the optimum use and operation of the product? If there are questions between the closing of the sale and the receipt of the product, to whom do they turn? What are the linkages between the sales department and the other parts of the organization to ensure that a smooth transition occurs as someone moves from prospect to customer? How do you foster a long-term relationship with customers who have been in the system for a while? Does the sales team consider it their job to resell the company and products when subscriptions, services, and products are up for renewal? Are they rewarded as heavily for continuing sources of revenue as bringing in a new source? The metrics that people are conditioned to perform tend to be short term and offer immediate gratification. It will be a challenge to get used to a new world where the work will pay off not in months but sometimes in years.

## A Kickstart for Integrating the Customer into the Sales Power Core

To get traction in the world of the sales power core, the first steps need to be tactical, supremely clear, and with a return as soon as possible. But first things first. There will need to be a great meeting of the minds to gain agreement that you are not only a customer acquisition company but also a customer retention company. You need to secure a strategic commitment to recognize and promote continuing sales and relationships as the same holy grail as bringing in a new account or closing a new sale (Table 2.8). The challenge here is getting the time on the agenda to discuss these shifts. Sales organizations are constantly on the move. They're in for ten minutes and then they're gone again. Pull out all the stops to get the time at the highest levels to have the discussions where this conversation will receive the attention it deserves.

You need to gain consensus that the move from being an acquisition company to a retention company includes specific new actions that the company will become good at. Lay out what these things are. Then gain agreement with leadership across the company that this is the direction you are all committed to. This will take a while. Slate at least six months to get to this point. During this period, work on defining and rolling out the guerrilla metrics (Chapter Five) to boost the shift and create more clarity for the organization on the direction.

Next, lay out the connection points between the sale and the overall customer relationship. Make this a simple exercise. I'm not talking process maps here. These are bullet points with questions such as these:

- What is the handoff between sales and service?
- What is the communication between the sale and the ownership experience?
- Where is there vulnerability in the customer life cycle?

### Table 2.8.  Sales Power Core Kickstart

1. Commit to focus on customer retention, not just acquisition.

2. Establish a defector pipeline.

3. Commit to no more than five new actions to manage retention.

4. Begin to track and manage retention performance.

5. Introduce guerrilla metrics.

Then establish something I've done with success in many different industries and cultures, which is to create a defector pipeline (Figure 2.2). This is one of the best ways I know to turn what seems like a huge concept into a plan of action for the sales organization. It engages them immediately, connects them to specific actions to take, and expands the role immediately beyond sales to relationship. At Allstate, I observed two power cores: the vertical insurance power core, followed closely by the sales power core. Knowing this, it became clear that the way to gain momentum was to rejigger approaches to the customer work in the context of sales-speak.

Here's how to accomplish this. Plot the stages of the customer experience visually so the organization can see and identify the stages. Then identify the places where your research indicates that you are vulnerable to losing customers to defection. For example, a classic area of defections for the insurance industry is right after a new policy is purchased. Connecting with customers prior to renewal is critical for resolving issues and increasing positive renewal decision making, as is reaching out to customers after pricing increases. This is all pretty commonsense stuff you could recite based on your own experiences, but it needs to be laid out clearly to encourage a large corporate entity to move in unison. By identifying these points in time along the life cycle, you can take the concept of managing the customer relationship out of the clouds and down to points that are tied directly to sales. More important, you will be able to turn that pipeline into a series of actions and tactics. For example, at Allstate, using that pipeline, we created and executed a reliable way to

## FIGURE 2.2.  DEFECTOR PIPELINE CONCEPT

**Managing Across the Defector Pipeline**

| New Customer | Service Call | Warranty Claim | Service Contract Renewal | Winback |
|---|---|---|---|---|
| Address questions or issues two weeks after purchase | Follow up after inbound service call or poor feedback on outbound survey | Follow up midstage and after claim is closed | One month prior to renewal; resolve issues before reselling | Contact customers who left to resolve their issues and regain their business |

hold the sales force accountable for contacting customers prior to renewal. These contacts put us in a position for resolving the issues that were uncovered during these calls for the individual customer. We then were able to use the information to dive into company operations, driving the issue to reoccur for other customers. Goals were set to increase the existing customer renewal rates as a result of helping customer through these calls, and targets were set for regions and the company to achieve. We created incentive for performance with what I call the "friendly horse race" by posting every region's performance so everyone could see how their across-company colleagues were doing. While this is definitely what I call a kind of starter-level of customer management, it got traction with the sales force. Before then, some had felt, to a certain degree, that the customer stuff was a lot of hooey.

## WHEN A VERTICAL BUSINESS IS THE POWER CORE

When a vertical business is your company power core, you have deep competencies in an area of business, such as hospitality, or insurance, or accounting. And you have become known in the marketplace because of this competency. Table 2.9 identifies the typical areas of strengths and vulnerabilities for companies with a vertical business as their power core.

### Areas of Strength

Companies with a vertical business as their power core are long practiced in their discipline. This competency has yielded a strong set of metrics to guide the operational execution, such as how to run a hotel front desk or how to execute a tax return. Real clarity exists around the execution of that competency. You continue to develop and stay abreast of the movement in the marketplace around your competency. The products, sales, and services created are connected to your perspective of what customers need from you based on your long tenure of executing the discipline.

For example, the deep real estate background of the founders and ensuing leadership of Coldwell Banker drove the development of the deliverables of the franchise system. The vertical discipline of the practice of real estate was the cornerstone of what was provided and how it was provided. As the market shifted and the business

**TABLE 2.9. Vertical Business Core Strengths and Vulnerabilities**

| | Products, sales, services based on customer needs | Integrated customer experience | Metrics drive reliability in key interactions | Recognition based on action-able operational metrics | Clarity in handoffs and integration between silos | Customer feedback drives ongoing development |
|---|---|---|---|---|---|---|
| Strength | Products, sales, services based on customer needs | Integrated customer experience | Metrics drive reliability in key interactions | Recognition based on action-able operational metrics | Clarity in handoffs and integration between silos | Customer feedback drives ongoing development |
| Vulnerability | Products, sales, services based on customer needs | Integrated customer experience | Metrics drive reliability in key interactions | Recognition based on action-able operational metrics | Clarity in handoffs and integration between silos | Customer feedback drives ongoing development |

*Note:* Typical areas of strength and customer vulnerability are shaded.

became more complex, Coldwell Banker brought more disciplines in to round out the business and cater to the franchisees' shifting world. For example, the largest franchisees had excelled in the practice of running a real estate business and had grown tremendously as a result. What they needed were leading-edge ideas and resources for running a burgeoning business. They needed to know how to move from running a mom-and-pop operation to running a corporate entity. They had transition issues and merger and acquisition questions. They needed help with capital investment and software and Internet listings.

These requirements expanded the scope of our role as the franchisor from providing support singular to the vertical of the practice of real estate and accelerated the position we would move to as partner and resource manager to the franchisees. So in addition to supporting the execution of the practice of real estate, we became partners with them in developing their business, no matter what the area in which they were looking for support. That inflection point required us to change our course to continue to be relevant to customers. We expanded from our vertical focus as real estate practitioners to become a customer-focused partner to ensure the growth and success of franchisees. We put the customer's success at the core. And although the real estate vertical focus that developed the business was still a critical part of the deliverables, it was just one of many things offered.

## Customer Vulnerability and Hot Spots

Companies with a strong basis in a vertical business can lose sight of the customer along the way. The thing they are best at becomes the definition of the business. An understanding of customer needs is frequently internal: the people who are the practitioners believe that they know the business so well that they speak for customers. There's a risk of looking too internally and not externally to define the deliverables. The interactions that are created are by the book for the execution of the operation. However, there may not be customer experience woven into them. For example, a travel company that knows travel can plan, execute, and deliver on ticketing efficiently. But it may have lost sight of the fact that customers look to it as a service for a family vacation. The company has inadvertently pigeon-holed itself into the role of ticket vendor.

Therefore, the metrics are around that view of what it does: measure tickets sold, revenue per ticket, ticket changes and cancels. There's much less thought (if any) on customer needs, meeting preferences for how options are presented, or changing the way the ticketing process is completed by customer travel need. Connecting the experience across the business is likely to be less than robust. In this type of environment, each of the silos tends to look at its part of the operation as separate and distinct. Execution is therefore separate and distinct. The experience is the jumble that emanates from it as the customer experiences each silo's output.

### A Kickstart for Integrating Customer Focus into the Vertical Business Power Core

There's a good first step to take here: initiate a companywide conversation to establish clarity on what you want to be to customers (Table 2.10). Since this may or may not ever have been a discussion at an operational level, it's important to bring together those who run the business into these decisions. Many times "who we are" is a marketing branding exercise that doesn't cascade throughout the organization or is ignored with the hand wave: "That's marketing's work. We're running the business." Remember learning about the demise of the railroads? Those that faded away had defined themselves as being in the railroad business. Those that moved forward thought of themselves as being in the transportation business. In order to move past the execution of your vertical business discipline, you need to recast your purpose for supporting customers. Making the operational areas part of this discussion is key to inspiring people to think about the business differently.

#### TABLE 2.10.  Vertical Business Power Core Kickstart

1. Scrub your business to understand your relevance to customers.

2. Clarify what you want to deliver and why. Gain consensus.

3. Identify the experience and top ten interactions for delivery.

4. Begin to track and manage performance in top interactions.

5. Introduce guerrilla metrics.

It's important if you're a company that has been good at one thing for a long time to take stock of your relevance to customers. Is what you're delivering keeping pace with the way their lives and needs have evolved? How do you know for sure? Is the answer, "We know because we know"? You need to really find out the answer by investing in the research and customer information to shed light on how you're doing. Have you become a product or solution in search of a customer?

Then move into the guerrilla metrics (Chapter Five). Get your arms around the ebb and flow of who your customers are and how they are responding to you. You'll then be in a strong position to define the customer experience across the organization and start the nitty-gritty work of changing what you delver and how you deliver it.

## WHEN INFORMATION TECHNOLOGY IS THE POWER CORE

When information technology (IT) is the power core, the ability to weave customer management into the organization is also a bit of a wild card based on leadership, its ability to bring the silos together, and the organizational appetite for delivering a unified platform to customers. Table 2.11 identifies the typical areas of strength and vulnerabilities for companies with IT as their power core.

### Areas of Strength

When IT is calling the shots for the business, investments are often allocated by jobs and projects and what can be executed by quarter. You have a clear idea of what you can expect to roll out each year. Metrics are specific to operational execution areas. With a strong IT power core, you could be fortunate to be far along on the continuum of collecting and using customer data and feedback. Strong IT departments push very hard for the business leaders to provide clear requirements for the application of resources. So that means that people have to justify what they're doing to get funding.

### Customer Vulnerability and Hot Spots

The great vulnerability is the decision-making process to determine what defines the company priorities. Most processes for getting IT funding aren't comprehensive to the point of seeing how the

**TABLE 2.11. Information Technology Core Strengths and Vulnerabilities**

| | Product differentiation in the marketplace | Integrated customer experience | Metrics drive reliability in key interactions | Recognition based on actionable operational metrics | Clarity in handoffs and integration between silos | Customer feedback drives ongoing development |
|---|---|---|---|---|---|---|
| Strength | Product differentiation in the marketplace | Integrated customer experience | Metrics drive reliability in key interactions | Recognition based on actionable operational metrics | Clarity in handoffs and integration between silos | Customer feedback drives ongoing development |
| Strength | Product development based on customer needs | Integrated customer experience | Metrics drive reliability in key interactions | Recognition based on actionable operational metrics | Clarity in handoffs and integration between silos | Customer feedback drives ongoing development |

*Note:* Typical areas of strength and customer vulnerability are shaded.

pieces connect to deliver the brand. They don't begin to put the puzzle together for how it connects for customers. Therefore, what gets done in any given year may not amass to something greater for customers. In this power core, as we have seen in others, there is no glue bringing the silos together to connect the operations. Each creates its own annual plan, IT requirements, and budget. The result is customers receiving uncoordinated contacts automated within databases. How many different ways for sorting customers exist in your company? How many individual databases do you think have sprouted up to run the engines for each individual department? Each one of them undoubtedly was argued for in a specific and intelligent way. The risk here is that now we're not only delivering a disjointed experience to customers, we've automated it. I call it "automating mediocrity."

## Customer Vulnerability and the CRM Hallucination

And then there's this: How many of us waited for the world to change after the ceremonial big red CRM button was pushed in our organizations? After months of mapping processes and lining up data flows and software and hardware configuration, we finally reached the day when we would achieve the hallucination of "sales force automation." There were two things that didn't get done in the process of doing all of this work. First, we didn't take the time to think up new processes designed to differentiate us for customers before we started automating. And second, we didn't work out what needed to be done to motivate the sales force or other silos to change their behavior.

Nothing changed. There was not much to motivate the sales force to remember to plug in the customer information that would pump out the answers to the "who-what-where-and-when" of the marketing campaigns that would now miraculously find the right customers to receive them. And salespeople didn't get better at customer relationships with the push of that big red button. There's no shortcut to achieving the customer focus competencies. And while IT and automating customer data is a huge part of the solution, they just can't do it alone. Ironically, most of the IT people I know realized this all along and were practically begging for more people to be involved in sorting it out. During the CRM frenzy, they were actually muttering this under their breath.

*Hope in a Case Study: Harrah's Flying Lesson*

Handling the customer work for Harrah's meant digging deep into the data to understand the customer issues, categories, and priorities for building loyalty and profitability. That information had to be translated to actions that cut across the organization, causing silos to work together in new and unfamiliar organizational configurations. Harrah's eventually got it in spades. But just like every other company, it experienced that phenomenon that occurs when the data is ready and handed over to people to begin to use for the customer work. John Boushy, Harrah's senior vice president and chief integration officer, described his emotions during this stage: "I feel a lot like I've built an F-14 and I have Piper Cub pilots to fly them, and what I'm most concerned about . . . is that they're either going to inadvertently crash and burn, or worse yet, they're going to fire a missile and . . . take down a friendly airplane" (Gulati and Oldroyd, 2005, p. 7). This was not just about using data for Harrah's. Those data would shoot off a series of actions to, for, and with customers. Too many things, and they would become ineffective. Conflicting messages would have Harrah's losing credibility with customers. It had to learn to integrate the new competencies for working across the organization before it could declare success. And that took intensive work and commitment.

There's no silver bullet here. When we are trying to source positions for clients, I'm frequently told, "Go get me someone from Harrah's!" Hiring someone who touched their data is somehow considered a silver bullet. The reason that the Harrah's project worked and continues to thrive is that it wired the necessary competencies for connected implementation into its culture, in addition to the data architecture and systems.

*A Kickstart for Integrating the Customer into the IT Power Core*

This is about the planning process, about the silos working together, and about someone integrating the pieces (Table 2.12). Trying to do this will feel like a putting together a Rubik's cube. Some of the best partners I have had in companies were in IT. The onus was on me to make them a partner by bringing them to understand what we were trying to accomplish. But once they did, there was an amazing enthusiasm for this customer work. The reason is that the data

**TABLE 2.12.  IT Power Core Kickstart**

---

1. Make information technology a partner in the customer mission.

2. Identify the customer priorities.

3. Create an oversight process for reviewing projects for IT funding.

4. Review projects in the queue to redefine priorities.

5. Establish a planning process to enable and fund priorities.

---

and levers that IT can pull can have huge benefits to the customer experience and customer profitability. They crave business requirements that amalgamate up to results, something that are often sorely lacking according to them.

The first job is making IT a true partner in this mission. People make the mistake of bringing IT in way too late in the game. Starting this process is similar to starting the process when a strong vertical is your power core. You've got to define what you're all about, and IT needs to be sitting at the table when this happens. You'll see them become animated and involved and committed to the mission. They'll begin to develop the intuition you need them to have as they become arbiters for deciding where the work falls on the priority list. As their role is elevated to custodian of the customer relationship, this power core becomes a powerhouse for driving the customer agenda.

Next, you've got to see how what has been prioritized adds up for customers. There are a slew of projects in the queue that relate somehow to customers. These are the first things to go through to see if they all connect. You won't be able to change anything for this year, but this will be a training ground for building next year's plan. Using what you've learned, create the set of customer priorities that the company commits to. Focus on the few important things versus a mountain of small projects. Urge groups to work cross-functionally to create the plans for resource requirements, including IT. And don't forget to have IT on those planning groups. Create the specific questions that the projects must meet to get slated a priority. Continue to review quarterly as you foster the advocacy and IT ownership of the customer thing.

Web-based companies are relatively far along on cracking this code. Some of the biggest are centralizing the planning process in one place, on the business side. The business planning leader and staff are selected for their ability to speak the language of the silos in their own business-speak, but also for their ability to speak with IT folks in their language. This business planning function crosses the transom of the organization, puts everything in a bucket, interprets what they think people are saying, and then translates a draft plan for the organization. From there it's on to the collaborative process of getting a plan everyone signs up for. That role in the middle of bringing the pieces together ensures that resources are optimized and efforts add up to worthwhile commitments to advance the business. These companies are putting business planning in that role of bringing the silos together to create a unified plan, similar to the CCO role.

## PLAN YOUR POWER CORE STRATEGY

Take the time to think seriously and strategically about your company power core and what its impact will be on your ability to drive the customer effort.

### POWER CORE STRATEGY STEP 1: IDENTIFY YOUR POWER CORE

The first step in creating a power core partnership is to identify your primary and secondary power cores using the form in Exhibit 2.1. Take a minute to determine what these are in your organization. To do this, review these three dimensions of your business:

1. How does your company define success?
   What are the areas of strength the company prides itself in?
   What part of the company did the leaders of the company come from?
2. What does it excel at?
   What competencies are stressed?
   What competencies do the "stars" possess?

**EXHIBIT 2.1.  Identifying Your Company's Power Core**

**1.** Check the predominant power core in your organization that drives the action.
**2.** Rank the others to identify what determines priorities, focus, and resources.

☐ **Marketing**—The marketing department "owns" the tenor and tone of the relationship with customers.

☐ **Sales**—Quarterly targets and sales goals pull the weight in the company. "The sale" is the focus, sometimes at the expense of the rest of the experience.

☐ **Product**—Resources and success metrics center on product development, not necessarily customers' focus.

☐ **A Vertical Business**—Execution in the vertical business (such as insurance) is how success is defined and measured and forms the power core.

☐ **IT**—Technology projects and planning define the priorities and staging of project completion for the business.

☐ **Other** _____

3. What are people rewarded for?
   What metrics are called for the most in meetings and during reviews?
   What are the memos, pep rallies, and bonuses about?

POWER CORE STRATEGY STEP 2:
ASSESS YOUR POWER CORE AND THE JOB AHEAD

Determining how to proceed requires you to identify not only what the sources of power are within your organization but their impact on the work. Take the time to think through the strengths and vulnerabilities in your organization. List the most recent decisions that were proposed regarding customers, and review how those decisions were made. What affected them? How much of a struggle was it to make them happen? Now think through the things that are easy to get done? How are those decisions made? Who drives those? Take stock of this information, using Exhibit 2.2 to plan your course for moving forward with your customer agenda.

**EXHIBIT 2.2. Assessing Your Power Core and the Job Ahead**

**Your Company's Power Core Is:** _____

**Impact of the Power Core: Are Customer Competencies a Strength or Vulnerability?**

| Products, sales, services based on customer needs | Integrated customer experience | Metrics drive reliability in key interactions | Recognition based on actionable operational metrics | Clarity in handoffs and integration between silos | Customer feedback drives ongoing development |
|---|---|---|---|---|---|
| ☐ Strength ☐ Vulnerability | ☐ Strength ☐ Vulnerability | ☐ Strength ☐ Vulnerability | ☐ Strength ☐ Vulnerability | ☐ Strength ☐ Vulnerability | ☐ Strength ☐ Vulnerability |
| Why? Power Core Impact | Why? Power Core Impact | Why? Power Core Impact | Why? Power Core Impact | Why? Power Core Impact | Why? Power Core Impact |

**Net Out Your Distance from the Customer—How Much Work Is There Ahead?**

## POWER CORE STRATEGY STEP 3: DETERMINE HOW TO PROCEED

The idea of the company power core needs to be explored with others in your organization. Take the time to bring leaders into the discussion of identifying the company power core and evaluating its impact on the customer mission. Use the examination of the strengths and vulnerabilities of your power core to define the scope and scale of work ahead of you in driving the customer agenda. Before you jump into the customer work, make sure that you pause to understand the realities of the pull of your company priorities. Putting yourself and your company through the paces of identifying and integrating the power core into your plan will be well worth the time you invest to ensure that you proceed in a manner that will resonate inside your organization.

## CONCLUSION

The power core is the place of strength from which the business emanates. Frequently it is the strongest skill set in the company or the most comfortable to senior executives. The power core can be the most influential in directing the silos and is one of the biggest determinants of how success, metrics, recognition, and company growth are defined:

- The power core has great influence over the complexity and scale of work required to drive customer profitability and loyalty into the business model. Complete these three steps to put you in the best position for driving the customer agenda ahead within your organization:

1. Understand the most common power cores and their strengths and vulnerabilities.
2. Identify your company power core.
3. Evaluate its impact on your ability to drive a customer profitability culture.

- The complexity of retrofitting the customer inside the company power core is dependent on how far the power core is from the customer in your organization. Distance from customer to the power core can be determined based on customer metrics and considerations that are woven into the way the power core is developed, invested in, and measured. For example, if it's full steam ahead in developing products at the expense of understanding customer needs and resolving or removing known customer irritants or issues, the distance between the customer and the company's power core is formidable, and so is the work to reconcile them.

• Distance between customer and the power core is the most important determinant in planning a realistic approach to weaving customer perspective and a focus on customer profitability into the organization. This distance says everything about how hard the job will be and how aggressively you can plan your actions. Push it too fast, and the effort will die a quick death. Go too slow, and it will surely be lost in the shuffle and sucked up into the autopiloted workings of the corporate machine.

• Because most companies don't begin with the customer experience or customer profitability as their power core, an action that is required (but little understood) is that the customer experience needs to be fit into the company's power core strategy. Understanding and reconciling the power core in relation to the customer is critical to driving customer focus, loyalty, and profitability. I believe this has become one of the reasons for failure inside corporate machines where a big hoopla has been made around customer focus with little to back it up. Integrating the customer to mesh with the power core has not happened successfully. Too often the corporation has viewed customer objectives in opposition to business objectives. Too often customer work as been seen as the extra work layered on to the business at hand of driving the strength of the corporate machine's core of power into the marketplace.

# CHAPTER THREE

# DUELING SILOS
## Competing Metrics,
## Mechanics, and Motivation

The silos don't work together well, and it's not their fault. Now that we've got that off our chest, let's move on. It's true that as soldiers of the corporate machine, we've not been compensated or rewarded to work together. But let's get over ourselves. Our inability to play together in the sandbox has largely gotten us in the bad state we're in with customers. None of us has to read yet another article or book to know that our independent ways of working aren't cutting it with customers. We all suffer from silo dysfunction.

Silo dysfunction is the inability or lack of collaboration inside the corporate machine to link together what it does for and to the customer. Working together is unnatural for people inside the corporate machine because they're simply not led or motivated to do this. Recognition has been within the individual silos. How many team awards have you seen that were truly meaningful? The metrics used to define success drive us more deeply into our own silo. Our inability to connect the operations of the corporate machine is widening the chasm between us and our customers. As we try (or don't try) to figure out how to work together, customers sink further and further out of our sight. Down they sink, into the quicksand we've created.

## THE CUSTOMER BERMUDA TRIANGLE

Customers are lost in the handoffs between our departments. We lose sight of them when they fall in the cracks between the silos.

Because we don't purposefully observe or measure how the customer traverses the jumbles of our organization, they sink deeper and deeper out of our viewfinder. And for the customer, we slip further and further away from any place they want to be associated with. We annoy customers in a seemingly orchestrated dim-witted chain of events as we make our attempts to serve them.

## STRANGER THAN FICTION (THIS STUFF REALLY HAPPENED)

An automotive company began to charge customers for loaner cars regardless of what car they had purchased, how old or new the vehicle was, or how many vehicles the customer had purchased from them. An insurance company cancelled a customer's service for nonpayment, then solicited that customer the next day for a different product. A packaged goods company sent out empty boxes to customers who had purchased out-of-stock products and then sent the product later under separate cover. Each of these occurred as the outcome of separate silo objectives intersecting and falling in an awkward heap on customers' laps.

In the automotive business, one accountant becomes a hero by running the numbers on savings to be had by disallowing free loaner cars without the benefit of knowing the customer assets they're being taken away from. In the insurance example, one part of the business makes actuarial decisions about whom they will and will not insure. Another is doing acquisition marketing to add its line of business to customers' portfolios (even those asked to leave by another part of the company). For the packaged goods company, the operations department had its incentives tied to fulfillment rates. So as long as they sent something out to the customer (even an empty box), they could say that they had achieved them. And the perplexed customers? Well, they burned up the phone lines wondering what was going on and thought twice about buying again from that company.

The grand result of all this clashing and clanging of silos coming together haphazardly is customer disbelief. "What are they thinking?" "Do they talk to each other?" and finally, "Why should I continue to take this?" The company may never know the impact of these decisions. But good customers will begin to sow the seeds of doubt as they feel that their value to the company has been downgraded. Our inability to work together has our customers voting with their feet. And they stay or leave depending on how well we're doing in ironing out our differences.

## FEET ON THE STREET: RESEARCH VALIDATION

Knowing this is happening everywhere else besides our own organization is strangely comforting. This lack of ability to work together is running rampant across our corporations. In 2003, the American Marketing Association's Survey on Leadership Challenges found the number one challenge reported by its members was "getting people to work together who have different agendas or goals." Sixty percent suffered from lack of company collaboration. Not that we needed someone to tally that sentiment up for us. We live it every day. And the outcome is the gift we give our customers.

# CUSTOMER QUICKSAND

Customer quicksand is borne out of three things we just can't seem to coordinate among ourselves:

- *Motivation—The beacons people follow.* People follow the path laid out before them by leaders that looks as if it will bring them the greatest reward. They want to know what is of the greatest importance to the organization and want to be a part of it. These messages are usually sent loud and clear, with little need to read the tea leaves and interpret what side your bread is buttered on. And although it'd be nice to think that customer focus is swimming in that butter, it's usually not the motivating factor driving people to do their job.
- *Metrics—How success is defined.* Metrics cast the culture. The metrics that are called for the most by leaders send a clear direction of where people should focus their efforts. Few organizations have clear customer metrics that elevate managing the customer to the same frenzied level as quarterly sales goals. Rarely are habit-forming customer-centric counts asked for. We simply don't keep track of customers or have metrics to demand performance improvement in this area.

- *Mechanics—The customer experience across the silos.* This is an indication of how well the corporate machine is oiled. It's about our ability for passing the customer along our organizations. *Mechanics* refer to our lack of process causing customer pain and the absolutely mind-numbing time we have in working together across the silos. Rarely can we connect the efforts to mean something to customers more than the sum of our parts. No matter how hard we try, we seem to lose the customer in the handoffs.

Here's a classic example of customer quicksand creation: the dance that goes on between sales and service. How robust is the relationship between these two groups in your company? We use Figure 3.1 to bring clarity to the relationship between sales and service in many (if not most) organizations. In my foray into the franchising business, this is what we experienced for a time between the sales force who sold the franchise and the service field force then responsible for serving them. The sales force was on-point to bring in new franchisees. Their job was to be the best closer on the planet, selling the reason that an independent and successful business should become a franchisee. Sales described services that they were sure would be available, but they didn't always bring the service people in on those conversations to ensure that what they promised could be optimally delivered. Why? Because the service field force had a mountain of other things on their plate!

When it came time to renew the franchise agreement, sales would have played a highly beneficial role by stepping back into the

**FIGURE 3.1. Classic Organizational Divide
Between Sales and Service**

Unclear customer expectations
Suboptimum customer growth or achievement of objectives
Suboptimum renewal process and outcomes

franchisee relationship to help resell the value to the franchisee. But they had already left the building. More important, we found that franchisees were creating a burgeoning need for growth through merger and acquisition. This was a skill set more naturally in the bailiwick of the sales organization than the service organization. However, there was not a graceful way to bring sales into the process, even though they would bring the greatest value, because they weren't compensated for such activity.

So here's the bottom line on what we were doing with sales and service: sales and service lacked the *motivation* to work together. We hadn't clarified or stressed not only that this was okay, it was also preferred. *Metrics* didn't push sales and service to work together for the good of the customer. We actually prevented them from working together with our compensation systems and the way we asked them about their performance. A sales and service partnership wasn't something sanctioned and ballyhooed as great for customers and the company. Therefore, the *mechanics* of working together as teams were not thought through. Sure, some folks worked together because it made sense, but this was a pretty clunky process, and they did it swimming upstream. Everyone didn't work together, and of those who did all, they did it differently.

By motivating sales and service to work together, we opened a floodgate of opportunity. Not only did the two groups of people want to work together, they thought we had been nuts because we had made rules that motivated them *not* to. To fix this, we created a partnership between sales and service where both participated in the orientation process and the new franchisee saw all of the products and services of the franchisor they just became affiliated with (Figure 3.2). This eliminated many of the hiccups we had experienced in over-promising throughout the previously disconnected sales and service process. The sales team was given the opportunity and was rewarded for growth activities for existing franchisees. And both sales and service benefited in compensation and recognition when a franchisee renewed. Besides the powerful business results, there was a great boon to the human spirit of these teams. The esprit de corps created was priceless. Most important, this showed up in spades to the franchisees, convincing them that they had joined an organization they were proud to belong to.

**FIGURE 3.2. Sales and Service:
The Revised Organizational Partnership**

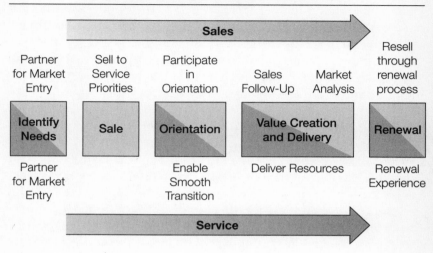

## MOTIVATION:
## THE BEACONS PEOPLE FOLLOW

There is a yearning for clarity on exactly what top executives want people to do when they say, "Go focus on the customer." Many CEOs aren't clear themselves about what they want as a destination for their brands' customer experience. They simply haven't had the chance to do the deep thinking about it. That's not to say that they aren't verbal zealots telling the company to focus on customers. It's just that it doesn't often go much past that.

### WHY MOTIVATION MATTERS

Without real clarity from leadership on what they want, it's hard for people to be motivated about doing the work. Achieving this clarity requires leaders to rethink how they plan, listen, and request information about customers.

In most companies, leaders take their information on the state of customer relationships and customer profitability in loose and anecdotal reporting from the leaders of the silos. Squeaky-wheel customer issues get their attention. And with the time pressures that leaders operate under, it is typically more efficient to deal with the parts of the organization and their accountability. This is just more achievable than seeing things from the customers' perspective—of viewing and managing the outcomes of the corporate machine collectively. People need and want a beacon from their leaders regarding customers (see Figure 3.3). They want permission to take the hill. And they want to know that when they do, they have their leader spurring them on to do the hard work that it takes to get there.

Without clarity of purpose around customers, the company's feet stay firmly planted in the realm of functional leadership. And functional leadership is part of what got us here in the first place. Each officer presents to the CEO what and how he or she is doing and the results being achieved. There is rarely a point of connection from one presentation to the next about customers or how their related issues are being handled across the silos. It's nearly impossible for the CEO to keep straight all the ways customers are being taken care of, contacted, or ignored.

## WHY PEOPLE AREN'T MOTIVATED

Two things get to the heart of the lack of motivation for doing the customer thing. First, there is no scoreboard. We don't know what we're going for, and no one's keeping customer score. Sure, the silos have all taken a stab at their own metrics related to their operations, but in terms of something everyone gets, that's pretty uncommon stuff. Will your career take an upward trajectory if you

FIGURE 3.3.  Motivation: The Beacons People Follow

| **Motivation**<br>The Beacons People Follow | **No One's Keeping Customer Score**<br>• Unclear customer profitability goals<br>• Imbalance between corporate goals and customer goals<br>**There's Not a Customer Game Plan**<br>• Recognition doesn't encourage alignment of customer deliverables<br>• Inconsistent accountability for customer experience delivery |
|---|---|

perform here? Who's keeping track to even know? Second, the game plan for customers is murky. So even if people do want to do the customer thing, it's hard to know what the "thing" is.

### No One's Keeping Customer Score

Managing customers is not placed front and center as a priority like quarterly sales. Without a simplified and focused approach on customers as assets, they continue to be considered a by-product of the work, not the reason for the work. The "real" work is the work of the silos; of the operations. But we're all missing the point here. It's the lack of keeping customer score that's pushing customers down on the agenda. And the more we don't keep track of them, the more we will stay in our mode of throwing money out the door to try to find new customers as we wonder why sales aren't what they should be. We don't know how well we're doing with our customers because we're not zealots about keeping track of them or the health of our relationship with them.

Getting to the basics of customer counting doesn't have to be rocket science. In fact it's better if it's not. Chapter Five on guerrilla metrics outlines the basics for keeping customer score. Not many organizations can answer yes to these questions:

- Does anyone know if the CEO and senior leadership care about the volumes of customers who come and go?
- Do they ask frequently for not only the numbers but the reasons behind the numbers?
- Is the customer usually part of the conversation? (And I don't mean some twenty-minute item that's wedged into a meeting because the survey results are coming in.)
- Is there a rigorous process for knowing the state of the relationship your customers have with you by trending the issues? For example, does your company track and report on customer losses on a regular basis?
- Can the CEO and leadership recite the top five things that really bother them about how your company is treating customers?
- If so, do they ask about these things regularly?
- Are the CEO and leadership an absolute broken record about determining when customer issues will be fixed and by whom?

Even if companies are running the numbers, they've got to do something with the information. Few are making that actionable. Here are a few more questions that painfully few corporate machines can answer yes to:

- Do the CEO and the other leaders make a point of rewarding and recognizing operating areas whose performance assists customers?
- Are there reliable systems for holding people accountable for customer performance? (Or is it mostly "atta boys" that happen only sporadically?)
- Has real thought been put into how these leaders can motivate people for their performance with customers?
- If the company leadership is this committed, does the rest of the company feel it and believe it?
- Does this customer commitment seem real to the organization, or does it ring hollow as some program a consultant rigged up?

### There's Not a Single Customer Game Plan

Clarity of purpose regarding customers and how to translate the mission operationally is usually very murky in most corporate machines. There is not a universal and clear understanding or belief that the customer experience and customer profitability are pivotal to the success of the organization. If there is, the clarity of what the experience should be, what the brand stands for, and the point of differentiation to customers has multiple interpretations throughout the corporate machine. Beyond that pie in the sky stuff, people around the building can't consistently cite the true value the brand brings to customers, the one or two things delivered that clearly make that point, and what keeps them on track with the work they do. Go around the halls, and ask ten people those three questions. The mix of answers may astound you.

Poor alignment across the organization stems from lack of clarity on the customer mission and how that translates to accountability and actions. People will naturally translate what they believe the brand values are based on their opinion of what's important *from their vantage point.* Frequently there's no unifying force bringing people together to translate the purpose of the company together and define the key interaction points with the customer and the objectives of each. Multiple personalities get delivered to the customer because multiple parts of the organization are defining what it should be and what the standards are for its delivery. Because of this, there is no bar of reliability for what customers can expect across the company.

There was a strong and powerful home builder I was doing some work with. At a lively workshop I stuck my microphone in a number of people's faces and asked, "What's your job?" The sales reps answered, "To get the customer to sign the contract." Another department said, "To get customers to upgrade their options." We went through the room as the departments counted off what their job was. Then I asked, "How about delivering the American dream?" Silence. (They were thinking.) Suddenly idea balloons started flying.

In that one afternoon, we got people thinking past their tick sheet of action items to the emotional journey customers go through in the process of building their house. They had a lot of work to do after that moment, but this was a jolt they needed to get everyone to start thinking about the universal purpose they all shared with every customer they touched. Try doing an exercise like this in your organization. You'll be surprised at how potent this can be in beginning to bridge the silos.

## IS YOUR GAME PLAN CLEAR AS MUD?

Want to know how connected your company is for customers? CEOs, try this: walk the halls asking two simple questions: "What's your job?" and "What's our collective job?" This walk will give you a clear picture of the experiences your customers receive from your company. With each answer, you'll hear the fractured things that people spend eight hours doing every day that end up as a jumble in your customers' laps and you'll hear the multitude of purposes that people think you're in business to accomplish.

When walking through companies doing this exercise, I write down the answers in a notebook as I hear them. At the end of the day, they are strung together to see if there's any connection to the various statements. Sometimes prior to going to a company, I ask a leadership team to do this, and we string all of their answers together in our initial meeting. A revealing picture emerges pretty quickly of what's being doled out to customers. Try it. The answers may give you pain. But sometimes that's exactly what you need to nudge that rock out of that rut it's been nesting in.

### Hope in a Case Study: How Baxter Healthcare in Germany Established Clarity and Drove Momentum

Just like those home builders, Baxter Healthcare Corporation's Germany operation would benefit from a mission boost. Leaders drove their organizations in the execution of a series of functions "to provide postoperative nutritional products to hospitals." Once patients went home, Baxter delivered a few more of the basics of home care, such as dispensing nurses or wheelchairs. It was proficient in this role, but it lacked a higher connection to customers. It lacked a greater purpose for people in the company to believe in and deliver against.

Then a light bulb went off for the country manager of Baxter Healthcare Corporation Germany. He moved Baxter past its role as product supplier to partner in meeting a greater need for hospitals and their patients. The role was redefined to be a partner with hospitals to provide rehabilitation services for their patients. Baxter Healthcare Germany redefined their purpose as providing *home recovery enhancement* for patients and hospitals. This put things in a different light. Home recovery enhancement as a purpose meant understanding customers and supporting them in their homes. It meant creating a connection and partnership with the patient, hospital, health care providers, and the people welcoming the patient home. The redefinition of what Baxter really wanted to do with and for patients created a clear and connected purpose across the organization. Now called "Home Supply and Care," this move to redirect actions from a series of tactics to meeting a customer need comprehensively became the catalyst to create a new, profitable market space for Baxter (Vandermerwe, 2004).

## BEGIN TO CLARIFY YOUR CUSTOMER EXPERIENCE

Companies don't usually share a common language for how they define the customer experience. No wonder there's a disconnect regarding who does what and where the hand-offs are. No wonder customers fall into the equivalent of the Bermuda triangle as they traverse our organization charts trying to get out of what we say we're in business to offer them.

One of the first things I try to do with organizations is to get a respected braintrust in the room to define the customer experience. Take a look at Exhibit 3.1 to get a better understanding of what I mean here.

A good first action is to gain cross-company agreement on the stages of your customer relationship. I've been in companies where marketing had a customer life cycle that they defined. Then service had a more narrowly defined set of customer stages limited to its purview of customer contacts. Operations didn't think in terms of customer stages or experiences. And sales sometimes thought in terms of customer stages, but it usually ended once the sale was made. After making the sale, they tossed the customer over the wall, and that was then end of thinking about that customer!

You need to gain cross-company agreement on the stages of your customer experience to ensure everyone's working on the same customer experience. Then define what you need to accomplish in

**EXHIBIT 3.1.  Defining the Customer Experience**

Does your company consistently define the stages of your customer experience? Use this diagram as a litmus test. Put this in front of ten people in your organization, and ask them to label the stages of the experience that you purposefully create for customers. You can also use this as a tool to develop a single continuum that you adopt as a company.

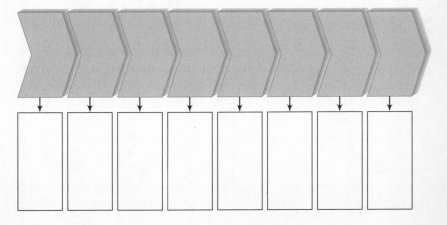

each. Use your research, foster debate, and get people to really talk about the emotions and the experience customers need to have in each stage. The whole purpose of defining the stages is to understand what the operational responsibilities are across the company to deliver a customer experience for each. Identify what hand-offs must occur across the silos and gain consensus. This is important to clarify work and agree on the deliverables. From there, make sure that cross-company leaders agree and that operating areas will adopt the stages in a unified manner of defining the customer experience. Once these stages are in place and agreed on, you'll have a far better time trying to move ahead with metrics because everyone will be working from a common framework of what metrics they're working to define and manage.

# METRICS: HOW SUCCESS IS DEFINED

Metrics are the elusive behavior-changing, culture-shifting critical dimension of driving the customer thing. If you were to ask people, "Do you have metrics around customers?" the answer you'll frequently get is a resounding yes! The problem is that there are multitudes of metrics created separately across the organization. At the end of the day, they don't aggregate up to send a message about how to treat customers or manage their profitability. And because there's no real clarity about which ones are important, leaders lack a clear platform for driving behavior change and focus on customers and customer profitability.

## WHY METRICS MATTER

People go where they smell the green. They go where they feel the glory. But glory around customer performance is just not very common. Leaders don't think to ask regularly for key customer flow metrics (customers coming in, customers going out, and the net effect). They don't hold up exceptional examples of customer leadership and applaud the performance. Rarely does anyone bring the silos together to truly define what they will mean to customers and how they will deliver it with actionable and accountable metrics. These actions are all too often considered to be extra work to the running of the business.

Integrating customer-focused compensation, recognition, and reporting on key metrics is spotty at best inside most corporate machines. Although getting to this state does take work, I can't identify one organization where focus on the customer wasn't embraced by the organization once they saw that executives were serious about it with money, resources, and the firepower of accountability and personal passion. People inside organizations want to be a part of a company that has a significant positive impact on the customers they serve. And what I have seen is usually a collective "Finally!" when people see the metrics and money finally line up with mouthing the words of customer commitment (Figure 3.4).

### Hope in a Case Study: How Enterprise Rent-a-Car Defines Success

Enterprise Rent-a-Car puts the power in customers' hands for the growth and development of the talent that runs this company. Enterprise surveys millions of customers every year to ensure that the focus and accountability is on serving them. If customer ratings are low for an Enterprise branch, no one in that branch, including vice presidents, gets promoted. This is absolutely motivating behavior. Because it is crystal clear about what they have to do (everyone starts out washing cars and listening to customers at Enterprise locations), managers and leaders have it in their best interest to hire the right people and develop them to deliver a great customer experience. Is this brand of motivation and accountability working? It sure seems so. In 1980, revenue was $78 million. They've grown now to over $7 billion (Powers, 2004).

#### FIGURE 3.4. Metrics: How Success Is Defined

**Metrics**
How Success is Defined

**Power Core Impact on Customers**
- Sets the tone for the customer experience
- Can compromise customer focus competencies

**Disjointed Goals and Metrics**
- Varied and uncoordinated metrics
- Lack of customer experience metrics
- Recognition out of sync with customer priorities

## WHY METRICS ARE MURKY: THE IMPACT OF THE POWER CORE

The base of power in your organization sets the tone for what people care about for what they pay attention to. All eyes seek approval from the power core. As seasoned veterans of the corporate machine, we've learned which side our bread is buttered on and know where to perform for greatest glory and compensation. If the power core isn't necessarily customer-centric, its pull drawing people's attention elsewhere will play havoc with integrating the customer work. Even those brave souls pushing grassroots reform will usually have to fall in line when their pay and ability to rise within the company become compromised.

Strong, honest conversations must be held with those who lead within the power core to lay out the customer implications with existing power core priorities. Remember that it doesn't work to try to change the power core. It is what it is from history and the growth and development of the company. Thinking it can be morphed into something else is like a woman thinking she can change a man after she marries him. And we all know how well that works! Power core leadership can and will integrate the customer work into the business plan when it is delivered in a pragmatic way, with clear tactics and a clearly understood payoff.

## A POWER CORE DANCING LESSON

To dance with the power core, you've got to know its priorities. And you've got to get the dirt of the business under your fingernails. This means that if you don't know the inner workings of the business, you'll get laughed out of the room. This might not happen to your face, but lack of credibility is the death knell to someone wanting to drive change. So here's a power core dancing lesson that you might find handy.

### Step One: Know the Business of the Business

If you're in the automotive business, for example, go to dealerships, spend the day in the service department, and learn how to fulfill a warranty request. Read everything you can get your hands on and become a student of the business. Make the rounds of the power core leaders. Ask them what they need to accomplish in the next six months and what the business needs to do to flourish over the next year and the next five years. Ask them what metrics they use to keep score and what the five most important places are that they want to know about when they get status reports. If they state that the customer is a priority, drill deep to ask what they mean by that and how they measure performance and the business around customer treatment.

You need to get past the superficial hand wave here and push for answers with substance. (This is what I mean by getting dirt under your fingernails.) Find a way to get these kinds of meetings regularly or get a seat at enough meetings where you can surmise this information. The key is to be able to encapsulate the business and power core priorities in your own words, and you've got to get it absolutely right.

### Step Two: Outline Customer Implications in Current Power Core Priorities

It is very important that the customer implications of company decisions be brought to the forefront. If you can create an elevated understanding of the impact of business decisions on customers, people will begin to understand what the job of driving customer focus really means. The implications have to be clear so everyone grasps them the moment they are laid out. Here are two examples illustrating how to explain the impact of their decisions to power core leaders:

- "The emphasis on locking customers into a five-year contract puts sales reps out of touch with customers for extended periods of time. Such a long-term commitment has the high potential to drive customers away to more flexible options for their service providers."
- "There is unbalanced focus of new product development versus resolving issues in existing products."

### Step Three: Address the Bottom Line

Proving the return on investment (ROI) of better customer experiences and eliminating customer issues will increase the bottom line. This is critical in partnering with the power core. However, the key here is to engage them in a partnership in gathering this information. I've found that sometimes collecting the bad news first and then delivering it right between the eyes of the power core leaders does not have the right end result. Here are some examples:

- For the five-year service contract illustration, run the numbers to see the impact of customers who have not renewed since the policy began. If this is a new policy, talk to customers about their intentions. Tape incoming calls into customer service where customers explain their annoyance with the situation and play these back frequently to the audience that needs to hear the words of customers.
- For the product development example, graph the trends of the issues and problems around existing products. Show the correlation between escalating unresolved problems and a northbound problem trend line showing no signs of declining. If you've got a robust database and complaint-handling system, you're in even better shape because then you can assign complaints to customers and point out how the impact of those customer complaints shows up in buying patterns for repeat business.

*Step Four: Partner with the Power Core to Identify New Metrics*

Partner with the power core to share the leadership of establishing customer accountability metrics. Take a systematic approach and engage the power core with relevance to the business and process. Definitely leave the jargon outside the door. The new customer-based metrics should be practical, tactical, and flexible. This is a key to moving forward. The key is to create a partnership where the power core begins to seek your involvement. You want the power core leaders to lean on you to add the missing dimension of all things customer oriented.

## WHY METRICS ARE MURKY: THE SILOS HAVE DISJOINTED GOALS AND METRICS

"Score" means different things to different silos. Each area of the company has its own operating plan that dictates its successes. This seems natural, except that it leaves a mess of disjointed metrics that don't add up to a good experience for customers. These disjointed goals and metrics come as a direct result of the lack of clarity across the organization. This breeds a lack of alignment around what's important to measure regarding customers. And true to operational form, separate silo-specific operational objectives are created. These usually don't link the parts of the organization together to understand the net effect on the customer relationship.

Success metrics are typically operational goals rather than customer goals that tie back to the flow of customers, the profitability of customers, and reasons for retention or defection of customers. The president and other executives are put in the position of gauging performance standards from these separate goals and metrics. So naturally metrics are around the operations of the business, not the customer. There's no clear way to map the customer experience end to end to define if the company's doing well, great, or poorly. Usually a common customer language to define customer relationship and profitability success is lacking or spotty at best. You'll find hot spots of zealots who've gotten customer focus and created a language around the customer, but it's not fully integrated or accepted as the common way to talk about the business.

Business objectives tracked at the highest levels and defining success for the company are more often than not inward looking. Typical objectives tend to be about the business outcome, not how to achieve customer outcomes. Among the outcomes I've seen measured are time to market, sales for the quarter, number of units sold, and number of units deployed. It's possible to identify the customer objectives that should also be considered, measured, and rewarded in defining the outcome for the business, but historically these process or customer experience metrics haven't been considered. It's a lot easier to put up the flag of success on how many widgets you've sold versus if they were sold in a meaningful way to customers. It's a lot simpler to rank sales personnel by those who sold most to those who sold fewest rather than by those who served customers from best to last. Merging these two is critical to digging the customer out of the quicksand.

Finally, the organization usually does not have a grasp on how to measure the movement of customer behavior down the relationship cycle with the company. Without someone pushing everyone together to understand how to define and measure these critical points, they will not be measured. Cross-functional metrics are unnatural to the corporate machine. As a result of disjointed goals and metrics, the brand and customer profitability are eroded, and customers leave due to service failures and lack of differentiation. What the corporate machine spits out is an unreliable customer experience attributed to these things:

- Separate silo-specific operational objectives
- Progress reports by operation versus by customer group or customer experience
- Inconsistent operational metrics created separately
- Little collaboration on companywide customer objectives and what that means operationally
- Lack of comprehensive metrics
- Lack of understanding what motivates the customer to increase their purchase behaviors, company loyalty and profitability
- Lack of measurement of customer profitability or customer metrics

### A Case Study: Continental's Mixed Message Metrics

To cut costs in the 1990s, Continental installed a series of metrics, recognition, and incentives. In one particular effort to cut fuel costs, no one connected the dots to understand the effect those metrics would have on pilots, customers, and Continental's ground crew. How much fuel cost reduction was achieved is uncertain. What is certain is that the effort cost Continental in decreased employee morale increased spending to allay the customer aggravation which ensued.

To execute their plan for fuel-cost reduction, management tied pilot bonuses to keeping the burn rate of engine fuel below a specified level. This did motivate the pilots to reduce their fuel consumption, but it had the side effect of motivating pilots to do certain things that affected customers. Pilots were skimping on air-conditioning to reduce fuel consumption. They were flying slower to use less fuel, which messed up customers' schedules, getting to their destinations late and making them angry, especially if they missed connections. As a result, the gate people had to work harder and longer to assuage overheated, cranky customers. Gate personnel's hours increased because planes weren't on schedule. And the kicker was that Continental spent more money to reconnect customers with other carriers due to missed flight connections. Continental reversed much of this during their heralded turnaround in the mid-1990s. But the lesson learned here is this: metrics without understanding how they course through the organization to the customer may end up giving you a result you had not intended. There needs to be someone who thinks through your metrics (especially the internally driven ones such as cost cutting) to determine how they affect decisions and to ensure you know how they end up in the customers' lap. Don't pull the trigger until you do (Brenneman, 2000).

## MURKY METRICS MAKING A MESS: CONFERENCE BOARD FINDINGS

The Conference Board wanted to know how aligned companies and their employees were able to translate strategies into plans and metrics and how they operated. It surveyed eighty-six corporations to find out what was going on in their 2003 strategic business alignment survey (Dell and Kramer, 2004). The results won't surprise you: 76 percent of the companies surveyed say that they consider alignment to be extremely important. However, just 39 percent believed they had strong alignment inside their company. All the respondents agreed that leadership support and engagement are keys to ensuring alignment. However, only one-third even expected or tried to get alignment before acting. Why? Because it's just too hard to do it. One-quarter of the respondents said that the organization made it too hard to achieve.

So it will take some diligence to get people to measure something related to customers and get the alignment to drive wholesale change throughout the company. This is not impossible, but I do think that people don't go into this work with their eyes open. And when they hit the brick wall of trying to align all the different factions, they abandon the task rather than pressing on (CEOs can help immensely by staying in the game and helping with the heavy lifting in this effort).

## HOW DO THE SILOS IN YOUR COMPANY DETERMINE WHAT TO MEASURE?

Each silo probably determines what it should measure based on what it deems to be crucial for the function of its operation. These metrics may or may not be tracked and measured in a consistent or reliable way. There is typically not a great understanding of which metrics are key to driving customer loyalty or profitability or if the right ones are even being measured. Moreover, the operational areas are rarely, if ever, linked together to present a comprehensive view of how the corporate machine is delivering to customers. The random experience that ensues is due to the following four factors:

- Every silo chooses the metrics it thinks are important.
- Each chooses its own standards of what defines great, good, and poor performance.
- Metrics typically aren't gauged, created, or tracked based on customer requirements.
- The linkages between the metrics aren't created so the company can see its overall performance in delivering a customer experience.

## A KICKSTART FOR CUSTOMER GOALS AND METRICS

The silos are going to have their own operating metrics to run the business, but you also need a set of metrics that runs across the company to tie everyone to the customer experience. A good way to begin doing this is to identify the top ten to twelve customer interactions with attached performance metrics you have to get right every time (Exhibit 3.2). Identify these across the customer

**EXHIBIT 3.2. A Kickstart for Customer Goals and Metrics**

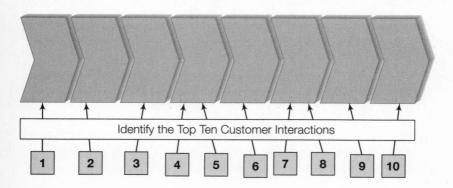

Identify the Top Ten Customer Interactions

| 1 | 2 | 3 | 4 | 5 | 6 | 7 | 8 | 9 | 10 |

continuum, and make them the first set of metrics that operations across the company have to work on together to achieve performance targets.

## MECHANICS: CUSTOMER TREATMENT ACROSS THE SILOS

The grand outcome of how we operate inside the typical corporate structure is the random and inconsistent experiences delivered to customers. It is our organization charts that emerge most clearly to them when they do business with us, certainly not a unified brand experience.

### WHY MECHANICS MATTER

Our lack of a unifying purpose for customer treatment across the silos and hodgepodge of inconsistent metrics means that different parts of the organization deliver to customers at varying levels of performance. Service providers and everyone else throughout the company can't get a grip on what their personal performance is supposed to be. Especially those at the front line are subject to performing based on their personal skill set and interpretation of what's important. And as we all know, people have better days than others. Without the guideposts of metrics to keep us in line, the service delivered frequently goes up and down based on the mood, competence, or opinions of the person interacting with the customer. This is what I call biorhythmic service because the front line, not the company, individually makes decisions on what the brand will mean to customers, and that changes from day to day, from person to person. There is no process inside organizations to work together and figure out how to move the customer through an experience versus a tour of our disjointed and dysfunctional organization charts. Being able to coordinate the mechanics of the corporate machine across the machine is important for two reasons: (1) to assign accountability and connect the functions of the operation that are delivered disjointedly to the customer today and (2) to bring the silos together to use annual planning in a strategic manner to drive the management of customers as assets (Figure 3.5).

**FIGURE 3.5. Mechanics: Customer Treatment Across the Silos**

| | |
|---|---|
| **Mechanics** Customer Treatment Across the Silos | **No One Owns the Customer** • Silo dysfunction—customer experience breakdown • Fractured and incongruent experience—brand erosion **Annual Opportunity Missed** • Lost strategic opportunity to manage customer asset • Cobbled-together plan doesn't target highest priorities |

## Mechanics Matter to Prevent Customer Experience Breakdown

In order to prevent customer experience breakdown, there needs to be an enterprise view of what is being delivered and a way to bring the pieces together in the development and execution of the customer experience. In most companies, each silo owns its cordoned-off part of its contacts with customers, but that's it. This leads to the fractured and incongruent experiences we amalgamate on the customer. And that's what it turns out to be for customers, isn't it? Today it's not a customer experience we deliver but rather an organizational amalgamation. Each operating area certainly needs its own goals and metrics for its function, but there must also be a connecting tissue of metrics that keeps track of how the customer traverses the operations. Most companies don't think out these factors. As a result, the brand experience becomes the sum of all of the parts—some good and some not so good. Without bringing everyone together to create a common set of customer experience metrics, companies continue to deliver random and defaulted experiences. And this absolutely erodes a customer's ability to define what sets one company apart from another. Most companies inflict customer pain. Sometimes the end game for customers becomes merely to pick the one that will inflict the least pain.

### Hope in a Case Study: The Sum of 3M's Parts

3M is a perfect example of a great company doing a bunch of great things separately. We can take solace in the fact that even this innovative company had a hard time creating a coordinated customer experience. But don't breathe a sigh of relief too fast; in 1997 it also committed to fixing it (Sawhney, 2001). To a large part, 3M thrived in its structure as a set of separate entities with intense focus on what it created. 3M leaders attribute this intensity to their ability to do the deep thinking that has put the corporation on the map with its innovative products. But the clanging and clashing of the individual units showed up in classic fashion at the point of customer interaction.

Sales reps from different areas each called on customers independent of one another, causing duplicative calls with different requirements. It is no surprise that each of these independent units collected customer information differently, all in different databases that didn't talk to each other. Each of these separate databases had to be managed separately. And customers couldn't understand why this company of deep thinkers couldn't coordinate schedules or databases.

The Internet experience exacerbated this phenomenon. The Web site reflected the organization chart, with each area setting up its part of the site. For example, a health care customer needed to navigate through the separate sites, log-ins, registrations, and password requirements of 3M's pharmaceutical, medical-surgical, medical specialties, and office supply divisions. Naturally, no cross-over of customer issues existed, so when customers called in for customer service help, they had to repeat who they were, what they needed, and what had happened in the past as if they were a stranger to the company (Edwards, 2000).

3M did step up and link all of this together beginning in 1997. It synchronized the customer experience and the company found a way to show a consistent face to customers through connecting databases, intelligence, and actions. As a result, you can't tell 3M's organization chart anymore by viewing the Web site. Although silos still exist to drive that creativity, they no longer impose themselves on customers.

## Mechanics Matter to Wire In Accountability for the Customer Experience

Picture this: a customer calls in with a question and concern about a notice she received from her bank. Customer service answers the call. The rep doesn't know the answer and doesn't have the authority to help her. So he tells the customer to call something called "bank operations." The customer is transferred to someone who really isn't set up to routinely answer customer calls and gets handed off again in a grand sequence of customer hot potato. After being bounced out of customer service, she is met with one of three endings in this scenario: (1) someone answers the call but can't help her; (2) she is passed on to someone who doesn't answer and therefore has to leave a message or the administrative assistant of the person who last handed off the customer takes a message; or (3) she is told someone will get back to her. Will someone? Maybe. Maybe not.

The bottom line is that *no one owns the customer* in the corporate machine. This customer hot potato occurs for a couple of reasons. Operationally, it can occur because the centralized system for taking customer calls is based on the old-school routing system. A customer's call is answered, just so the issue (not the customer) can be catalogued and put in a queue. It can also occur because the organization has a system that is no system: pass around the customer until someone relents and talks to the poor customer. The biggest question here is why those systems haven't been abolished. The answer is that owning customer problems and the customer experience is not deeply rooted in most cultures. This has to do with both culture and translating that culture to operational accountability. As you could see in the phone example, it's in the handoffs and the lack of an aligned approach to meeting customer needs that things fall apart.

The lack of motivation behind wanting to fix these things frequently is due to the lack of clarity that exists inside the corporate machine in understanding the revenue importance in keeping and increasing the number of existing customers and in understanding that simple customer interaction failures can drive even the most profitable customers away after years of service. The silos simply haven't internalized that they must own accountability for customer profitability through the customer experiences they have a hand in delivering. Customer ownership is unfortunately frequently relegated to the customer service department, which is the last stop for most free-falling customers on their way out the door.

This case study that follows is particularly useful to leaders and organizations contemplating this process because it's an eye-opener. Unless you go into the area knowing that it's this much work and committing to do it, you should reconsider.

## Hope in a Case Study: Royal Bank of Canada's Silo Connection

The Royal Bank of Canada (RBC), like most other organizations, was built to focus on operational execution or lines of business. But customers wanted the bank to reorder what it delivered according to *their* priorities. They didn't want to have to traverse RBC's organization chart every time they wanted to get something done. So RBC committed to figuring out how to work across the traditional execution areas of the business to offer integrated customer solutions. To make this happen, leaders executed a series of actions to ensure that employees understood and made the commitment, and were clear how they needed to work differently.

Like any other company that commits to working across the company for developing improved customer solutions, there was a period of confusion. People knew how to win inside their own operating area and had concerns that they wouldn't be able to perform in this new configuration.

Here's what Gordon Nixon, RBC's chief executive, did to turn the tide:

- Collaboration at the highest levels. From the start, he enlisted his top executives, called the Group Management Committee (GMC), to develop a statement of what they were trying to do. This went out to everyone in the company.

- Widespread leadership discussions. RBC Leadership Dialogues were initiated and run by Nixon and two members of his GMC. Thirty cross-company leaders were invited at a time, rotating through leadership ranks. They discussed the challenges, recognized issues, and opened them up to discussion.

- Companywide inclusion. A quarterly conference call with thousands of employees was held.

- Issues were dealt with outright. Task forces were created to work through the issues that naturally erupted at the personal and business levels.

- Leaders were developed for the new approach. Development of executives and new skills was focused on at the corporate level, given to GMC members to manage and be custodian of.

- Accountability was rewired. For a time until the reward and recognition system was changed, people continued to focus on their own independent goals and work independently. Once the system was reworked, behaviors changed because there were incentives that motivated the change and signaled its importance (Ready, 2004a).

Many companies want to leapfrog past the basic blocking and tackling of doing the everyday things right and move on toward loyalty programs. This just won't cut it. If a company can't get the basics down in the delivery of its products and services, other efforts will fall on the deaf ears of customers. How much beneficial impact is a points program going to have if you put a customer through an elaborate labyrinth of customer hot potato every time that person contacts you? The customer experience that will get you the most confidence with your customers is to get the basics right. First earn the right to customers' confidence and then move on from there (Figure 3.6). You've got to knit together the series of contacts you have with customers to bring a sense of reliability in what they can expect from you. Only after you've gotten past this hurdle can you go on to the highly touted but rarely achieved avenues of building a personal relationship with customers, where they feel strongly that they will advocate that others purchase from you. In my experience, that was one of the unfortunate fallouts of the CRM boom. The frenzy over CRM obscured the understanding that the blocking and tackling had to be done first.

## FIGURE 3.6. The Reliability Continuum

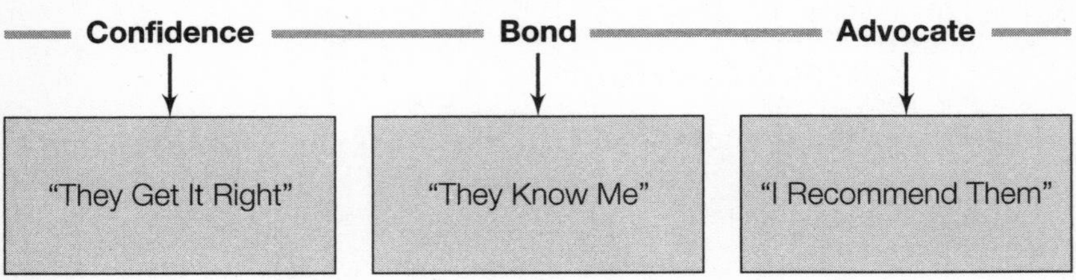

| Confidence | Bond | Advocate |
|------------|------|----------|
| "They Get It Right" | "They Know Me" | "I Recommend Them" |

## Why Metrics Matter: There's No Annual Planning for Customers as Assets

Ah, the joy of the annual plan. Those last three months before the fiscal year ends are spent rushing about trying to decide what you'll do next year. Each silo pushes its numbers around for head count, capital expenses, vendors, and programs. Programs? Is this where the customer comes in? Or is it vendors? How does all of this tie together across the organization? Tilt. It doesn't. This is perhaps one of the greatest missed opportunities regarding customers (Figure 3.7). Everyone's budgets and plans get cobbled together. We miss the opportunity to strategically forge ahead on key things that would have an impact for customers. Instead we do a multitude of separate things which don't connect. And therefore, neither does the customer experience. Ask yourself these questions to see if you're capitalizing on this annual planning opportunity to manage customers as assets:

- Do you time research and customer feedback results so you can use this information for planning?
- Do you make sure that the customer research you have is relevant to the problems you are trying to solve? Having customer research is great, but it can mislead and misguide the allocation of valuable resources if it's contorted to give

FIGURE 3.7.  Currently Ignored Annual Opportunities

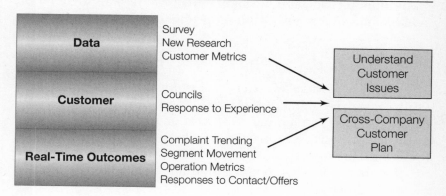

the answers to something different from what it was created
to capture.

- Do you do a loss review prior to planning to know which customers left and why?
- Do you evaluate the trending of customer issues prior to planning to identify priorities?
- Do you take stock of the segments of your customers and their
profitability prior to planning?
- Do you convene a forum of cross-company groups to determine the customer priorities for the upcoming year?
- Do you take the results of those forums and have them drive
annual plan investments?

Does any of this sound familiar? It's likely that the mad dash that
has caused annual planning in your organization is (like that of most
other companies) partly to blame for the lack of focus on the customer. It's a bit odd that in all the hand waving about strategy, a company's biggest asset, its customer base, is not yet viewed as critical
when it comes to the annual plan and what to invest in.

# CONCLUSION

Until corporate citizens are motivated and measured to work
together, they won't make the effort to get the mechanics of the
customer experience right. Customers will continue to be sub-
jected to the defaulted experience of the silos clashing and clanging together. The corporate machine must learn to incorporate
motivation, metrics, and mechanics to move the silos together on
behalf of customers and customer profitability.

## MOTIVATION

The ability of leaders to inspire and motivate an organization to
think collectively about its purpose for and with customers is critical to this work. Segmenting the operation into the silos may seem
a manageable way to a top executive, but it's not the way the customer sees the world. Look for these two symptoms in your organization to decide if you've got a motivation challenge around the
customer thing:

- You're not keeping customer score. It's not at the top of executives' talk track to ask about customers lost or saved and the reasons.
- You lack clarity of purpose of what you will achieve for customers. Everyone's doing his or her own thing. If you walk through the company and ask ten different people what the company is supposed to mean to customers, you'll get ten different answers.

## METRICS

People keep score on what's important to the company based on what the leaders ask for and care about the most. Ultimately this translates to the metrics you follow and track and the impact they have in people's paychecks. Two things tend to generate metrics that don't translate well for customers:

- The power core. Depending on what it is and its priority, the power core will play lead dog in determining what metrics people go after.
- Silo metrics are naturally built in individual vacuums. Without real clarity and someone pushing to bring people together in at least a high-level set of unified metrics, this will continue.

## MECHANICS

The corporate machine is clear about how to drive individual and departmental accountability. But the customer gets lost between the silo walls:

- No one owns the customer. There is no graceful way to execute the handoffs. The lack of motivation for performing cross-functionally ensures that not a lot of time is spent thinking about those handoffs and their impact on customers.
- Annual opportunity missed. We need to take the time to weave in managing customers as assets. A new section on the balance sheet needs to be added to force us to cover this area and be accountable for it across the organization. Then we'll see a new kind of annual planning.

## ARE YOU SLIPPING INTO CUSTOMER QUICKSAND?

Take a gander through the quicksand scenarios in Figure 3.8 to see if you recognize your company and your own leadership tendencies.

To figure where to go from here, first determine if you suffer from silo dysfunction. The next step is admitting it. And then finally, it's your choice to decide if you have the corporate tenacity to do something about it.

FIGURE 3.8.  Signs of Slipping into Customer Quicksand

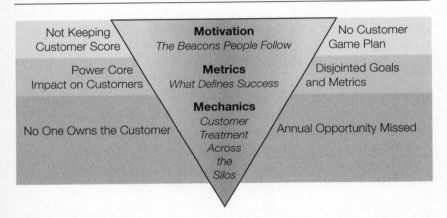

# PART TWO

# WRESTLING WITH CUSTOMER LEADERSHIP

# CHAPTER FOUR

# LEADERSHIP GUT AND GUTS
## Real Passion or Hand Wave

This work won't budge from hand wave to action without two leadership attributes: gut and guts.

**Gut.**

*Gut* leaders know the higher purpose they want to have for their customers. They have sharpened radar for seeing what's right and wrong and what's getting in the way. They've got an internal compass and instinct for how to get there. And they have a clear line of sight for where they want to take the company.

**Guts.**

Leaders with *guts* will absolutely take the hill to get there. They will make the customer agenda a priority of the organization. There will be no settling for mediocrity. They've got the chops to stick their neck out and will do it to make things happen. They will push the company and push back on the company until they get it right. Customer priority and issues will be known, understood, and thought about at all levels, straight up to the board.

The fact of the matter is that customer issues have still not earned a place in the boardroom. In fact, customer management issues being kicked upstairs are on the decline. Need proof beyond the experience of your own organization? A *Harvard Business Review* article reported on the level of exposure the boards of thirty large U.S. companies had with marketing issues or customer management (Court, Crawford, and Quelch, 2004). Among the companies surveyed, over a third of them said that their boards spent less than 10 percent of their time on customer-related or marketing issues.

Leaders who own the customer agenda don't stand for that. They elevate high-priority customer issues to the critical level, and they get their boards close to the customer and to understanding the investments required to keep them close. But this remains the exception and not the rule. That survey further reported that only a few of those thirty boards are ever in contact with major customers through visits or one-to-one contact. In the cases where customer councils exist, that face-to-face contact rarely exists in the boardroom. "Customer" is something which might only be discussed in an anecdotal fashion.

## GOTTA GET THE GUT

Leaders with a well-honed gut response have a clear idea about what they want to accomplish with customers. They've thought about it, stewed about it, and suffered over it. It is an idea that swims around in their consciousness. They don't relegate it to marketing. And they don't assume the silos will take care of bringing it together for customers. Their idea of what and how they will define themselves in the marketplace is so well understood that they become a lightning rod for the company. There is an internal compass inside their head that guides reactions to ideas and proposals. They use that skill like a sculptor, chiseling out the company's customer relationship by steering and driving decisions throughout the company.

Back in the late 1980s, Lands' End was asked to speak at the Direct Marketing Association's annual conference. Until that point, we had declined this type of invitation. We didn't want to risk clouding our thinking by peering over our shoulder at the competition. We sought to design the future for customers based on our own unique vision and promise. For whatever reason, we agreed to go, and I was tapped to speak. There must have been two hundred people squished inside to hear how Lands' End got close to customers. We offered up what I thought was a pretty benign prescription . . . unless you had the leadership gut and guts to make it live. Here are a few of the tidbits I passed along that day that came from our founder, Gary Comer:

"Think small."

"Worry about being better; bigger will take care of itself."

"Think one customer at a time, and take care of each one the best way you can."

After that, there were a lot of questions from the audience. One still sticks with me because of the reaction to the answer: "How do you make these decisions on what to do for your customers?" I answered, "Gut." And often that was the case. Comer trusted his gut and made it all right for all of us to do the same. For example, one time we put together a piece called "Out Our Way." It was an introduction to the company that went out in people's first orders. Comer was ready to move on it, but the circulation people wanted to test its effect on orders first. The numbers came in, and the piece had little impact on order size. "Do it anyway!" Comer said. His gut was talking, and it said, *"This is something we've got to do."* He wanted people to know who Lands' End was on a personal level. His gut told him that the return on that printing and ink would come in ways that could not be measured by average order size. And it did.

That piece humanized Lands' End at a time when customers still had some questions about catalogue shopping. Another great story is about the woman who had bought a garment from us with a red dye in it. The dye transferred the color from the garment to the new leather interior of the customer's vehicle. The customer service rep authorized the replacement of the leather interior— and was praised for it! These folklore stories among many others were widely circulated. They clarified that we were right to trust our gut and make decisions based on our instincts of doing the right thing. People could clearly understand these examples and model their behavior. Comer's gut was very important to Lands' End's growth in the marketplace.

## SALMON LEADERSHIP: CUSTOMER LEADERS WITH GUTS

Customer leaders need the guts of a salmon. Some might say delirium. Think about it. The salmon goes head first against the current. It pushes on to its destination, unscathed by resistant forces. The salmon leader turns the company from facing itself to facing its customers. Salmon leaders use business meetings to guide and challenge people to understand how what they're doing affects the customer. Salmon leaders constantly ask if the tactics being served up are connected across the organization. Salmon leaders are not afraid to trade short-term profits for long-term gains with customers. They know how to explain the commitment to the board, the stockholders, and the company so that they transfer this clarity to everyone else.

One day Gary Comer went into his office, and he emerged carrying with him a yellow pad on which he had written "The Lands' End Principles of Doing Business." These were an important beacon for all of us. They have stood the test of time and remain on the Lands' End Web site. There are eight principles covering product creation and pricing, why returns are accepted at any reason for any time, and the power of the guarantee (Exhibit 4.1). The guarantee alone was an amazing lightning rod to help us know what we had to do. When you tell customers that there are no ifs, ands, or buts about the service they'll receive from you, you'd better deliver. The "Principles of Doing Business," went even further to guide us as they translated Gary's gut and guts about the business into actions we could follow. It galvanized us as an organization.

## REAL PASSION OR HAND WAVE?

Too many times when I've been handed the customer thing by the president of a company, I'd swear a box gets checked on a to-do list next to the word "customer thing." I have repeatedly seen this

---

**EXHIBIT 4.1  The Lands' End Guarantee**

---

**Guaranteed.Period.**

The world is full of guarantees, no two alike. As a rule, the more words they contain, the more their protection is limited. The Lands' End guarantee has always been an unconditional one, It reads "If you are not completely satisfied with any item you buy from us, at any time during your use of it, return it and we will refund your full purchase price."

We mean every word of it. Whatever. Always. But to make sure this is perfectly clear, we've decided to simplify it further.

**GUARANTEED.PERIOD.®**

---

huge sigh of relief come from executives when they feel they've pushed it off their plate and onto mine. The tried-and-true formula we've all seen when there's a problem area in a company is this: hire someone, staff up, and let them run. But just throwing head count won't cut it for this work. This isn't the same as telling someone to build a great advertising campaign or rev up the sales force or build a great new product to sell on their own. This work cannot be held inside a single department in the organization. It will cut its way across the organization, getting in people's stuff and stirring up the pot. This work will challenge conventional thinking about how to approach the business and about what's important to manage and measure. It's big—really big. And the executive sponsor has to know what he or she is signing up for and agree to be in for the duration. And that's the rub: in the quest to check the customer problem off the list, there's usually not enough thought given to what's being signed up for.

Here are the high-level items you must know about when thinking about taking this journey with a company. These are the questions to ask your leaders or yourself about the intensity of your gut and guts to take this work forward. Are you ready to sign up for the work? Knowing what you're taking on and still wanting to do it will be required . . . and that takes guts.

## ARE YOU CLEAR IN YOUR MIND ABOUT WHAT YOU WANT TO ACCOMPLISH?

Why is it that you are pushing the customer agenda now? If it is an old subject you're bringing up again, think through how you will make it work this time. Have clarity on where you want to take this. You don't have to have all the fine points figured out, but you do need to be clear enough that people understand what you're asking them to sign up for. Lay out this commitment with your leaders. Reconcile the issues, and gain agreement to move ahead.

Different parts of a company have different answers for what they are trying to accomplish with their customers. How many times do you hear the answer that even *who* the customer is becomes open to debate? How can a company expect to be in sync under these conditions? Take the time to do this. Enlist marketing and the gurus to help you think it through, and make sure you include the front line. Get customers to give you feedback. And do the deep contemplation about what you want the business to be to customers.

People respond to a lightning rod message that will give meaning to their work. The clearer you can be here, the better the results will be. The less you leave open to interpretation, the less others will try to read your mind, leaving them to fill in the gaps with their own view. And don't interpret this to mean that you don't want people's creativity in getting you to the end game. It's just that you've got to be perfectly clear on where you're headed. The more cryptic and loose your translation is, the more versions of your company your will customers receive.

A mentor once quoted Benjamin Franklin to me when he said: "I would have written you a one page letter if I had the time, but instead here's three." It takes longer to crystallize your thoughts into meaning that can be delivered simply. It means that you have processed your intentions down to their critical points. Take the time to do that. Write that one-pager for your company to follow. They'll thank you for it, and you'll get a return from that investment over and over again in saved time and resources and course corrections.

### Hope in a Case Study: Samsung Clarity in the Customer Mission

Samsung is no shrinking violet when it comes to building their brand and delivering it to customers. In May 2005 it was recognized for the fourth consecutive year by Brand Keys, Inc. as the manufacturer whose devices consumers intended to buy over the next eighteen to twenty-four months. Samsung also holds the top spot for customer satisfaction among cell phone manufacturers for the second year in a row according to the American Customer Satisfaction Index (SprintUsers.com, 2005; Conlon, 2002). So when its leaders decided to turbopower their effort to build even closer relationships with customers, they were postured well. They have a sort of chant that everyone seems to know. It starts with the acronym CRM, which to Samsung means, "Customers Really Matter." Anyone around the company can recite back not only that little ditty but what it means in particular to Samsung: *Every form of customer interaction and every touch point is CRM.* This is a reminder that the customer experience is not about a piece of software. It's about the processes that need to be changed, the commitments that need to be made, and the constant evaluations that need to be made to determine how customers want Samsung to interact with them.

## DO YOU UNDERSTAND THE SWEEPING SCOPE OF THIS WORK?

CEOs and companywide leaders: you need to understand and commit to the sweeping scope of this work before jumping into it. Are you willingly taking it on, knowing that it will cut across the organization and take multiple years to take effect? Are you willing to have the organization live in the pain of shaking up how the company does its work, what's important, and how to measure success? Is the company in a place right now to take on this work? Is there any impending issue that will overshadow your ability to focus on this work? Do you have the strength of leadership who will band together to work on this? Will you be able to enforce openness in questioning processes that worked for individual silos but don't work collectively for the customer? Will you be able to get people to come together to collectively understand the entirety of the contacts with customers? Do you have the tenacity and persistence to manage people's impatience at wanting to see results? Are your leaders ready to take on this minimum of five-year journey?

## WILL YOU DEVELOP THE NEW SKILLS REQUIRED FOR THE COMPANY TO THRIVE WITH CUSTOMERS?

This will require the hard work of process and change management. It's likely that the skill sets of the front line will be challenged. You will need to question the job descriptions and requirements for some jobs. One of the hardest skills will be for the company to learn to work cross-functionally. This means that silos will need to make a part of all they do a collaboration to ensure that the handoffs across the organization are executed for optimum customer interactions with what they deliver. This will seem to slow people down. They will feel frustrated that they can't own the entire job as they did in the past.

As a leader, you'll need to ask the questions constantly about whether people are engaging in this important collaboration. You have to ask regularly about the customer touch points that are affected and question if they were all thought through. And you'll need to figure out a way to motivate teams of people across the organization to pull in the same direction. This will challenge even the way you meet with the leaders of the functional areas. You'll need to be thinking about the handoffs they affect, not just the function they perform.

## Is the Company Willing to Commit the Time and Resources to Make This Happen?

In the beginning, this is going to feel very much like new work layered on to existing work. This view will change, but it will take a couple of years. Are you willing to commit resources from every part of the organization to participate in this work? Are you willing to dedicate the head count for facilitators and change management people to do this work? Can you ensure that your leadership will be collaborative partners in this work? Do they believe in it? Are they convinced of the return on the work that is ahead of them? Do they take accountability for the state of the customer relationship and understand their part in improving it? If there are outliers, do you have an approach for bringing them into the fold of the work?

## Does the CEO Sign Up to Be a True Partner?

This is especially important in organizations where a chief has been named to lead the customer effort at the behest of executives. For example, if one of your best performers won't participate or support this work, what will you do? Will you hold your ground when people push back and question the importance of this work? Will you make this your personal platform? Driving the customer agenda and customer profitability has got to be at the top of your agenda. If you have to be reminded to speak about it or prodded to bring it up, reconsider. Being a true partner at the highest level means this:

  • You make the leap to change the way people think about the business. For example, the leader reinforces that a trucking company does more than move things from point A to point B: it is a service provider. CEO questions on the state of business performance are as much about service and service delivery as financial performance. A spa company impassions the front line's sense of purpose by expanding the scope and title of their job, changing it from "spa technician" to "customer escape artist." Driving the business from the perspective of delivering a pleasurable escape for a customer inspires the organization to move beyond tactics to the delivery of a memorable experience that will make customers want to return.

• You keep customers top of mind. You take ownership for making customers a priority of the business. If proposals are lacking in customer perspective or customer considerations, you send everyone back to the drawing board. Leaders who are committed let it be known that this is a personal priority for them.

• You hold people accountable for their performance with customers. Will you force the tides of change to make customer metrics your company metrics? This means that what's important transcends the traditional metrics of operational performance. You'll need to push the company to figure out a way to know which customers are being affected and how and the outcome on customer profitability. People will have to come to expect these questions. They'll need to prepare for them and in doing so will begin to develop their own sensitivity to what this effort is all about. This may be rocky at first, but with clear questions come clearer metrics, and the reality will set in that this is not the priority of the month.

## WILL YOU INSIST ON CORPORATE PATIENCE?

This work is not for the mild-hearted or the quarterly inclined. People need to understand that this is a multiyear endeavor they are taking on. They can't bail in the first year, which would be a huge waste of human and financial capital. There is major impatience for seeing progress and something measurable.

Think about all the different types of customer solutions that have peeled their way through corporate America in the past twenty years. Each time a new one came out, the last try was abandoned. Customer Satisfaction, Total Quality Management, Six Sigma, CRM (customer relationship management). Each of these could have driven more change if they had *really* been incorporated into the way people do work. But the patience timer for seeing results lies somewhere between six months and two years. The corporation will be quick to move to the next big thing if it doesn't see the numbers turn fast enough. Some of this is based on the completely arbitrary goals submitted in an annual plans. Don't abandon the work if something the scale of turning around the *Titanic* isn't completed by a date selected during the pressure cooker of annual planning! This work is not like a marketing campaign where you write something, have it printed, and can track the results within three months. This is a multiyear process. You will begin to see progress in the first year as people come together and work collectively. Chapter Nine outlines the stages and landmarks that companies can use to track and celebrate progress in addition to hard-and-fast metrics so people stay motivated, especially in the first year. These are changes in attitudes, approaches, and how people work together. For example, when proposals move from spinning a campaign to meet sales number to creating an experience to improve customer interactions, a shift has occurred. Celebrate that! The delineation of these points must be understood, looked for, or tracked. You will need to give people tangible evidence that things are happening, that there are results, and that you support them. You will need to stay tuned in to the organization and its capacity to change to ensure that you make sure that one dimension of the work sticks before layering on the next. Over time, as you do the things you say you'll do, people will step up. A company usually needs at least five years until it is part of the corporate ecosystem.

It takes a steadfast leader to help everyone survive through the chaos of the shift to arrive at "the new normal." This means not rushing. This means having the fortitude with the board to set expectations that the process takes time. And it takes discipline not to back down when the pressure to move faster sets in—and it will.

## ARE YOU READY TO PUSH HARD FOR STRATEGIC CUSTOMER METRICS?

You need to get the point across as soon as possible that customers must be managed as assets. Chapter Five is singularly focused on strategic customer metrics, which I call "guerrilla metrics." It covers what the commitment to strategic customer metrics entails and how to get started using them to drive your customer commitment. Guerrilla metrics can be an important first step to help your organization take the customer work seriously and create corporate consistency for how you define success in the management of customers. Moving to the focus of managing customers as assets will require a shift in how leaders define success for the organization and in how they demand accountability to include strategic customer metrics. The management of customer profitability is a vast area, and it is critical that you establish the skills in your organization for this. Some organizations have complete teams to drive this work. Make sure before you proceed in pronouncing your commitment for driving the customer agenda that you are willing to incorporate some version of the guerrilla metrics and that your organization has the talent to drive this critical discipline.

## DO YOU HAVE THE GUTS TO DRIVE RELIABILITY IN COMPANY OPERATIONS?

Think about your path this way: there is a mess of things you already know are broken about the experience you're delivering to your customers, but you haven't been able to get your arms around the volume and inventory of the issues. More important, you haven't tied the different operations' accountability, compensation, or recognition to whittling down the list. This is your Achilles' heel to getting the organization to delivering a great experience. This is about the voice of the customer, *not* about surveys. You have all the information you need right now, from your customers, about what's broken and what's getting in the way of their wanting to do more business with you. Every day thousands of comments and feedback come in through your company pipes. But you're not tracking it, prioritizing it, or attaching accountability by area to the problems.

To get traction for a financial services client, one of the first things we did was to collapse all of the incoming customer complaints and comments into a monthly trending report. Looking at that information was enlightening, but it was also confusing because every customer service operator chose a different way to catalogue the issues heard from customers.

The next thing we did was create uniform categories for reporting. We automated the collection of this information into the call center operators' software program for consistency, and within a month we had a pretty decent tracking mechanism to identify the issues bugging customers. Somewhere along the way, we came up with the term "cracks in the foundation" to define this ever-growing list, and it stuck. People could make the connection that the foundation of our offering to customers was being constantly compromised because of these lapses in how we executed the different functions of our business. Once that was understood, we determined how many of the "cracks" we could fix each quarter or year. Then the operating vice presidents responsible for improving these issues were made accountable for erasing them from the issues being reported by customers.

You can't leapfrog over fixing these issues. Resolving these day-to-day bugs in the system are critical to creating reliability of the experience your customers feel they can get from you.

## DO YOU HAVE THE FOCUS TO DEFINE THE DIFFERENTIATED VALUE YOU WANT TO DELIVER?

Once you build the organizational muscle for fixing the existing problems that inhibit reliability, you can take on the more glorious work of defining a better future for your customers. This will be a large-scale undertaking that will involve all parts of your organization. It will stretch and challenge your ability to foster and repeatedly push people toward cross-functional working relationships. This is where those new skill sets of process change will especially need to be developed and honed. If you are serious about this, you will need talent to facilitate this work across your organization. Chapter Eight will help you to determine if you have the staffing and organizational mind-set to make the push now.

### Hope in a Case Study: Wegman's "Telepathic Levels of Customer Service"

Saying that the way you want to differentiate your grocery store by delivering "telepathic levels of customer service" could either have people looking at you sideways or mark you as one of the most admired leaders whose stores have customers clamoring for a return visit. For Danny Wegman, the telepathy has paid off. Customers gravitate to the theater that he's created in his grocery stores, and they even drive out of their way to get there because going to Wegman's is not like any other grocery store experience you might know.

Becoming the knowledge purveyor about foods is the way that he chose to differentiate in the marketplace, and it is working in a spectacular way. There's bread baking in a brick oven. Around the corner from the breads, you're greeted by a cheese expert in a black beret who can introduce you to more than four hundred kinds of cheese.

In his interview with *Fast Company* (Prospero, 2004), Danny Wegman tells a few of the secrets of his success. It's all about knowing what Wegman's will be to customers and giving employees the opportunity to own that differentiation. For example, he sent Carol Kent, who runs the cheese department for the Pittsford, New York, store, to Italy several years ago to see how parmesan cheese is made. It was important that Kent not just sell the cheese but also sell the culture and pass on the importance of the mystique of that culture with every hunk of cheese that she sells. She's not selling hunks of cheese; she's selling a little piece of Italy, of the love of the Italian family who made that cheese possible. Wegman makes sure that each of his employees has this deep knowledge with which he chooses to differentiate the business. Employees must go through programs and pass tests on each of their different areas so they can impart their knowledge (and love) for the foods on to the customers.

Revenue for Wegman's stores grew 9.1 percent from 2003 to 2004 to equal $3.6 billion across sixty-six stores in the northeastern and mid-Atlantic states. That's a lot of clams for delivering telepathic food service no one knew they wanted (Datamonitor, 2005).

## CONCLUSION

Leading a charge for customer profitability takes passion, fortitude, and the belief that it can be achieved. It takes gut and guts. It's easy for leaders to say they want to focus on the customer. But most do it without knowing what they're signing up for. Some don't realize that they need to personally have skin in the game. If you are making the push inside your organization for customers, it's absolutely critical that the CEO and leadership team know and agree to what they're signing on for. If you are a leader or part of a leadership team contemplating this work, here's what it's all about:

- Gut = Instinct about customers. Committing to drive customer focus and profitability is not a casual commitment. It must be a personal passion that stays with the leader and remains top of mind. Leaders driving this action need to have thought enough about where they want to take the organization that it's clear in their mind. They need to be able to translate their vision into clear priorities and actions. They need to describe so accurately the hill they want people to climb that there's no question about where people are headed and how they will get there.
- Guts = Courage to make customer commitment happen. People inside the organization need to know that focus on the customer is a steadfast position. There are no compromises, gaming results, or going halfway. Decisions will be scrutinized, and accountability for customers will be absolute.
- Real passion and commitment. Leaders need to know the scale and complexity of the work ahead. They need to knowingly take it on having asked and answered these questions.

Do you have it clear in your mind what you're trying to accomplish?

Do you understand that the scope of this work will cut across the organization and take years for it to take effect?

Will you be willing to have the company learn and adopt new skills necessary to managing profitable customer relationships?

Is the company willing to commit the time and resources to make this happen?

Do you sign up to be a true partner?

Will you insist on corporate patience?

Are you ready to push hard for strategic customer metrics?

Do you have the guts to begin the drive for reliability through operational accountability and metrics?

Do you have the focus to move the work along to define the differentiated value you want to deliver?

# CHAPTER FIVE

# GUERRILLA METRICS

We're all now zealots of "what gets measured gets managed," right? I don't think so. Judging from the piles and reams of scorecards and countless customer satisfaction reports I've seen piled up all over offices, this is just not the case. There is so much information that our eyes are rolling into the back of our heads. Company analysts can run cross-sections of customer satisfaction scores until it's possible to refute almost any survey result. One company I worked with had this frequently occur as they gave people access to their survey scores and verbatim comments online. They were made available by functional area, geography, and numerous other ways. People spent an astounding amount of time sorting results to find the silver lining of a good score rather than "fessing" up to results they didn't like ("Wait a minute; let me cross-tab number 25,435 on the satisfaction score results. Ah, yes, I can refute that!").

To drive the customer action, we need traction that we're just not getting naturally. That's where guerrilla metrics come in. These are the metrics that will simplify, clarify, and kickstart the customer effort, and they'll make the connection to revenue fast. Why call them "guerrilla"? Because getting them into your organization as a regular part of the discipline and conversation is a campaign you'll need to forge.

Here's where the sales guys have us customer types over a barrel: they know exactly what they need to define and measure. I have to hand it to them: they keep it simple. Of course, we'd like to integrate some customer-based goals into their widget-oriented scoreboard, but they know at all times which way is north. There are tick-sheets and meters and some kind of quarterly clicker that's going inside their head that keeps them on target. They've got simplicity wired. It's clear what they're going for. The revenue connection is crystal clear, and so is the payoff.

Customer Land is something completely different. Where is our goal line? How do we figure out if we're making progress? Because the customer is not owned like a discipline, customer metrics come and go, but not much sticks. Occasionally the customer becomes a hot topic in meetings, but that thinking disappears as people return to their respective corners. In the absence of real leadership, all parts of the organization churn out their version of customer information. Just how many ways are there to calculate "customer lifetime value"?

## Get an Abacus

If we could take a lesson from the sales force, we might find the answer to all this. It's too hard to see how simple this is: just start counting customers. That's it. The fact is that customers have simply not made it into our scoreboards. Customer survey answers have made it there, but not customers themselves. Why should a company ask customers if they're going to stay when they can track who's actually staying and going? Counting the flow in and the flow out of customers has evaded us as a simple way to keep score. In our quest to be smart about all of this, we've simply overanalyzed ourselves out of our common sense. You've heard this before, but it has to be said:

- If you lose more customers than you keep, this is not good.
- If you don't know how many you're losing versus keeping, this is even worse.
- If no one's asking the question or caring about the answer, you're sliding down a slippery slope.

So let's get down to basics. Are you counting your customers? Do you know the new ones and the old ones? Do you know which stay and which leave? Do you know why they're coming and going? Do you know which ones came because someone told them to? Do you know how many people are calling your service centers and why they're calling? As you fix those problems, do the call center numbers go down?

# WHAT ARE THE GUERRILLA METRICS?

Those previous questions form the foundation of guerrilla metrics. Guerrilla metrics establish a new language for your organization so that you can consistently manage customers as assets. Guerrilla metrics will give your leadership a platform to drive the customer agenda from. And guerrilla metrics will at last clarify the end game of what is trying to be accomplished with this customer work. Use guerrilla metrics to kickstart your customer effort or to breathe life into a stalled effort.

Guerrilla metrics have five components that establish a customer scoreboard for your organization. Using this simple scoreboard, you can get things started. Just getting your company aligned to track these things will let you know how well the hand wave to customers can turn to action. And once you're measuring and tracking these, you'll be on a strong path to drive the action ahead. When I work with presidents, they often begin by simply asking for this information in a meeting. Then they ask about it again at the next meeting. They keep asking until someone finds a way to capture and measure it. Lo and behold, the president now has a customer platform. And the company takes its first step in defining a common way to interpret and report how it's doing with customers. Because these are simple, they're powerful. Guerrilla metrics give leadership five simple things to care about and demand knowing about customers (Figure 5.1).

## METRIC 1: NEW CUSTOMERS—VOLUME AND VALUE

There's a decent likelihood that someone in your company is keeping track of this metric, and it most likely is marketing. You may find that this is happening in a multitude of areas with possibly conflicting definitions of what it means to be a "new" customer. The wild card here is if you have achieved alignment in how customers are classified inside your system. Companies still tend to be acquisition companies, and "how many new customers have you

### FIGURE 5.1. Guerrilla Metrics

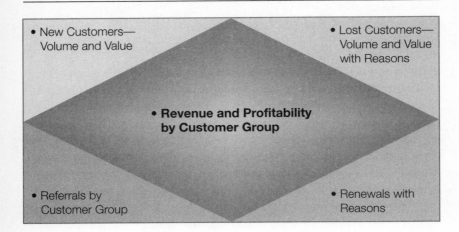

- New Customers—
  Volume and Value

- Lost Customers—
  Volume and Value
  with Reasons

- **Revenue and Profitability
  by Customer Group**

- Referrals by
  Customer Group

- Renewals with
  Reasons

got?" is like counting widgets. Incoming customers are fairly easy to identify as long as you count them consistently and sum them up throughout the organization.

The part that's not likely tracked is the *quality* of incoming customers. This is especially important as the market becomes more saturated and the pickings for customers are harder to come by. But just knowing how many new customers you get through the door won't tell the company if it's heading toward peril in its long-term revenue stream. This one-for-one approach is what has gotten companies into the mode of becoming acquisition focused in the first place. They match one customer in the door to one customer out. So you've got to track and measure two things:

- How many new customers did you reel in this month (or quarter or year)?
- What is their potential contribution?

## METRIC 2: LOST CUSTOMERS—VOLUME AND VALUE AND REASONS WHY

The volume and value of lost customers needs to be paired with the new customer information to lay out the true situation for your company. This is just about math. Call it what you want—the revolving door theory or the leaky bucket approach. You've got to reconcile customers in with customers out to know what kind of job you're doing with managing customers as an asset of your company. One business-to-business client was counting the number of customer accounts but not the flow or the quality. The sales team was led by an ex-fighter-pilot who "just wanted to take the hill." So off the sales force went to do what they actually called "speed kills." They were fired up to get as many customers as they could and as fast as they could. But the thing is, they weren't keeping track of the differences in the value of business each would bring to the company. To them, one unit was one unit: customers had become widgets. Each speed kill carried the same weight on the tote board used to measure success.

During this time, the market was competing fiercely, and high-quality prospects to bring into the business were harder and harder to find. So the salespeople had to dig pretty deep into the prospect pile to make their speed-kill goals. They exceeded their goal for new customer accounts that year, but sales became a drag on profits, which actually declined. Bringing in a mediocre new customer account took just as many resources and field personnel as a great one, and sometimes they took more time. The new customers just couldn't bring in the same volume of business as existing accounts, and the ones they had lost were replaced with customer accounts of lesser value. No one had an eye on the profitability of customer accounts, just the number of them.

In addition to knowing which customers left, you need to know the reasons that they don't care to do business with you anymore. Without knowing or caring about this, the organization misses a massive opportunity to galvanize people into taking action. To gather this information, you need to know which customers did not pony up to stay with you. You have to create a purposeful way to enable customers to inform you they're cutting you loose. And you need to care enough about the potency of this information to find a way to collect their feedback.

Think of garnering this information in terms of an exit interview for your customers. You'll need to take time to think this through to figure out how you'll be able to acquire it in your business model. If it never occurred to you to have this type of intervention, this will seem a difficult thing to set up. Communicating with departing customers is most easily executed in a subscription- or service contract–based business because the customer contacts you to end the relationship, but there are other ways to know when customers leave you and to find out why they are departing. If you are database driven, you can review your data and define defection as customers who have not purchased within a certain period of time. There is a multitude of creative ways to start chipping away at acquiring this information once it's prioritized as important. People will find a way to get it if there is a mandate for it.

One potent approach for making the customer defection information come alive is to hold a monthly "customer loss review" meeting. To prep for this meeting, compile the data on customer defections so that you know which customers left and why. In addition, assign executives to each make outbound calls to ten customers who have left during the month under review to find out how and why they left. There's nothing quite as compelling as a customer speaking right to an executive who has accountability for making something happen. Customers are often so amazed by the effort that they consider trying the company again.

Shortly after the calls have been completed, convene a meeting to discuss what's happening with your customers and what is driving them away. In that meeting get alignment on how to prioritize the issues and assign accountability. Use subsequent loss review meetings to track progress on resolving issues, continuing the process with executives calling customers who defected. Hour for hour, the return on investment for this loss review process is one of the best in terms of driving action. The process of establishing a reliable discussion for identifying customer defection issues and having executives constantly involved in speaking to defecting customers gets people moving more rapidly than any twenty presentations I've seen on customer satisfaction statistics. It's real-time information, it's operational, it's relevant, and it puts people's skin in the game.

## METRIC 3: RENEWALS WITH REASONS

For this metric to have relevance for your company, you'll need to define *renew* according to your business model. Again, pick a target, and start to track it. Definitely do some analysis to determine what the target should be, but don't go into a analysis paralysis on your data preparation. The main thing is to get started. Once you begin tracking numbers around customers, you can course-correct over time as your data mature and become more consistent and reliable. The key is to understand the patterns of your customers and see which ones are loyal to you based on their continuous purchase habits with you. By flagging and attaching these data to customer records, you will know what this trend is. A good database marketer is crucial here, but you must keep this person focused. Without clarity of specific deliverables, the data are so delectable that they can spend hours and hours slicing and dicing them. The only thing is that frequently no one uses the data. Keep it simple. Keep it simple. Keep it simple.

## METRIC 4: REVENUE AND PROFITABILITY BY CUSTOMER GROUP

Your crackerjack database person will be able to sort and segment your customers by customer group. Getting to this classification of customers is not a trivial project and is critical to getting guerrilla metrics up and running. The key is to come up with labels and categories for these groups that are simple yet meaningful.

In the quest to define the behavior of the customer, there is something akin to a branding exercise that occurs for each group. I've seen customers sorted as "Fighters," "Indifferents," "Likers," and "Lovers!" Sheesh. I like simpler categories defining customers by clearer buying patterns, but it's completely up to you. What you want to do with this is show the movement of customers from one group to another. You also want to see your costliest customer group declining and your most profitable customer group showing signs of growth. This will take some time to accomplish, but stay the course. Having this information is a key ingredient in the optimum effect of guerrilla metrics within your organization.

### Hope in a Case Study: What Harrah's Has Its Eye On

Harrah's Entertainment, the renowned casino and hotel company, has become a model for how to integrate metrics and action across a company to drive the growth of important customer segments. Harrah's particular talent is keeping loyal customers, whom they call VIPs, and for its scientific approach to executing appropriate actions for each customer to drive growth, loyalty, and profitability. Harrah's has created a sophisticated database system that tracks transactions and customer behaviors to keep a finger on the pulse of the relationships by segment, down to the individual customer level. Those data translate the business to key customer metrics that everyone has come to understand, appreciate, and act on. Harrah's highest segments are assigned a VIP host whose job it is to manage and strengthen the relationship. Using the database information, Harrah's provides all hosts with potent customer data so that they can target and manage performance in their own version of guerrilla metrics for each of their VIP customers. For example, hosts are provided with a customized list of daily activities for building relationships with loyal customers (Ulfelder, 2003).

Harrah's tracks each host's customer performance, which includes host revenue goals, revenue from host-initiated calls, host expense goals, host profit and loss, contacts made by the host for each segment, penetration rate by segment, and trips per guest. By instilling this level of rigor, Harrah's has a consistent set of its own version of guerrilla metrics, defined as customer segment growth, successful host contacts, the first-year return on investment by property, and overall VIP customer number growth. The results from this level of focus have been impressive. The business achieved 30 to 60 percent revenue growth depending on the customer segment ("Harrah's," 2005).

This translation of guerrilla metrics illustrates their purpose and power as a concept in driving the customer agenda. Harrah's metrics get the business down to the customer level. These are recognizable, and they drive action. And they define the business in customer terms and create a common language from which the business defines success.

## METRIC 5: REFERRALS BY CUSTOMER GROUP

You have to earn the right to a customer referral. A referral means that you're firing on two important cylinders. First, you've done enough things right that they meld together into an experience that's more than the sum of the parts of your organization. Your products, services, people, locations, and contacts present themselves beyond the ho-hum of our daily lives as consumers. You've gone beyond the execution of actions and tactics. You create memories customers want to have again and again. Second, the connection you've created with customers through the delivery of this experience compels them to tell others about it. Your customers become your marketing department, relating their experiences and convincing others to try you. Consider the referral as the true money question; it's the final frontier of loyalty. If your customers are willing to stick their neck out vouching for you, they are truly powerful to your organization and the potency of its revenue stream down the line. Keeping and developing these customers, and developing other customers like them, is the key.

You need to know how far you are down this path of building a customer base that would refer you. If you can track the rate of referrals in general and by customer group, you'll know the strength of your ongoing revenue stream before you even spend another dollar on marketing. The examined company will also spend just as much time wringing its hands over why customers aren't referring it and how the referral rates differ by customer group. You need to use this information to dig into the reasons behind the numbers and drive change as a result of what you learn.

When I get preachy about this, I'm usually met with the "we can't do this" chant. Of course, you can't track referrals if you haven't thought about referrals as an indicator of how well you're differentiating yourself in the marketplace. Of course, you can't if you haven't considered the power of having a customer refer you to someone else. Of course, you can't if you haven't figured out how to encourage customers to forward referrals or haven't figured out how to track and measure them. Find the way. It costs you only the time and commitment to get it done.

## How Far Along Are You with Guerrilla Metrics?

You may be tracking some of this information in pockets of your organization, but you probably don't have a consistent system to manage this information as critical metrics to define business success. Use Exhibit 5.1 to check how your company is doing by

EXHIBIT 5.1. Gauging How Far Along You Are with Guerrilla Metrics

## New Customers—Volume and Value

☐ Yes, we track          ☐ No, we do not track

**Barometer of Difficulty**

| Relatively easy | Moderately difficult | Hard but possible | Impossible right now |

## Lost Customers—Volume and Value with Reasons

☐ Yes, we track          ☐ No, we do not track

**Barometer of Difficulty**

| Relatively easy | Moderately difficult | Hard but possible | Impossible right now |

## Renewals with Reasons

☐ Yes, we track          ☐ No, we do not track

**Barometer of Difficulty**

| Relatively easy | Moderately difficult | Hard but possible | Impossible right now |

## Revenue and Profitability by Customer Group

☐ Yes, we track          ☐ No, we do not track

**Barometer of Difficulty**

| Relatively easy | Moderately difficult | Hard but possible | Impossible right now |

## Referrals by Customer Group

☐ Yes, we track          ☐ No, we do not track

**Barometer of Difficulty**

| Relatively easy | Moderately difficult | Hard but possible | Impossible right now |

reviewing the components of guerrilla metrics and circling the barometer of difficulty to assess the current state of your tracking and management.

## CUSTOMER TOTE BOARD

In order to have guerrilla metrics mean something, you have to make them become part of the everyday language of the corporation. You need to get them front and center. Don't bury them in the report; don't even waste the effort if that's how they'll end up. In the beginning, you'll especially need to get the guerrilla metrics in people's faces until they become part of the language of meetings and part of how success is defined. Some may find this unwavering persistence annoying. Don't back down! Driving hard is part of the passion package that's required to keep weaving customers into the everyday workings of the corporate machine.

Here's an extremely powerful way to get the guerrilla metrics front and center: create a customer tote board—something large and posted permanently where people pass frequently. A key is making this visual and simple, so people can see the ebb and flow of the customer numbers. Employees need to understand the impact their actions have in moving those customer numbers up or down, and that is tied directly to revenue and profit. These numbers need to be talked about, and they need to become part of how you define the success or challenges with your brand.

When the automotive industry began compiling retention numbers by brand in the early 1990s, this began to put customer retention rates on the map. I kept thinking that there had to be a way to use this information to jolt people into understanding the competitive battlefield. Then the idea of the customer tote board emerged, which did have an impact in reframing the problem (Table 5.1). By establishing a competitive tote board based on the repurchase loyalty among brands, we were first able to collapse our performance down to a ranking among other automotive brands. This simple math showed the amount of extra work and investment that companies with lower retention rates had to expend to replace customer losses to get back to the baseline number. The lower the retention rate, the more customer acquisition dollars had to be spent refilling the customer bucket. Smart people got this

**TABLE 5.1. Automaker's Tote Board**

| | A | | | B | A - B = C |
|---|---|---|---|---|---|
| | Original Owner Base | Number Still Owning the Vehicle | Number Who Disposed of Vehicle | Number Who Replaced with Same Brand—Repurchase Loyalty | Revised Owner Base | Number of New Owners Needed to Get to Original Owner Base |
| Company A | 50,000 | 30,000 | 20,000 | 5,400 (27%) | 35,400 | 14,600 |
| Company B | 50,000 | 30,000 | 20,000 | 12,400 (62%) | 42,400 | 7,600 |
| Company C | 50,000 | 30,000 | 20,000 | 8,800 (44%) | 38,800 | 11,200 |
| Company D | 50,000 | 30,000 | 20,000 | 6,000 (30%) | 36,000 | 14,000 |

concept, of course. But once the numbers were front and center with each competitive brand listed, we got the word *retention* to mean something. Companies with the lowest rates could see that they were reprospecting to replace lost customers over and over again. It was as if they were running in place. Automakers with higher retention rates could use their prospecting dollars to add new customers and bring in incremental sales. The realization of the importance of retention did not magically drive action, of course. But we were able to nudge people into understanding that something had to be done about it.

## How to Get Started with Guerrilla Metrics

The key to making guerrilla metrics a success is to do three things right. First, introduce them the right way. Sell that guerrilla metrics provide the clarity and revenue connection that's been missing. Next, get a commitment for involvement in gathering the data, and secure the resources to do it. Putting these metrics together will take some doing. Complete the legwork first to define the size of the undertaking then ask for the necessary resources as part of the plan. Third, secure leadership commitment in integrating the metrics as a key part of business reviews and definition of business success. Define the forums that you want to include them in up front and have a plan for how they will be rolled out and the accountability forums around them.

## The Grand Hallucination

Here's the grand hallucination we customer zealots have in the back of our mind about how this is all supposed to go. The president of the company owns these numbers. Every important meeting begins with them. People talk about them and rally to understand what affects them. Smart people dig inside the databases to see how these can be flagged, tracked, and measured. Questions about the flow and quality of customers become as important in monthly meetings as those about the number of widgets sold. A long shot to achieve? Maybe. But a girl can dream, can't she?

## CONCLUSION

Guerrilla metrics are a potent first action to take to kickstart or reenergize your customer effort.  They will immediately propel your organization into understanding the customer end game and supply leaders with a platform to stand behind and reinforce. They work because they clear through the clutter usually encountered in the drive for customer experience and profitability. Here are the important points about guerrilla metrics:

- Few companies have a consistent manner for defining, reporting, and managing the state of relationships with customers.
- Companies frequently get stuck in administering surveys and negotiating survey results rather than tracking and managing their customer performance scorecard.
- A new way to simplify the elements of the customer scorecard and gain traction is to introduce the practice of managing guerrilla metrics, a set of five targets that define outcomes companies have with their customers:
  New customers—volume and value
  Lost customers—volume, and value and reasons why
  Renewals with reasons
  Revenue and profitability by customer group
  Referrals by customer group
- Senior leaders who commit to the practice of managing guerrilla metrics take ownership and create a personal platform for driving the customer agenda.
- Guerrilla metrics demystify and simplify the customer work.

# CHAPTER SIX

# HERDING C-A-T-S
## Customer Accountability Targets

## ELUSIVE ACCOUNTABILITY

It's no wonder we keep trying over and over again to do this work to no avail. In the absence of a clear accountability process, leaders manage with what they've got. They ask the silos how they're doing with their separate jobs. They get a presentation and a report. The beat goes on. Nothing changes. Accountability is plain and simple the sticking point for this work. Check to see if you recognize these three culprits for lackluster customer accountability inside your corporate machine:

• "It's everyone's job to own the customer." How many times have you heard that one? The fact is that when "everyone" owns the customer, no one does. Everything "customer" is up for grabs. And with all that hand waving, the customer falls between the cracks. Things don't get done because it's assumed someone else is taking care of them. Customer hot potato issues run rampant when this accountability softball is thrown into the air. Either no one catches it, or everyone catches it. When no one catches it, customers go into voice-mail hell or must nearly have a fit for someone take the accountability for resolving their issue. When everyone catches it, efforts trip over one other. Do a quick inventory of the duplicitous contacts you've got going to your overstimulated customer base. You'll see what I mean right away.

• No one's connecting the mess of company metrics. Does anyone even know what the metrics should be? Who is the point person for all of these metrics? No one knows. Each area has its own spin on what it owns, what's important, and how to measure it. Everyone's got a version of success that they trumpet to leadership. There's not much in the way of metrics that holds multiple operating areas responsible for the same customer contact. Frequently, there is no clear sequence of metrics for executives to scan to see how their company is doing with customers and customer profitability. There is no companywide annual plan for setting customer targets and moving that along. Each silo creates an annual plan and metrics for its own operating area. When these are presented separately they make sense. But if you tried to connect them, the metrics most likely wouldn't connect. The sum of the parts wouldn't add up to managing an end-to-end customer experience.

Strategic customer metrics are often in the remedial stage. Counting customers is hard to do because everyone defines "customer" differently. That's why getting the guerrilla metrics will have some pain associated with it. Just sorting through all the derivations of how customers are defined is a chore. Follow-through on issue resolution is murky because companies don't make a science out of tracking these things. And even when they are tracked, the reports don't often make their way onto review schedules to demand accountability in their resolution.

• The silos are disconnected and compete for resources and priorities. The silos are going to compete. Even when they're all focusing on the customer, they all have different agendas and priorities. Each area knows what's important to them. Its leaders have pitched their projects, which are now budgeted, and scorecards are created to reward the commitments. In the planning process, each silo has had its plan approved separately, so the resource competition wages in full force. Each silo vies for resources to get its projects accomplished. Each believes its projects should be the priority. This frenzy of activity leads a lot of companies to have a misplaced sense that there is real focus on the customer. There may be a lot of plates spinning, but they're going at different speeds and in different directions. Unless someone has the time and the inclination to herd the cats and get them all to agree to unify priorities, resources, and metrics, this surge of energy will have a questionable impact for customers and the bottom-line impact you hope to achieve. It just won't happen.

# THE ACCOUNTABILITY TARGETS

Managing accountability for what you'll deliver to customers is not rocket science, but it is overwhelming. This work is all about herding cats, and finding the metrics for accountability is a big part of it. With all this in mind, offered up now is a method for managing customer accountability across your organization. To remember the different things you've got to think about and harness for customer accountability, just remember C-A-T-S: customer accountability targets. What C-A-T-S does is skinny the accountability formula down to four things. C-A-T-S links together the mish-mash of metrics bouncing around the organization to tell a cumulative story of customer treatment and its effect.

C-A-T-S is a comprehensive approach. My recommendation is to first take it in. Read the recipe. Then think about what ingredients you've got and which you're missing. Prepare yourself; there is a lot here.

To demand accountability for the four C-A-T-S components, people inside the organization need to know that there will be purposeful and planned reviews for each of them. And it needs to be explicitly stated and understood with leadership follow-through that goals and reviews will be attached to tracking and understanding the progression or decline of their performance. This means:

- Don't send a memo with a corporate mandate that these are the new metrics the company now cares about. This won't accomplish anything. First, everyone will interpret them differently. You'll immediately have a mess of disconnected actions taking place. Second, especially if the company has been "committed" to the customer before, these new metrics will seem like the latest hoopla around the customer thing.

- Create a reliable system for measuring and managing the C-A-T-S. Connect the C-A-T-S components with a series of accountability forums and processes that are recognizable and reliable for people to perform within. Set deadlines for gathering the first set of data. Establish consistency in how these meetings will go and the process for presentations. Make them be a big deal.

- Translate the targets into metrics that people learn to track and report on as much as the hallowed quarterly sales goals. Keep it simple, and people will start to integrate these into their vocabulary and priorities. Make them complicated, and they'll never sink in. You'll get perfunctory gathering and reporting because leaders have commanded them, but they won't sink in as a way to look at and manage the business.

C-A-T-S has four components (Figure 6.1):

- Customers gained and lost as a result of our actions—guerrilla metrics
- Ability to serve customers and rescue customers at risk—service performance
- Targeting and resolving issues driving customers away— customer listening metrics
- Silo connectivity and metrics for optimum experience delivery—operational metrics

You'll note that guerrilla metrics are listed as the first component of C-A-T-S. I dedicated a chapter of this book to guerrilla metrics because of their potency in kickstarting the work. Focus on these initially. Use guerrilla metrics to get the momentum going and insert the language of customer management into your orga-

**FIGURE 6.1. The Components of the Customer Accountability Target Metrics**

| | |
|---|---|
| **Guerrilla Metrics** | **C**ustomers gained and lost as a result of our actions |
| **Service and Frontline Performance** | **A**bility to serve customers and rescue customers at risk |
| **Customer Listening Metrics** | **T**argeting and resolving issues driving customers away |
| **Operational Metrics** | **S**ilo connectivity and metrics for optimum experience delivery |

nization. They will form the foundation that the organization needs to move the customer work out of something foggy to something they can work to manage purposefully with cause and effect. However, using guerrilla metrics alone will not get you the operational accountability required to manage the customer work in its entirety. The logic in how the pieces link together to create a management story of accountability for the customer work is set out in Table 6.1.

TABLE 6.1: Purpose of Each C-A-T-S Metric

| Metric | Purpose |
| --- | --- |
| Guerrilla metrics | Show the gain and loss of customers. |
| | Identify how loyalty is paying off in referrals and customer spending. |
| | Establish quarterly and annual customer management targets. |
| Service performance metrics | Show the trend of customer-facing-personnel performance. |
| | Identify the trends for customers at risk, and reduce them. |
| | Set targets and goals for quarterly and annual performance. |
| Customer listening metrics | Target and prioritize issues driving customers away. |
| | Assign and demand operational accountability for issue resolution. |
| | Set targets and goals for quarterly and annual performance. |
| Operational metrics | Determine silo requirements and connections for experience delivery. |
| | Assign and demand operational accountability. |
| | Set targets and goals for quarterly and annual performance. |

# C-A-T-S Component 1: Guerrilla Metrics

Guerrilla metrics, the first component of the C-A-T-S system, form the new language you will introduce into the organization to propel managing customers as a revenue priority. These metrics will give your leadership a platform to drive the agenda from and will serve to clarify the company's targeted end game for this customer work (Figure 6.2).

Guerrilla metrics give leadership five simple things to start to care about (see Chapter Five for in-depth information on guerrilla metrics):

- New customers—volume and value
- Lost customers—volume and value
- Renewals with reasons
- Referrals by customer group
- Revenue by customer group

## Customer Referrals as the Loyalty Payoff

The goal here is to enforce customer referrals as the loyalty payoff. There's nothing more compelling and simpler to understand than the trending of customer recommendations as an indicator of growth and growth potential. It's been proven that customers who recommend you are the most fiercely loyal. You can count on them

**FIGURE 6.2.  C-A-T-S Component 1: Guerrilla Metrics**

| C-A-T-S Component 1 | Customers Gained and Lost Due to Our Actions |
|---|---|
|  | **Guerrilla Metrics** |
|  | • Customer and profit impact from our actions |
|  | • Baseline of customer profit and relationship |
|  | • Consistent metric for managing and setting targets |
|  | • New reporting metric to define the business |

for build your revenue stream. It's not just if you're getting referrals or not that's important. It's the power of the customers who give the referrals and their impact on your business. And it's the power of knowing what you've done that is so wrong that your customer would not subject anyone else to your organization with a referral.

I am a huge fan of the work that Fred Reichheld has done in the field of loyalty, especially his most recent work. We've all known for a long time that it's a good idea to ask customers if they'd recommend you. But Reichheld put a system behind it to make this actionable. He classifies customers as "net promoters" and "net detractors." Promoters are the people you want all your customers to develop into. Promoters are customers advocating a company and recommending that others experience them. By developing your strong base of promoters, you can build a promising future for driving long-term growth for your organization. That's because your customers are the strongest voice you have in the marketplace. They toot your horn. They convince people to buy from you. Most important, it is the trend of your pool of net promoters versus net detractors that tells you if you are on the path for growth.

To implement the enforcement of referrals, you need an automated daily system for collecting the information, attaching it to customer records, and reporting it in real time. This obviously will draw on your technology and database people from an execution standpoint, but leadership here is the most critical. To put the focus on this that will make it the simple beacon that it's meant to be, someone needs to own this. The other leaders in the company need to commit and agree to this metric and take it seriously. Most important, compensation and recognition need to be wrapped around the real performance tied by geography and operational area.

## RESOURCES ABOUT NET PROMOTERS

Reichheld addresses this concept extensively. His material is also accessible over the Internet. A place to begin is to read his article, "The One Number You Need to Grow" (2003), which summarizes and explains the concept. In addition, find out more on this topic on Reichheld's Web site, http://loyaltyrules.com.

# C-A-T-S COMPONENT 2: SERVICE PERFORMANCE METRICS

Some companies make this metric the major one they focus on regarding customers (Figure 6.3). Customer service exists to deal with the fallout from the dysfunctional experiences we deliver. To manage these disgruntled customers, a sea of operators is assembled to take calls from them. The irony is that the focus becomes how these operators are doing in calming down disgruntled customers. This is in lieu of resolving the systemic things causing the customers to call in the first place.

Customer issues too often are collapsed down to the nonperforming front line, and "service" is defined narrowly as the customer service people. Certainly the performance of the front line is an important part of understanding how your company treats customers, but it is just that: one component of the brand experience. Don't make the mistake of hanging the burden of improving customer loyalty and profitability solely on the backs of the front line.

There are some simple ways to get a perspective on frontline performance. My guess is that what you do now is one of three things or a combination of them: you track operational metrics such as talk time, do an outbound survey, or listen in on calls.

## MY TAKE ON THE OUTBOUND SATISFACTION SURVEY

I'm in agreement with getting feedback about how customer service is doing. I just don't believe it has to be as complicated as it has become, and that it can be more effective. Outbound surveys are

**FIGURE 6.3.  C-A-T-S Component 2: Service Performance Metrics**

**A**bility to Serve Customers and Rescue Customers at Risk

**Service Performance Metrics**

C-A-T-S Component 2

- Service performance improvement
- Service channel net promoter "detractor" calls
- Feedback by account executive on issues and call experience
- Dashboard for immediate feedback with improvement recommendations
- Aggregate data by call center/comparison across call centers

frequently not done immediately after the contact, so in effect you are using the fading memories of customers to define the performance and rating of your customer service reps and company service levels. You're asking people with busy lives to try to remember back to a company contact and tell you what you did and what you can do to improve. Then there's the issue of what to do with the miles of paper that come from the survey results. The bottom line is not to overrely on your busy customers' answers on after-the-fact survey questions to rate and change performance or build the next new wave of products or services for you. There are many other engaging manners to garner and use customer feedback to drive improvement for your company. For example, in addition to survey results, use the immediate feedback given to you daily through customers' comments and feedback about how you're doing. Capitalize and categorize that information. Then get inspired. Great products or experiences customers crave often stem from passionate companies that could see a new reality in their mind's eye. Then they executed on it until they made it happen.

## IDEAS FOR PUTTING SERVICE PERFORMANCE METRICS INTO PLACE

If you are asking customers if they would refer your company, you have an automatic system for understanding some things about the service relationship with those customers. For example, you can track the trend and volume of type of customer by service representative. Through having the rep ask if the customer will refer others to you during each contact, you know where the customer stands. From that information, you can do focused outbound calls immediately after the contact to find out what is happening with the customer relationship. To those who would not refer your organization, you want to find out why they would not and try to pinpoint specific issues and reasons. This is a rich source of information about both the service person's ability to rescue the customer and the company's ability to do the right things right. To those customers who would recommend you, you want to be able to reach out to thank them and ask them what is going well and continue using those skills and approaches. Most important, you want to keep the customers who hold you in such high esteem that they would refer you. Reach out to them; they will respond to you because it is likely they have a strong attachment to your organization. For example, these are the customers to ask for feedback and get involved in the heady area of new product development, even giving them early access to new products. These are your company zealots, and they will respond when you reach out to them.

Take a lesson from the net promoter idea introduced by Fred Reichheld (2003). Begin asking service customers if they will recommend you. This is your sorting mechanism for understanding immediately which bucket they fall into. You can then probe customers to see the variances of the referral answer by service personnel. Next, trend and track "recommend" and "not recommend" by service personnel. Right off the bat, you have a high-level bar for performance across the board. Make outbound calls to a good cross-section of "recommend" and "not recommend" for each service employee, and collect actionable information from customers on what they like and do not like about your company and performance. Specifically probe why they would or would not recommend your business. For customers to recommend, they feel so strongly about a company that they have created their own words to describe it. Customers who would not recommend you are also very vocal. It's likely they will have no trouble spelling out the reasons. On inbound customer contacts, take the opportunity to ask continuously about how it's going and what they like and do not like and if they'd refer you.

### Hope in a Case Study: How Wachovia Listens and Act

Just about anyone can conduct a customer survey or check with those in customer service to see how they're doing. It's what you do with this information that matters, and how you do it that is even more critical. Consider Wachovia, for instance. The bank purposefully reaches out to twenty-five thousand customers each month to find out about service performance. They call it the "service experience," and it sends the message to the phone reps that their job is elevated to delivering a customer experience. (That label is a whole lot better than being called a "problem solver" or the "complaint department.")

The key to what Wachovia does is getting the feedback down to the individual employee and use that information for one-on-one coaching. The information gets rolled up to the branches for the traditional summary of results by locations, but what Wachovia cares about is the personal interaction between the rep and the customer. Wachovia leaders recognize that in those few moments, a relationship can be mended or severed. Now we've all been the recipient of what I call the "customer fluff" feedback. This is not that. Wachovia has thirty-three employee behaviors to ask the customer about. Then based on this feedback, the reps are coached individually (McGregor, 2004).

The lesson here is that there is no need for a quest to seek out the best whiz-bang system to use. Simply find a way to hear what customers have to say about your reps. Then determine how to translate that into feedback that fundamentally helps them know what to change to improve. Finally, learn from feedback. For Wachovia, since 2001, this process has helped contribute to its position holding the number one spot among banks in the American Customer Satisfaction Index.

## RESOURCES FOR SERVICE PERFORMANCE METRICS

A multitude of resources exists for you to choose from. The call center and frontline performance space is rich with methodologies, metrics, and dashboards. As you look for the right partners to help you with the metrics, make sure they go beyond the traditional metrics like talk time and checking off the completion of tasks and fulfillment of schedules. They need to understand and support you in fulfilling both the "customer experience" management side of the equation and the customer profitability dimension. Include your IT and telephony systems folks from the start to make sure there's compatibility with your planned approach and what is being proposed. Be sure to manage for scope creep; don't buy a soup-to-nuts solution too soon from any vendor. Pace the work, see how it's going, and then plan the next phase of systems, competency development, support, and tools. Know your own strategy, keep it focused, and find the right partners to help you execute.

## C-A-T-S COMPONENT 3: CUSTOMER LISTENING METRICS

Add the trending and tracking of customer issues to your management of customer growth (Figure 6.4). This is where you get the granularity of information to understand why you don't have

**FIGURE 6.4.  C-A-T-S Component 3: Customer Listening Metrics**

| | |
|---|---|
| **C-A-T-S Component 3** | **T**argeting and Resolving Issues Driving Customers Away<br>**Customer Listening**<br>• Recovery of customer revenue loss through outreach and resolution of issues<br>• Categorization and trending of issues from all customer channels<br>• Flow back to accountable operational areas<br>• Outbound contact to net promoter "detractors"<br>• Net promoter "detractor" issues trended |

more customers who want to recommend you. Through this information, you also can get operational very easily. You should take the time to organize the customer information, assigning operational accountability for the trend of the feedback and the resolution of the issues.

## IMPLEMENTING CUSTOMER LISTENING ACCOUNTABILITY

Implementing customer listening accountability is prescribed often, but very few do it well. Most don't make it a part of a system of tracking and management. You'll need someone to shepherd this through. This person will need to catalogue the customer feedback you receive, understand how it clusters into areas of the customer experience, and then translate those elements to the operational areas that are accountable.

Every piece of incoming feedback has to have an operating area that will be held accountable for reducing, eliminating, or justifying (and I mean *really* justifying) that piece of customer frustration. This is a most critical part of the work—and the part that companies fail to do. Without the clarity of which feedback goes to what area, you've just collected more data to add to the piles you already have. And without agreement and commitment to own the feedback they get, you won't get traction or change. Don't shortchange yourself on the amount of time or dedication it will take to get through this stage. People will be likely to hand-wave it away with the "of course we will" comment. But I've found that you need to put down on paper exactly the type of feedback that they will be receiving, in exactly the format, showing exactly the volume. The commitment needs to be made with full disclosure, and executives need to be present when the commitment is made. Finally, leaders need to know how they are going to be held accountable for their progress in the identified problem areas.

After you've done the legwork on defining the arena of customer feedback, you will need technology support to create a scaleable approach and solution. This can be as simple as putting a prompter with back-end screens on your main Web page for collecting the data. The complexity will be dependent on the cleanliness and synergy among your databases. You'll need to grapple with the basics: classification of customers, nightly processing to merge the data, and ensuring that the data fields talk to one another, for example. From a resource standpoint, I've never seen this work successfully as an add-on job to an already busy docket of work. My recommendation is to make this a focused project for a minimum of six months to do the research and work to get it up and running. Here are the major action items:

• Organize the categories of incoming customer information. I have seen customer feedback reports with page after page of verbatim comments on a menagerie of subjects. While these might engender some gasps about the way customers feel about your company, they're not going to push anybody to make changes to their operation. This is where the beleaguered crusaders hit the wall. But they can't blame the operational areas for pushing back here. Customer feedback has to be classified into something that is actionable. Even back in the Lands' End days, we did this. It took about a week of listening on the phones until we knew all the categories; then we simply copied pages with the categories. When the phone reps got customer feedback, they documented the volume by category manually.

• Track the volume and trend of comments and issues, and separate them into operational areas. There are many tools available that will enable the automation of this information into action reports and dashboards for you. Separating this feedback helps identify simple targets to take action on (just like the sales force).

For example, tracking and trending customer comments indicating what they don't like about your return policy is quantifiable, understood, and actionable, and it can be assigned operational accountability.

• Accountability can be assigned immediately for the resolution of issues with high feedback counts. Assign the categories directly to operational areas, and send them information about what's broken.

• Drive accountability metrics and compensation around the reduction and resolution of issues. Create public accountability forums for recording and reporting. Formalizing monthly reviews where the visual depiction of this stuff is posted is truly powerful.

• Make reliability performance part of the ongoing leadership talk track.

### Hope in a Case Study: Capital One's Customer Accountability System

Taking the resolution of customer problem seriously is the mantra of Capital One, which has gone to great lengths to make sure that the people who talk to customers know who they're talking to and what they need. And then they give them their trust and the latitude to do the right thing.

Capital One exercises "microsegmentation" of its customer base (Day, 2002). When a customer calls in, a complete history of the customer relationship appears on the customer service rep's screen. The information is almost instantaneously cross-tabbed with data that classify the customer for routing in the service system. Prospects routed to the voice-mail system are those whom the company doesn't see the financial win on rescuing and hence doesn't block any attempts to close their account. Others are connected to one of Capital One's representatives, who are immediately provided two dozen pieces of data about the caller and why he or she might be calling. Then the screen is filled with offers and other information to assist that operator in making the right call and the right offer to that customer.

This is not just about database marketing and segmentation alone. These representatives are trained, trusted, and rewarded for the resolution of issues and the retention of high-value customers, and they have the confidence of a company that is organized to provide them with the data and other support in sync with how the customers contact them.

This passion for advocating for the customer has pervaded corporate culture performance standards as well. Representatives are measured not only on their performance with customers but also their ability to be supportive to their fellow reps.  Something must be working. Capital One enjoys only a 5 percent turnover rate per year among reps versus the industry average of 30 percent. Who knew that something as simple as holding people accountable and then giving them the tools to be successful in the job would make people feel good about where they are? (As the kids in my life say to me all the time, "Duh.")

## RESOURCES FOR VOICE OF THE CUSTOMER ACCOUNTABILITY

You'll need to find a resource to build the instruments for collecting the customer information. This will take place in two ways. First, the customer-facing employees need screens and systems to enter unsolicited customer information they receive. Next, you need to create a system for customers themselves to enter information. There are many ways to get this information, so don't limit it to the Web site. For example, a company that sends out bills has an ongoing way to get feedback that can be a powerhouse of information. With just two questions printed on the return portion of the bill, such as  "Would your recommend us?" and "Please tell us of any issues with our products or services," you can get actionable information flowing in the door in your next billing cycle.

A number of companies offer software solutions to capture customer information. In looking for a supplier that's right for you, make sure of a few things:

• Keep the supplier focused on the task at hand. This is about creating a supercharged engine for customer feedback and information. Don't let scope creep get in the way.

• Ensure that the engine drives back to operating areas and accountability. It's critical that the operating areas get the information they need to make constant change. This cannot become yet another thick management report.

• Ensure there's flexibility. The data fields and information collected will be dynamic and constantly changing. Ensure that whatever you use gives you that flexibility and can be managed by your administrator to do the updates required.

# C-A-T-S COMPONENT 4: OPERATIONAL METRICS

By far this is the most gnarly and complex part of managing customer accountability (Figure 6.5). Without measuring the interaction points and operational execution of them, you will continue to look only at the disparate activities by silo. That's not to say that you are going to focus on every contact. There is a prioritization to those contacts that are most meaningful to customers and you need to know what those are. I like to cut a company's teeth on managing this level of accountability by having them focus on the top ten contacts the first year. As the ability and desire for this work increase, you'll be able to add more on these contacts to your priority list.

## CREATING ACCOUNTABILITY FOR OPERATIONAL METRICS

You can begin creating accountability for operational metrics by consistently defining the customer experience. It's likely as you travel through your organization that if you can ask three people to define the stages of your customer experience, you'll get three

**FIGURE 6.5.  C-A-T-S Component 4: Operational Metrics**

**C-A-T-S Component 4**

**S**ilo Connectivity and Metrics for Optimum Experience Delivery

**Operational Metrics**

• Metric identification and cross-silo accountability by customer experience
• Accountability for proactive development of new experiences
• Accountability for reactive improvement to issues identified by the voice of the customer

different answers. Not only will the answers be different; the interpretation won't even mean the same to all three. The first job here is to define the customer experience in stages that characterize the customer relationship with you.

Once the customer experience is defined, get granular on the contact points. From my early days doing this work, I have used the discipline of defining these contacts as the "moments of truth" of the customer experience. The "moments of truth" were established when Jan Carlzon was CEO of SAS airlines and the airline was facing losses of $20 million after seventeen consecutive years of profitability. He came up with them as a way to elevate the purpose of the business and the importance of each individual moment with customers. He catapulted the company to profitability in part by focusing on identifying and taking accountability for the delivery of the moments of truth. He said, "They are the moments when we must prove to our customers that SAS is their best alternative." Carlzon (1986) defined *moment of truth* in this way: "Anytime a customer comes into contact with any aspect of a business, however remote, is an opportunity to form an impression." This logic holds true today because the discipline required to identify each contact point forces an understanding of what you want it to deliver to customers at that contact point and what it will take to it. The process of defining the moments of truth is a great inclusive exercise to bring the company together. Once you've got the stages of the experience defined and everyone agrees, hold a brainstorming session to frame out the moments of truth.

## IDENTIFYING THE PRIORITY CONTACTS

Once you have established the moments of truth, you identify the priority contacts. Understand the critical customer-facing contact points or moments of truth that make or break it for customers. One helpful way to classify customer contacts is to identify four categories which they fall into:

- *Rescuing* a customer in distress
- *Revenue* building to increase the sale of goods or services
- *Responding* to a customer request
- *Relationship*-building contact to strengthen the customer bond

We did this exercise with a pharmaceutical company for one segment of its customers. It was a great way to approach the contacts for this segment because it aligned marketing, operations, IT, the call centers, and the regions around clarifying what they could deliver in a consistent way. We created a series of contacts called "triggers" to define the contacts that should happen to give a comprehensive experience. They were numerous and way too many to execute. But we overlaid the four categories noted above on the contact totals and were able to identify the top ten contacts to make for this customer segment. This gave us a good first list of tactics and actions in building the relationship with them. It drove how we initiated the relationship, what data we needed to service them, and how to track the renewal of their account. Doing this kickstarted a consistent approach for managing the customer relationship.

Canvass your moments of truth to understand where they fall in the categories. You will need some quantitative and qualitative research validating the priority contacts for relationship and long-term revenue generation here. Gut is important: there are some things you'll want to do because those contacts are a big part of delivering the passion of your brand. But make sure that you know the customer perspective. Make sure that the important things are known and that you can identify which ones you need to get right every time.

Once you have a list of the priority contacts, the challenge is to develop what the ideal customer experience should be for them. This is an unnatural exercise, as it will require multiple silos to work together to define, develop, and execute the end-to-end experience. Your research will help you validate the metrics you need to measure within each contact.

### Hope in a Case Study: How Canadian Pacific Hotels Wired In the Moments of Truth and Won

By focusing on the moments of truth and delivering an experience catering to business travelers, Canadian Pacific Hotels increased its share of Canadian business travel by 16 percent. It did this in a flat market without adding properties.

To establish an experience for business travelers, the hotels began by practicing the discipline of learning about this segment of customers and their particular needs and what they valued from a hotel. Then they took the work further by mapping each point of contact, or moment of truth, of the business traveler's guest experience. These began with parking through check-in, with every step leading to the check-out experience. Performance standards were established for each, and services were identified for the priority touch points and times of the experience.

This was somewhat foreign to Canadian Pacific employees who weren't seasoned in providing special attention and the level of personalization that business travelers required. (Many of the hotel's guests were on group tours that were fine with mass check-in and group services that the frontline was accustomed to.) Canadian Pacific took the time to educate and train the employees who would interface with these business guests. They helped them use tools of technology as a support to remembering and delivering the "corporate memory" about the preferences these important business travelers expected. Taking no chances, each hotel also had a cross-functional champion who worked throughout the property to ensure that the new disciplined approach was being delivered. They locked in behavioral change by instilling incentives and systems that complied with the new processes and delivered on the performance standards (Day, 2002).

## RESOURCES FOR MAKING OPERATIONAL ACCOUNTABILITY A REALITY

Conduct an Internet search on "customer experience" to identify the consulting organizations and methodologies available to assist you in this work. Begin your understanding of customer experience development by reading a few good books on the subject and sharing them with company leadership. Here are a few:

*Managing the Customer Experience: Turning Customers into Advocates,* by Shaun Smith and Joe Wheeler

*Customer Experience Management: A Revolutionary Approach to Connecting with Your Customers,* by Bernd H. Schmitt

*Clued In: How to Keep Customers Coming Back Again and Again,* by Lewis Carbone

Then determine whether you and your company have the fortitude for this work. Leaders need to weigh in on their commitment for beginning new work of this scale and if they will apply the resources to ensure its success. This is a big decision, so know what you're committing to before you jump in. In most cases, you should consider implementing this as one of the final stages of your customer accountability effort. It makes sense to get the other three accountability plates spinning before you take this one on.

# CREATING AN ACCOUNTABILITY AGENDA

All of this work will be for naught if you don't establish reliability on how and when you ask for this information. Companies that excel with customer relationships have scheduled forums where customer accountability is formally addressed. But the conversation does not stay cordoned off for just those moments of focus. In fact, that's the difference with the really great customer companies. The conversation about customers is not relegated to a meeting or an agenda item. It is part of nearly every conversation. Here are some actions that will work to get you to that first stage of reliability.

## THE POWER OF PUBLIC ACCOUNTABILITY

After spinning my wheels to get some traction, the idea of public accountability came to me. With the support of my executive sponsor, we created two potent ways to turn the work on its ear: putting people on the spot and pulling them together in a friendly horse race for performance on the customer metrics that we put into place. We acquiesced to doing what resonated with the sales force. But it worked. If it works, it works. And these things will deliver for you in spades.

## FOUR ACCOUNTABILITY ACTIONS

### Customer Accountability Room

One of the most rewarding accountability forums is the customer accountability room (Figure 6.6), which has these goals:

- Drive continuous learning and understanding about the impact the company has on customers
- Assign accountability and drive urgency for improvements

## FIGURE 6.6.  Customer Accountability Room

### Status: Customer Relationships

| Incoming Customers This Month | Outgoing Customers This Month | Customer Growth or Loss This Month |
|---|---|---|

| Year-to-Date Customer Growth or Loss Trend | Year-to-Date Customer Count |
|---|---|

### Status: Customer Quality

| Incoming Accounts Size This Month | Outgoing Accounts Size This Month | Account Size Growth or Loss This Month |
|---|---|---|

| Year-to-Date Account Size Trend | Year-to-Date Customer Net Present Value |
|---|---|

### Status: Customer Experiences

| Key Customer Touch Points | In-Process Measures | Complaints |
|---|---|---|

| Year-to-Date Complaint Trending | Customer Survey Touch Point Feedback |
|---|---|

### Status: Customer at Risk

| Volume of Lost Customers | Reasons for Losses | Critical Customers Lost |
|---|---|---|

| Potential Customer Losses Identified | Reasons for Potential Loss |
|---|---|

- Execute ongoing modifications and improvements
- Create awareness and manage the customer profitability pipeline and risk

In the customer accountability room, the walls are covered with the priority metrics you have identified to track and manage customer relationships and profitability. At regular intervals, all the operational leaders and the president meet in the room. The group moves around the room, which has been set up to traverse the customer experience. The first wall encountered depicts metrics on overall outcome: the flow of customers and other guerrilla metrics. The next wall has the volume, flow, and nature of customer issues posted. Finally, the last part of the room identifies operational accountability and performance in executing the customer experience at priority contact points. At each section of the room, the leaders are asked, "Why is this like this?" "When will it get better?" and "How will you improve it?"

This level of public accountability is potent. The reason this works is that people know the accountability meeting will regularly occur, they know they will be held accountable, and they know that good results will be rewarded. When leaders focus regular account-ability and reward on performing for customers, traction and progress is advanced.

As an example of a customer accountability room in action, we took over a large meeting room and around it posted the out-comes of the metrics. These included guerrilla metrics, account-ability metrics for the operations, and the other metrics in the accountability action chain. Wherever it was possible, we stacked ranked performance for each of these items. In addition to the outcome metrics, which were enlarged visually and posted on the walls, we listed customer quotes, reproduced letters, and set out regional and departmental rankings where applicable. We started with the wall on the left, explaining the outcome metrics of refer-rals and customer counts using the guerrilla metrics. At the back wall, the trending and tracking of customer issues were blown up to show who had done what to fix them and how long it was taking to get the counts down. The priority customer contacts were mapped and visually depicted whenever possible. For example, if receiving a shipment was a key priority, the packaging and com-munication were hung up there along with the results on how these were being executed and customer responses.

The customer room brought the concept of the guerrilla met-rics alive and pushed them from concept to accountability that peo-ple could manage. On a quarterly basis, we walked that room with the top executive and his lieutenants. We stopped in front of each of these stations. Then the questions would begin. Why is this like this? Who is performing best and worst? Why? When will you fix this? Why are we ignoring this? As the commitments were made, they were noted immediately at each station. At the end of the walk, customer management in its entirety was discussed. Each quarter, the room was revisited along with the results and the commitments.

This is an accountability forum! It is simple, and it is clear. Most important, it is public and in front of peers. We got additional trac-tion as the room became a major attraction during recruiting. In addition, since this was the visual and public depiction of a department's performance in the customer thing, it became an interesting competitive place where people popped in to see how others were doing. They also became quite creative at showing the depiction of their customer experiences. At last we had something that took this conceptual customer work to a place where people got it and passionately participated in it.

## The Quarterly Report

Complete a quarterly report documenting what's in the customer room (Figure 6.7). This is a visual depiction of the impact the company is having on customers and customer profitability created for widespread distribution. Consider getting it out in both paper and electronic form. Because questions are asked of and references made to it, people will become ardent readers of it. And because it publicly depicts who is winning the horse race, it prompts the same action-oriented response that the customer room and the daily screen tally create.

## Put the Guerrilla Metrics Front and Center

The guerrilla metrics will give you your voice for consistently talking about managing customers throughout the company. But these have to be internalized by those asking for the performance here.

### FIGURE 6.7. How to Tell the Customer Story in the Quarterly Report

| Front Cover | First Page | Second Page |
|---|---|---|
| Why a Quarterly Report—Why We Care | Companywide High-Level Customer Feedback—Quotes and Statistics | Area-Specific Customer Feedback—Quotes and Statistics |

| Third Page | Fourth Page | Fifth Page |
|---|---|---|
| Key Customer Issues in the Quarter/Trending from Past Quarters | The Guerrilla Metrics: Customer Relationship and Quality Statistics | Action Being Taken, Accountability, and Progress |

They can't be listed as an agenda item and referred to as something like, "Okay, now we have to go through the guerrilla metrics." To be effective, the guerrilla metrics have to be owned and understood and must become part of the fiber of the questions and just as important as quarterly sales goals.

### Enforce Creation of an Annual Customer Plan

Make the process of annual customer commitments have the same level of public accountability. Give annual planning the same type of competitive chord as the customer room. This can be done in the customer room because you'll need to create targets for each of those elements. It would be dramatic to have people commit publicly to the dimensions of performance as you make your way around the room. I see spirited discussions at each station of information. I see a leader named for each and the commitments for the following year recorded on the spot. These can be researched and revised for the final plan. But the important thing is to make managing these customer targets have great energy.

## CONCLUSION

Figure 6.8 and the following points provide a summary of herding C-A-T-S:

- Managing customer relationships and profitability requires clear and actionable accountability across the organization. Until this is accomplished, the customer work will remain elusive to the well-intentioned soldiers of the corporate machine, who will be left to do their own silo-based interpretation of the command, "Go focus on the customer." Progress will continue in fits and starts depending on the leader, the time, and the passion levels of the people inside the organization.
- CEOs and senior leadership need to expand their understanding of customer performance past the metrics presented by the individual operating areas. Leaders need to demand accountability from their organizations around customers. They must have a plan for how to link the functions of the organization together to review performance with customers. An accountability plan should be established which clearly outlines how the company will be held accountable for customer performance and in what forums.

## FIGURE 6.8. Herding C-A-T-S: A Summary

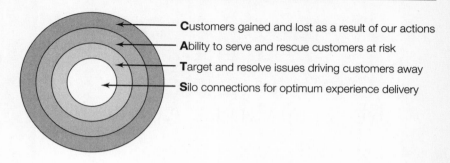

**C**ustomers gained and lost as a result of our actions

**A**bility to serve and rescue customers at risk

**T**arget and resolve issues driving customers away

**S**ilo connections for optimum experience delivery

- The C-A-T-S approach gives leaders four customer accountability targets to drive the action (Figure 6.8).
- Begin the accountability effort by making guerrilla metrics the customer language of the organization.
- Take stock of the organization's ability to grasp and manage each of the other components. This will require a great deal of cross-company work to sort through and reconcile the many versions of customer counting that have sprung up across the silos.
- Don't commit to more than you realistically have the resources to handle and stage the work. Recognize that to get a comprehensive system for customer accountability typically takes three to five years.
- At every stage, make the metrics clear and understandable. Leaders should adopt the language as their own and begin to use their own version of the customer accountability targets to tell the story of how the company is managing customer relationships and profitability.
- Establish accountability forums that people count on and know to perform to. Use the tool of public accountability to drive the action.

# CHAPTER SEVEN

# REALITY CHECK AUDIT

## TACTICS BEYOND THE HAND WAVE

The failure of the customer work is taking it past the hoopla to action. Progress must be measured in how an organization takes action, and in how those actions are stitched together to make a difference in the running of the company.

The reality check audit takes the concepts and ideas of Chapters One through Six and rolls them up into a concise to-do list that defines the task ahead. The manner in which it is organized and used will perform three functions for you.

First, the list of tasks will give your collective management team and organization an understanding of the scope of work and efforts required to lead and manage customer profitability and how customers experience your brand. It will give you the tactics required to take the effort way past lip-service. The audit is in actuality your to-do list. The questions of the audit comprise the actions to undertake if you're serious about managing customer profitability as part of the regular course of your business.

Second, the audit function will allow you to measure what work you have accomplished and the scale of work left to do. It will provide you with a baseline of performance for you to measure progress. The audit also offers the option of measuring the difference in perception of progress made in these activities between management and company members. Understanding if there is a chasm in perception of commitment and action will be important as you move forward in the work. It will clarify how locked in the rest of the organization is with the customer commitment and could help to point out gaps in communication requiring improvement as you progress with the work.

Finally, the process of completing the audit gives you the opportunity to reflect on your organization and its ability to get this work done. Think about your organization and the relationships that exist today. What are the dynamics that will help or hinder the progression of the customer work? You'll be able to apply this thinking later in Chapters Eight through Ten. These chapters put you through the paces of applying this knowledge to determine if a chief customer officer is right for your organization, if you have the strong leadership commitment and partnerships to make it successful, and what organizational structure might be best suited for the mission inside your corporate machine.

The contents of the audit in sheer enormity of tasks may seem daunting. It's easy to understand why the customer ecosystem in most companies is out of whack: there are so many moving parts. That's why few companies really excel with their customers. But don't let the scale of the work stalemate you. The audit provides a comprehensive list of tactics to execute over time. If you did one-third of these suggestions, you'd likely come out above most of your competition. As a first step, simply use the audit to demystify the work ahead of you. From there you can create a plan of action. And from there you can actually *take* action.

## Audit Components

The reality check audit contains fifty-eight questions covering the seven dimensions of building customer relationships and managing customer profitability shown in Figure 7.1. The fifty-eight question audit is provided later in this chapter for you to complete for your organization.

### Section One: Customer Leadership

This section probes for specifics. Have you committed to customer profitability? Can people across the company translate it into action? As leaders, do you have the clarity to steer decisions toward customers? Do you know what customers will value above all else? Have you provided your organization with that clarity of purpose? How

**FIGURE 7.1.** Reality Check Audit Components

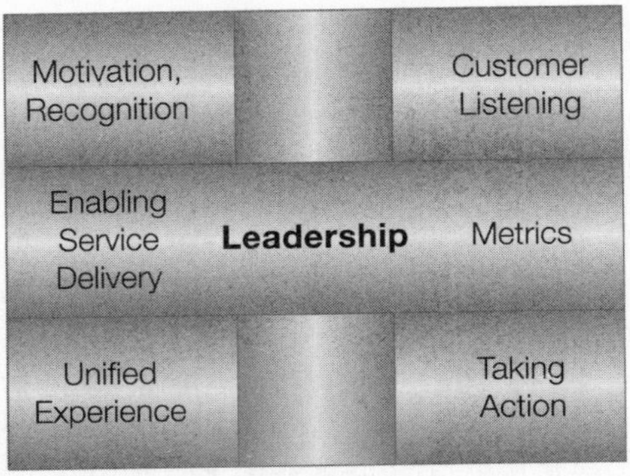

clear is your vision of the brand value you want to deliver to customers? Do you know which customers you should value? How does the organization understand your direction? Are you inspiring the movement past operational execution to experience delivery? Do you let people know what you are trying to accomplish?

Here are two examples of where customer leadership worked and where it didn't. A home builder moved the company focus from getting a customer to sign the contract to delivering their family dream home. As the company shifted its purpose, it went from executing a tactical list of actions to execute to becoming a partner in people's lives. It went from selling one house to providing a family their homes throughout their lifetime. It went from being a home builder to establishing a "family home partnership."

Their revenue stream and customer profitability grew as the builder expanded beyond building the family home to providing an ongoing list of goods and services to families to help them to enjoy their new home. Under this new umbrella of services, the company needed to expand its supplier and partner network. When proposals were brought forth, they were scrutinized through the lens of how well they contributed to the family home partnership direction. It was a little like bumper cars in the beginning: people wanted to go in this direction but weren't completely sure what it meant. There were many ideas bounced against the wall that were bounced back. But the leaders consistently upheld their beliefs. People eventually got it, and the company became a market leader and is thriving today.

In contrast, a retailer never got past the quarterly yardstick of sales. Some efforts were made with proclamations about customer service. Even reward programs were wired to incorporate frontline performance. But leadership personally never stayed consistently focused on the customer. When compensation time came around, a blind eye was turned when a high sales performer didn't quite make the customer performance numbers. There was no consistent messaging about the greater purpose for the customer experience and relationship. The focus of the business continued to be about making the sales targets. Cost cutting, promotions, and product were frequently modified, but the overall customer experience and relationship were not differentiated. Customers shopped them on price and product and were therefore seen as a commodity, exchangeable with stores offering similar products and promotions. Customer and employee attrition rates became among the highest in the industry.

## Section Two: Customer Listening

This section measures the organization's muscle for listening and responding to customer issues. Optimizing customer feedback is one of the most straightforward ways to garner the momentum for customer focus, yet most companies don't do it in an organized way. But all you have to do is listen: listen to what your customer tells you is broken, and then fix it. That's what this audit section probes for. It won't measure how well you're compiling customer input or what great piece of software you've bought to do it. Rather, it asks, Do you use the information? Does the customer feedback you receive keep you awake at night? Are you persistent in driving the trend of persistent issues down so that you don't spend your time refixing the same problem for scores of customers? Are you holding people's feet to the fire to continuously use this information and value it as a way to fix what ails your customers? You don't need to spend millions on a "satisfaction" survey. You have the information right at your fingertips if you'd only listen for it. This information your customers are taking the time to give you are the broken things getting in the way of your reliability. They are inhibiting your ability to take it to the next level.

## Low-Tech Listening That Works

Once a month, take one chair and put it in the middle of the room. Put twelve chairs in a circle around that chair. Seat twelve people from one part of the company in those chairs. Let them talk. The person in the middle listens. Someone takes notes. The people who talk are taken seriously. The person who listens is the president or highly placed executive who will champion and drive the company to change. A facilitator (a CCO-type person) works throughout the company to drive the organization to establish solutions to the things brought up. There's a tote board and accountability. The president continuously presses for resolution of the items. People do things to change the company. This is simple, and it works. But it takes a leader with gut and guts.

### Hope in a Case Study: Continental's Gutsy Low-Tech Listening

As Continental initiated its transformation in the mid-1990s, it began what it called a "forgiveness campaign." There were two parts to the campaign. First, all top executives through everyone who had the title of vice president were given a pile of letters written by angry customers, with the responsibility for calling each and every customer who wrote one. The customer was to be listened to and then given an apology and explanation. The apology was meant to be heartfelt and the explanation of actions that would be taken to rectify the situation, not just proclamations that good things would happen soon. The executives also had to give the customers time to vent. And did they ever! Calls would often run from thirty minutes to an hour, and in that time leadership learned about customers and the company and how their operations affected customers. That time was more valuable and had greater impact than any focus group or research results could have delivered. The voice of the customer was now resonating in their ears, and it came to mold decision making and gave impetus to the actions being taken (Brenneman, 2000).

Continental continued the forgiveness campaign with travel agents and corporate clients in every city that the airline served. This was an important step for the company to commit to, with results that paid off. The many resulting improvement actions helped to pull the airline out of the tailspin it was in and contributed to its transformation. According to Continental's Web site in August 2005, *Fortune* magazine named Continental the No. 1 Most Admired Global Airline on its 2005 list of Most Admired Global Companies for the second consecutive year. Continental again won major awards at the 2005 OAG Airline of the Year Awards, including "Airline of the Year" and "Best Airline Based in North America" for the second consecutive year, and "Best Executive/Business Class" for the third consecutive year.

## Reality: The Corporate Conundrum on Customer Listening

Here's what usually happens with corporate customer listening. Customer service hears the complaints day after day, year after year. A decision is made that *surely* the company will want to know the volume and trend with which customers are delivered these sub-par experiences. So some kind of system is rigged to track calls and record customer feedback. This material is compiled in a report and sent to executives, yet little action results from the compilation. And the reason for the inaction is that what executives receive is often a litany of quotes with no tracking or trending of the issues and their volume. They need to understand how widespread the issues are and this information is not provided. For example, operations won't be inclined to change a process that involves twenty-two hundred employees because of a list of quotes. That information is just not actionable or operational enough to gain attention or drive accountability. As much as we'd like comments alone to compel operational change, it isn't going to happen. You need to offer people a way to account for the issues in a reliable and automated manner for them to take hold and be taken seriously enough to drive change.

## Get People to Listen Through Technology

To interrupt quarterly sales goals with customer issues, you must translate them to include numbers, totals, counting, and competition. Unless you're in a place where the leadership shares your customer passion, you need to find a way to collapse masses of information acquired from customers into a system of issues that can be tracked and accounted for.

Software is now available to capture and tally this potent customer feedback into an electronic customer issue reporting tool for your company. This tool will provide you with the mechanism to track and hold people accountable. And the process to getting there can also be a beautiful thing.

What happens is that the process of defining the software requirements for the tool presses the organization into categorizing customer comments into a system. In order to be able to count issues, people first have to take the time to recognize the customer issues and categorize them. There must also be an exercise that clearly assigns the categories of comments to operating areas of the company. This is so that as the results are reported, the operational areas can be held accountable with the ebb and flow of customer issues attached to their area. Now *this* is a reliable and public forum for who is doing well and who's not. *Now* you will turn some heads and drive some action.

### Scale Reliability Across the Organization

There are a great many options to buy versus build software and tools to help you to scale this type of application across your organization. The complexity of channels has created a built-in excuse from some organizations I've spoken with on how they're stalemated on this work. But that's just not the case with the tools that are available today.

How you approach the identification and implementation of such a tool is critical and will take thought and consensus across the organization. Think CRM. The same problem that exists with that software can exist here if what the tools are for is not agreed on from the start. The good news about this new set of tools is that operations gets hard and fast numbers that they can track, and they can see their numbers go up or down based on how well they're doing at listening to comments and taking action. Best of all, the numbers appeal to the competitive streak that operations naturally has for performance. The type electronic reporting tool shown in Figure 7.2 offers customers an opportunity to give feedback in real time about the experience he or she just had with the organization. It's not intrusive, and the customer can opt out simply by not completing it. The feedback spans across the channels and provides immediate performance guidance that helps operations know how they're doing day in and day out.

## FIGURE 7.2.  A Screen Shot Example of a Customer Issue Reporting Tool

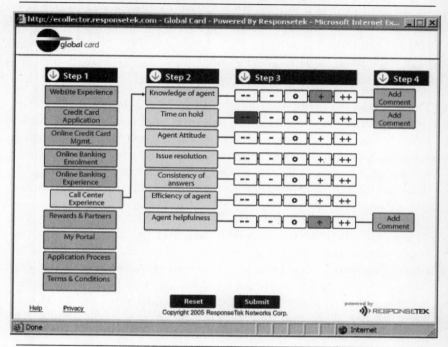

*Source:* Used with the permission of ResponseTek.

## Section Three: Metrics

This section evaluates how well you've executed a metrics system people understand and use to manage the business and customer experience.

### Guerrilla Metrics

For the guerrilla metrics, the questions push the respondent to evaluate the level of rigor being employed to manage the flow of incoming and outgoing customers. People are asked to rate their perception of how strategically the company is managing customers as assets. It will ask if they believe you have a handle on the levels of your customer retention and defection. For example, do you know if you are keeping customers or pushing them away? Are you still an acquisition company, where the lion's share of re-sources are pumped into getting new customers? Have you taken segmentation past a marketing exercise to enable you to person-ally know your best customers? Do you really understand the ebb and flow of customers in and out of your business and the impact they are having on your profitability?

### Diagnosis and Issue Resolution Metrics

These questions probe to find out just how real the muscle for cus-tomer listening is. Questions ask respondents how much discipline exists around trending and resolving the issues. Are these metrics asked as a part of key questions during quarterly reviews, for ex-ample? Just how well does the company track customer issues and drive performance improvement based on the reduction of issues?

### Operational Customer Experience Metrics

These questions get to the root of whether the company is work-ing as one unit to deliver to customers. They ask respondents to determine if there has been a purposeful identification of the key contact points and to evaluate the level of performance manage-ment metrics in place for managing key customer interactions. They ask people to rate their perception of how much people are held accountable for these performance metrics and where they rank when compared with more traditional metrics defining busi-ness success.

## SECTION FOUR: ACCOUNTABILITY AND TAKING ACTION

This section of the audit tests how disciplined the process is to mea-sure and demand the new behavior required to manage customer profitability. It asks, Does a mechanism exist to cause operational accountability and action? How does the company use metrics and performance standards in meetings and in the planning process?

Counting on a leader to naturally switch from driving the busi-ness from a quarterly sales perspective one day to thinking all things "customer" the next is pretty delusional. There's got to be some kind of accountability forum that forces the issue with leaders on what they did and how they did it. And these need to be with all the leaders of the operational areas in the room so a connected picture of what's happening can be understood.

An important element of driving accountability for customer profitability is how strategic the organization is about determining and executing customer targets. Many companies that say they focus on the customer don't take the time to wire customer priorities into annual planning. The resources and prioritization of what to do in the next year do not include targets for incoming and outgoing customers. There are no specific plans to eliminate the issues. Executives don't ask how the operating areas will wire in the improvement of the operation to excel at critical customer interactions. It's exactly these areas that this section of the audit prods the respondent to think about.

## Section Five: Unified Customer Experience

This section is an examination of how purposeful the organization has been in determining what it delivers to customers (Figure 7.3). All too frequently the customer experience is the unplanned collision of deliverables between the silos. An experience that's knit together through the life cycle isn't really thought through. With the advent of CRM, there has been some good work done to define a customer life cycle.

However, these efforts fall prey to being inwardly focused definitions of contact points when customers can be solicited to up-sell, cross-sell, and so on. While companies may have dabbled in other

**FIGURE 7.3.  Examining the Unified Customer Experience**

How the organization works together in creating and delivering a cohesive and optimum customer experience.

Have You Created a Holistic Experience?

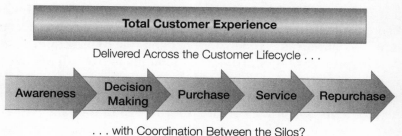

Total Customer Experience

Delivered Across the Customer Lifecycle . . .

Awareness   Decision Making   Purchase   Service   Repurchase

. . . with Coordination Between the Silos?

areas of customer focus, this idea of knitting the experience together takes some time to grasp. Who heads this? Is marketing the lead? Does operations call the shots? Is information technology inadvertently driving customer contacts because of what is being pumped out of the CRM system? If you took the tactics and pasted them side to side on a wall somewhere, what kind of experience would be delivered?

Achievement in the delivery of a unified customer experience is difficult because it requires that the silos drop their functional disciplines during the planning stages. It makes every project seem more complex because there are more people at the table participating in every aspect of the business. But the companies that are doing this well are the ones that customers continue to name as their favorites.

### Why the Moments of Truth Are Alive and Well

If you haven't identified the opportunities that exist to give your customers a good experience, then you can't manage it. Two key things happen to your customer experience: (1) the operational silos take over in determining what they're going to do to the customer and when, and (2) the customer experience happens by default, the outcome of the collision of your silos' interactions with the customer.

I believe in pushing people together to create a common language to define the stages of customer interaction and the moments of truth or customer touch points that define the experience for your brand. The moments of truth enlighten the organization to understand the stages that form their interaction with their customers. They push the organization to create a common language and framework for understanding the touch points with the customer that cross the organization. The identification of the moments of truth inspires creativity by opening people's minds to thinking through what should be delivered at key intersections with a customer to deliver value and experiences unique to the brand.

The process of identifying the moments of truth drives awareness about where a company can have an impact on a customer relationship and customer profitability. If there is no effort to identify the moments of truth, a contact prior to expiration of a subscription frequently is missed, along with revenue opportunity. Many companies don't purposefully plan an automated and consistent companywide renewal effort where they solve any issues with service prior to sealing the renewal. Finally, the moments of truth burst across the silos and push them to work together in the optimum delivery of the experience. Building an operating plan for the execution of the key moments of truth clarifies the organizational and operational handoffs where so much customer dissatisfaction and defection occurs.

## SECTION SIX: ENABLING SERVICE DELIVERY

This section audits how well the front line has been supported and prepared by the organization to deliver to customers. It's classic that defining the scope of customer work is frequently collapsed as being about customer service. But when people use the term *customer service,* they often mean problem solving. That's reactive, and this section is about much more than the ability to fix problems as they arise. Is your front line the last to know about most things? When they assist customers, are they dealing with a tangled mess of data that force them to toggle between multiple screens? Are you paying them to sell units while pontificating to them about serving customers? Do they have the skill sets to do the job? As the world has changed and you've changed what you want your company to be to customers, have you done the hard work to put those most likely to succeed in those positions?

### "If This Is Tuesday, I'm in Poughkeepsie"

Ah, the milk run of the field personnel. The duties of many people in the field are carved out as an autopilot series of stops along a geographical line in the sand: Tuesday in Chicago, Wednesday it's Indiana, Thursday St. Louis. Who cares if the customer in Chicago needs anything? It's the scheduled run for service. No wonder customers can sometimes feel disconnected from the field force who is assigned to serve them and that the sales force craves a higher purpose for their job. They've both been put on a schedule that drives their relationship and frequently an arbitrary set of tasks. The field force checks in at the scheduled date and time. And customers just aren't always sure what to do when these folks drop by.

Quite a few of the companies I worked with had the milk run down pat. At Coldwell Banker, the people whose job it was to deliver the value of the franchise system were our business consultants. These folks were on killer milk runs. They worked morning, noon, and night to show up at the franchisees' sites and make sure everything was okay. After spending a significant amount of time speaking to franchisees to understand what they valued, we came to realize that we needed to establish a consistent way for the franchisees to ask for, receive, and recognize service delivery from us. We also came to realize that in our quest to support customers, we needed to do a lot more listening to clearly understand the franchisee's priorities. The milk run was due for a change.

Based on what we learned, we modified our approach to establish an annual or biannual agreement between the franchise company and franchisee customer on how we would partner with them to help them develop and improve their business. This was quite a different approach from showing up on schedule to discuss the latest advertising campaign or check compliance on signage. It required a high level of listening from the business consultants, and it required moving the relationship to a strategic level. A major part of this shift was to establish the business consultants as partners and resource managers, thereby expanding their responsibilities and enhancing the meaning of their position. Now we wanted them to create a contract annually as an agreement to what the franchisee wanted to achieve and to the responsibilities that both the franchisee and us (the franchisor) had in making the achievements a reality. This was to shift the tenor of the relationship as we needed the business consultants to not only serve their franchisee customer, but to also hold them accountable for their end of meeting their goals.

As might be expected, this shift had a domino effect. We needed to develop new skill sets. We needed more resources to enhance business development and support. And we needed to leave behind the comfort of the milk run. Within eighteen months, this new approach was woven into the way we did business. Franchisees were able to understand and recognize what we were delivering to them through the resource management of their business consultant. Twenty-four months after rolling out this new approach, our performance ratings by franchisees increased three-fold. None of this would have happened if we hadn't paid serious attention to identifying and removing the significant barriers that stood between our business consultants and their ability to do their job. A big part of this became about listening to them and hearing them out to understand what they needed.

Too often companies see the front line as the deliverers of the good stuff they build at corporate. Who hasn't heard the line, "I'm from corporate and I'm here to help"?

## Section Seven: Motivation and Recognition

This section audits how well the company is motivating the drive for customer relationships and customer profitability. It probes to understand how you're using motivation and recognition to develop company behavior and culture. What are the questions in meetings focused on? Which people in the company are considered the emerging leaders? What areas of the business are they excelling in? Is there a blend of recognition for the many dimensions of running the business? As you've demystified the customer work, have you been able to create a method for recognizing achievement in the guerrilla metrics? How well are you inspiring and motivating people to work beyond the operational constraints of their area? Are people rewarded for working together and creating end-to-end customer solutions? Do you applaud the risk takers—those with the gut and the guts?

### Get Ready for the Wet Blanket

For a long time, I've been pushing back whenever someone asks me to help them tie compensation to customer satisfaction surveys. When companies get serious about managing customer loyalty or profits, or satisfaction, one of the first things they reach for is a way to tie bonus money to it. Cash is the first answer frequently thought of, but I caution the use of this type of motivation. Employees are going to look for leadership cues in a variety of ways to determine how serious the customer effort is. Jumping in too soon with the customer satisfaction score won't help and could hurt. Here's why: when reward works, it changes behavior. When companies tie bonuses to customer satisfaction surveys, they frequently pick the company performance in "top box" customer satisfaction survey results as the metric to track. Then they pick an arbitrary threshold that the company must meet to determine if the bonus will be paid. That "top box" customer satisfaction survey score is an aggre-gate of many things happening in the company, many which they can impact and some which they can't. It is extremely difficult to determine what each operation would do differently to contribute to the improvement of that score, so there's a flaw in assuming this number will steer or change behavior. Finally, customer satisfac-tion scores aren't a true indication that the company is doing a great or even a good job with customers. So if you're picking the moneymaker, it isn't necessarily satisfaction. When companies tie employees to satisfaction without changing what really ails the com-pany, they're inadvertently setting people up not to get their bonus. This breeds frustration and can fizzle out your effort pre-maturely as folks just don't feel they have any real control on that number. Want to breed even more frustration? Attach the front line and the field's bonuses, but not those of the top executives to those customer ratings. The "commitment" to the customer just won't take.

As an alternative to satisfaction scores, some companies are at-taching customer retention performance to compensation. That also has some sticking points to be aware of. If you're in a com-pany with long service contracts, for example, you may appear to have good retention numbers, when what you've really got is something I refer to as "captive loyalty." You also need to be very careful about the behavior you're pushing people to. By tying compensation to performance, customer service reps have been cajoled extensively to act in a certain way. And the customer un-fortunately takes the brunt of these well-intentioned brainstorms. For example, when a customer service rep's incentive is attached to talk time (for the operational purpose of keeping costs down), calls become clipped and rushed. When it's attached to incentives to boost cross-selling, operators sometimes feel pressured to pres-sure the customer.

### Case in Point: The Customer Retention Bonus

One company established a bonus system and minimum quota for customer retention performance. With this plan, customer service was motivated to "save" half of the customers calling the company to cancel their service. If they reached the target assigned, they got a bonus. What happened is that these service reps worked very hard trying to keep those customers from canceling. According to one report (Regan, 2005), a lot of customers didn't like how this was done. New York State Attorney General Eliot Spitzer stated that it was the incentives that solicited complaints from consumers: "These bonuses, and the minimum 'save' rates accompanying them, had the effect of employees not honoring cancellations, or otherwise making cancellation unduly difficult for consumers" (p. 1).

## Try a Well-Rounded Approach to Motivate Performance

Getting momentum and sustaining focus and excitement for managing for customer profitability require a well-rounded approach. If the only reward is monetary, people will see right through this singular island of commitment. A better choice is to add a series of actions that stress the privilege of working on the customer projects, recognition for new behavior, a focus on operational performance that people can really affect, and a series of recognition rewards that pump up people's chests, not just their wallets.

*Make Working on the Customer Projects a Privilege.*  Establish the customer work as the plum projects of the organization. Use the trump card of making sure that people know that customer profitability is a priority to senior executives. Then people will want to go there. If you're locked into the fact that sustainable growth comes from growing profitably within your customer ranks, you have the power to make the projects that advance that objective the ones to reach for.

Spread the wealth when you launch these initiatives. Some frenzied organizations have their people almost audition for spots on these coveted think tanks. They spread the wealth and don't keep participation to a certain level or job function. Because these projects are high-level priorities for executives, people are given a chance to present to them and achieve exposure they might not receive otherwise.

*Reinforce and Recognize New Behavior.*  If you're a company that really wants to make your mark through delivering great customer experiences, seek out the creative thinkers. Have you created an environment where gutsy ideas and actions are celebrated? Or do people feel that you say you want a great experience on one hand but sing out the "we can't do that" chant when new ideas are pitched? People aren't looking for a big program with banners and coffee mugs. They look for signs from leaders that they are on the right track. Sponsor brainstorming sessions where people are encouraged to throw out wild ideas that may expand the business. Work to create energy where there's not risk but reward in offering up ideas. The companies that really excel at this do it because they've figured out how to motivate people's spirit. The best companies for customers are the best ones for the people inside it. And the best ones making inroads in the marketplace have made idea generation the right of every person across every rank within the organization.

*Focus on Operational Performance People Can Affect.*  This takes more work than focusing on the one big number. But people need to be able to take specific actions that will yield recognition. That's why leaders and companies that have thought through key interactions can have more impact. They make the goals relevant to customer experiences. They explicitly identify the operating areas involved. And they put the collective teams to work in identifying the baseline and stretch performance metrics they should be working toward. This takes the customer work out of the clouds and into the day-to-day work of people's jobs. And it demystifies the task at hand. The "pie in the sky" aspect of customer work is one of the biggest deterrents to making traction.

*Use the Power of the Friendly Horse Race.*  Once you've got the operational metrics in place, show how people compare in common metrics across geographies or company areas. People want to see their name at the top of the list. Pride in performance is a very powerful thing to motivating customer-focused behavior.

*Celebrate Cross-Functional Successes.*  When groups collaborate to work out a gnarly problem, make their efforts a big deal. This is work that doesn't necessarily come naturally, so if you have people and groups who persistently reach out to others to identify and resolve problems, make them the example for what the company is looking for.

*Connect the Company with Customers.*  Put the people who care the most in front of customers. Have them tell the story of what they're working on and why. Have those folks be the people whom potential customers talk to and meet. Find a way to publicize who's on the spokesperson list. Others will clamor to have the chance to participate, especially when it's connected to senior-level recognition.

*Make Informal Recognition Purposeful and Personal.*  This has to be on the mind and in the consciousness of the company. There must be an ongoing stream of "attaboys" and pats on the back for people who are endeavoring in the customer work. A short penned note of thanks or notes on the margin of a report work wonders. I've seen people keep those tokens of appreciation for years. At Lands' End, we created something called the "Customer Correspondence Corps." There were so many letters that needed responding to that we pulled out the positive ones that basically needed a thank-you back and a personal response. Over two hundred people in the company at any given time were signed up to respond to at least five of these letters a month. After they had put in six months as a Correspondence Corps member, they were invited to a special meeting with the president. There they were given a personal thank you from the president and presented with a fountain pen with their name engraved to sign their name to the customer letters they sent. This had an enormous effect on employees and sent a message that this commitment was absolutely real and not some phony campaign we had thought up for "focus on the customer month." In today's wired world, I would venture to say that a hand-written note might have even more impact than it did back then.

*Make Executive Exposure Part of the Reward.*  Celebrate the conclusion of customer projects with the highest-level executives present. Bring customers to these celebrations if it makes sense, and have the team get another round of glory by presenting the work they've completed to deliver enhanced experiences to customers.

## Preparing for the Reality Check Audit

Consider two audiences to complete the audit. First, of course, is the leadership of your company. Next, give the audit to a cross-section of the company to complete prior to leaders' completion of the audit. Then back away as the sparks of reality and perspective fly! The differences will be eye-opening. You'll see how leaders rate themselves on customer leadership and commitment versus what the rest of the company sees as their reality. If you're going to take the time and resources to do the audit, then do it well. Make sure that people are honest, and use the opportunity to keep that ball of inactivity around the customer moving.

Keep in mind that the data provided by this diagnostic activity will be valid and useful only if people score current activities and not future activities in the works or planned. Prompt respondents to score for reality—not to achieve target scores.

## How to Distribute and Conduct the Audit

Having the audit completed as part of a meeting or workshop is very productive as it prompts thought-provoking discussion. I have seen this used as the jump-start for leaders' taking ownership of driving the customer agenda. It has been beneficial in bringing the silos together to uniformly understand and agree to the scale of the work. And it has prompted great debate as people get into the reasons that perspectives vary on the performance of the different elements. An effective approach for using the audit in a meeting setting is to send the audit out to leaders ahead of the meeting so they can think about the content. At the same time, send the audit to a cross-section of the company. Make sure you get the responses back from company members in time to have their scores tallied and summarized so you can use them in the meeting with leaders.

If you don't want to conduct the audit as part of a meeting, distribute the audit to leaders and a cross-section of the organization to complete. With this approach, set the stage for people to take the exercise seriously. The audit should be sent from the most senior customer champion in the organization, preferably the chief executive. There should be background on why it's being conducted, how people should be sincere in their responses, and what will be done with the results. People have taken way too many of these things that have disappeared with no follow-up. You need to commit to working this audit; otherwise don't do it. For this distribution option, the administrator of the audit collects the audits, tallies up the scores, and plots them for use in a meeting or other scenario for presenting the results.

# THE REALITY CHECK AUDIT

The reality check audit you are about to view contains fifty-eight questions to diagnose how you are doing in driving customer relationships and customer profitability. The following recommendations provide tips on how to execute the audit inside your organization. You can find the audit immediately following these instructions.

## INSTRUCTIONS

There are four basic steps in the audit process.

### Step 1: Answer the Questions

Respondents should read and give a performance rating to the statements in the audit. For each statement, respondents should think about whether they agree with the statement and how strongly they believe that the action is being successfully executed. Exhibit 7.1 shows the first section of the audit to illustrate how to answer each question.

### Step 2: Tally the Scores for Each Category

Go down each category in the questionnaire, and total the ratings for each using the form shown in Exhibit 7.2.

### Step 3: Plot Company Scores as a Platform for Driving Change

Plot the summary of company scores by placing an X in the box in Exhibit 7.3 for each audit component. The profile created with this summary provides a visual picture of the customer commitment that people believe exists for the organization. Scores falling in the range of 16 to 18 represent the targets for competency in each audit category. It would be rare for any company to be executing all seven categories in this target zone. This profile you create will become extremely useful in group discussions with leaders on how to advance your customer effort.

### Step 4: Group Discussion Settings

If you opt for a discussion approach to the audit, make sure that you allow at least an hour for this exercise. You need to allow time for people to complete the audit and total scores, discuss it in small

**EXHIBIT 7.1. Step 1: Answer Each Audit Question**

| | | Company Performance | | | |
|---|---|---|---|---|---|
| | | Never | Sometimes | Usually | Always |
| Customer Leadership | 1. You are aware of what drives value to customers. You have prioritized your deliverables accordingly. | 0 | 1 | (2) | 3 |
| | 2. You know your customers by groups of profitability and loyalty. | 0 | (1) | 2 | 3 |
| | 3. You are aware of what these differences are by customer group. | 0 | (1) | 2 | 3 |
| | 4. You have clearly defined the tangible and intangible deliverables of your brand to customers and to your organization. | 0 | 1 | (2) | 3 |
| | 5. You have a clear strategy, which everyone understands, on why your brand can be differentiated in the marketplace. | 0 | 1 | 2 | (3) |
| | Category Score | | | | |

**EXHIBIT 7.2. Step 2: Total Your Scores for Each Audit Section**

| Reality Check Audit Category | Company Performance for Each Category |
|---|---|
| Customer Leadership | |
| Customer Listening | |
| Metrics | |
| Accountability and Taking Action | |
| Unified Customer Experience | |
| Enabling Service Delivery | |
| Motivation and Recognition | |

EXHIBIT 7.3. Plot Your Score for Each Audit Category

| | 2 | 4 | 6 | 8 | 10 | 12 | 14 | 16 | 18 | 20 | 22 | 24 |
|---|---|---|---|---|---|---|---|---|---|---|---|---|
| | | | | | | | | | Competency Target | | | |
| Customer Leadership | | | | | | | | | | | | |
| Customer Listening | | | | | | | | | | | | |
| Metrics | | | | | | | | | | | | |
| Accountability and Taking Action | | | | | | | | | | | | |
| Unified Customer Experience | | | | | | | | | | | | |
| Enabling Service Delivery | | | | | | | | | | | | |
| Motivation and Recognition | | | | | | | | | | | | |

groups, pick a spokesperson to report each group's results, and then report and discuss it as an entire group. Don't skimp on time here. Short-changing time will keep the conversations at the hand-wave level. You need the time to get into the nitty-gritty of why the components are being scored the way they are.

For the optimum results, don't try to discuss the results of the audit in a large group meeting without first discussing it in separate smaller discussion groups of no more than ten people each. To do this, assign a category of the audit to each of seven discussion groups. As a result of their discussion, they should reach consensus on the company's current performance in their assigned audit category and plot the score (as shown in Exhibit 7.4). After each discussion group has completed its task, reconvene the entire group and discuss the outcome of the audit results. If you had company members complete the audit prior to your leadership meeting, you can also plot

### EXHIBIT 7.4. Plotted Leader and Company Scores

| | 2 | 4 | 6 | 8 | 10 | 12 | 14 | 16 | 18 | 20 Competency Target | 22 | 24 |
|---|---|---|---|---|---|---|---|---|---|---|---|---|
| Customer Leadership | | | | | ● | ■ | | | | | | |
| Customer Listening | | | | ■● | | | | | | | | |
| Metrics | | | | ● | ■ | | | | | | | |
| Accountability and Taking Action | | | ●■ | | | | | | | | | |
| Unified Customer Experience | | | ● | | ■ | | | | | | | |
| Enabling Service Delivery | | | | | | | ● | ■ | | | | |
| Motivation and Recognition | | | ● | ■ | | | | | | | | |

■ Leaders' Rating of Performance

● Company Members' Rating of Performance

their results on the form and compare how the folks in the trenches rated the company compared to leader ratings. If you've got the culture that lets people speak with candor, these conversations will be enlightening.

## THE REALITY CHECK AUDIT QUESTIONS

Following now is the Reality Check Audit. These fifty-eight questions should be answered with candor based on the respondent's perception of current company performance in each of them.

### Section One: Customer Leadership

The questions in this section (Exhibit 7.5) ask how people are inspired and held accountable for managing customer profitability and customer experiences. What level of clarity have leaders provided the organization on what they want when they say, "Go fix the customer thing"? How well are leaders able to bring the silos together and manage the multiple spinning plates to drive cohesive and meaningful outcomes for customers?

### Section Two: Customer Listening

These questions evaluate how well the organization categorizes incoming customer information to identify issues (Exhibit 7.6). How agile is it in assigning accountability and making changes that are meaningful to customers? How much does the organization make itself a student of the rich data coming from customers to manage improvements in an agile and timely manner?

### Section Three: Metrics

Section Three asks how well you are doing with the three types of metrics necessary to becoming a customer-committed organization: the "guerrillas," diagnosis and recovery metrics, and customer experience operation metrics (Exhibit 7.7).

### Section Four: Accountability and Taking Action

Section Four asks what is being done to cause operational accountability and action around customer profitability and customer issues (Exhibit 7.8). How does the company use metrics and performance standards to drive accountability and action to manage the experience? How does it ensure its delivery to profitable customers to build their loyalty? Is customer accountability an important part of leadership meetings? Is the customer discussed only occasionally? Is it difficult to get the customer on the agenda, and even then is it slotted in only after what some consider more important issues, such as quarterly sales, are discussed? Do you ever serve up accountability for customers to the board level?

### Section Five: Unified Customer Experience

Section Five addresses whether the company is defining a differentiated and unified customer experience (Figure 7.9). Is there a plan for its execution with accountability by operational area? Do people across the company understand and agree on what they are delivering?

### Section Six: Enabling Service Delivery

Section Six asks how well the organization prepares and enables customer-facing personnel to deliver the best experience to customers (Exhibit 7.10). Are their tools up-to-date? Do they have more on their plate than they can handle? Is the front line given mixed messages and conflicting priorities? Do they experience "frontline whiplash" where they are told the customer is important, then rewarded and paid based on business as usual? Is their mission and purpose understood and elevated so that they feel personal pride in their contribution?

### Section Seven: Motivation and Recognition

Section Seven is a diagnostic of the compensation, motivation, and reward systems of your organization (Exhibit 7.11). How do you reinforce and inspire the organization to be accountable and deliver the best experience to customers? Have you inspired people to take the chances necessary to trust their gut and have the guts to propel the work forward?

**EXHIBIT 7.5. Section One of the Reality Check Audit**

| Section 1: Customer Leadership | Company Performance | | | |
| --- | --- | --- | --- | --- |
| | Never | Sometimes | Usually | Always |
| 1. You are aware of what drives value to customers. You have prioritized your deliverables accordingly. | 0 | 1 | 2 | 3 |
| 2. You know your customers by groups of profitability and loyalty. | 0 | 1 | 2 | 3 |
| 3. You are aware of these differences by customer group. | 0 | 1 | 2 | 3 |
| 4. You have clearly defined the tangible and intangible deliverables of your brand to customers and to your organization. | 0 | 1 | 2 | 3 |
| 5. You have a clear strategy, which everyone understands, on why your brand can be differentiated in the marketplace. | 0 | 1 | 2 | 3 |
| 6. You have ensured that employees can internalize what your brand and desired customer experience are. They can translate how that vision and strategy affect their job performance. | 0 | 1 | 2 | 3 |
| 7. Business decisions are based on driving customer value and are clearly communicated inside the organization so people can internalize and role-model the customer commitment. | 0 | 1 | 2 | 3 |
| 8. You continuously inspire people to think of ways to meet customer needs and elevate the customer experience. | 0 | 1 | 2 | 3 |
| Category Score | | | | |

**EXHIBIT 7.6. Section Two of the Reality Check Audit**

| | | Company Performance | | |
|---|---|---|---|---|
| | **Never** | **Sometimes** | **Usually** | **Always** |
| **Section 2: Customer Listening** | | | | |
| 9. An easy mechanism exists for customers to give feedback. People across the organization can easily access the information. | 0 | 1 | 2 | 3 |
| 10. Leaders actively listen to customers and sponsor change to improve the customer experience. | 0 | 1 | 2 | 3 |
| 11. Leaders listen to the front line to hear their experiences and perspectives on improving the customer experience. | 0 | 1 | 2 | 3 |
| 12. Customer feedback is tracked and trended to resolve issues preventing experience reliability. | 0 | 1 | 2 | 3 |
| 13. Real-time data (comments and complaints) are used to know the pulse of the customer experience and make rapid change. | 0 | 1 | 2 | 3 |
| 14. The company survey system measures customer loyalty and retention and can be tied to operational changes required. | 0 | 1 | 2 | 3 |
| 15. You are able to segment your survey results by customer segment and in priority order for customers. | 0 | 1 | 2 | 3 |
| 16. You have a process to compile and use customer listening data to drive your annual planning priorities. | 0 | 1 | 2 | 3 |
| Category Score | | | | |

**EXHIBIT 7.7. Section Three of the Reality Check Audit**

| | | Company Performance | | |
|---|---|---|---|---|
| | **Never** | **Sometimes** | **Usually** | **Always** |
| Section 3: Metrics | | | | |
| 17. You track some level of guerrilla metrics to know the flow and quality of customers you gain and lose. | 0 | 1 | 2 | 3 |
| 18. You are as concerned with keeping existing customers as acquiring new ones. You vigorously follow metrics for customer retention and loyalty performance. | 0 | 1 | 2 | 3 |
| 19. Tracking metrics are in place to trend customer feedback issues, as well as their resolution and time to resolution. | 0 | 1 | 2 | 3 |
| 20. The organization has developed the competency for identifying and managing process performance metrics. | 0 | 1 | 2 | 3 |
| 21. Process metrics and performance standards are clearly established to manage customer experience delivery. | 0 | 1 | 2 | 3 |
| 22. You have identified priority customer interactions. Systems are in place to track the process performance for these moments of truth. | 0 | 1 | 2 | 3 |
| 23. You have assigned shared accountability for process metrics where multiple operational areas affect common customer experiences. | 0 | 1 | 2 | 3 |
| 24. You regularly hold reviews to gauge performance standard progress across operating areas. | 0 | 1 | 2 | 3 |
| Category Score | | | | |

**EXHIBIT 7.8. Section Four of the Reality Check Audit**

| | | Company Performance | | |
|---|---|---|---|---|
| | Never | Sometimes | Usually | Always |
| **Section 4: Accountability and Taking Action** | | | | |
| 25. Everyone can access an easy-to-understand reporting tool that pinpoints necessary changes and drives continuous improvement. | 0 | 1 | 2 | 3 |
| 26. Accountability and handoffs for operational performance in delivering customer experiences are clear. | 0 | 1 | 2 | 3 |
| 27. There are role clarity and accountability for managing profitable customers. | 0 | 1 | 2 | 3 |
| 28. Regular forums ensure accountability and performance standards for execution of experiences and managing profitable customers. These are considered critical—as much so as quarterly sales reviews. | 0 | 1 | 2 | 3 |

**EXHIBIT 7.8. Section Four of the Reality Check Audit,** *continued*

| | | Company Performance | | |
|---|---|---|---|---|
| | Never | Sometimes | Usually | Always |
| 29. Customer accountability is not limited to the forums but is part of regular conversation. Leaders continuously hold people accountable for operations performance, resolution of issues, and customer management. | 0 | 1 | 2 | 3 |
| 30. Processes are in place to continuously engage high-value customers who have a propensity to defect. | 0 | 1 | 2 | 3 |
| 31. The company runs quarterly and annual "loss reviews" of customers who left and why. Improvement efforts to remove the causes are executed. There is a sound system in place for ensuring that the same customer problem does not reoccur. | 0 | 1 | 2 | 3 |
| 32. Annual planning includes companywide discussions, targets and actions for customer profitability, and delivery performance. | 0 | 1 | 2 | 3 |
| Category Score | | | | |

**EXHIBIT 7.9. Section Five of the Reality Check Audit**

|  | Company Performance | | | |
|---|---|---|---|---|
|  | Never | Sometimes | Usually | Always |
| Section 5: Unified Customer Experience | | | | |
| 33. You have established a customer life cycle or continuum that the organization understands to define the customer experience. | 0 | 1 | 2 | 3 |
| 34. There is a clearly known performance objective for each segment of the customer continuum. | 0 | 1 | 2 | 3 |
| 35. You know the contact points, or moments of truth, with the customer and can identify the high-priority contacts for delivering brand value and keeping profitable customers. | 0 | 1 | 2 | 3 |
| 36. The organization works together to develop the experiences along the continuum that defines your brand. | 0 | 1 | 2 | 3 |
| 37. You have a process map for key interactions, or moments of truth, with customers, each with clear performance standards. | 0 | 1 | 2 | 3 |

**EXHIBIT 7.9. Section Five of the Reality Check Audit,** *continued*

| | Company Performance | | | |
| --- | --- | --- | --- | --- |
| | Never | Sometimes | Usually | Always |
| 38. The organization is clear about dependencies, handoffs, and performance accountability across operational boundaries. | 0 | 1 | 2 | 3 |
| 39. You organize company communication, performance reports, and improvement efforts around the customer experience. | 0 | 1 | 2 | 3 |
| 40. You conduct an annual moment of truth audit that summarizes the total customer experience, the operational handoffs, current performance, and where you can improve. | 0 | 1 | 2 | 3 |
| Category Score | | | | |

**EXHIBIT 7.10. Section Six of the Reality Check Audit**

|  | Company Performance | | | |
| --- | --- | --- | --- | --- |
|  | Never | Sometimes | Usually | Always |
| **Section 6: Enabling Service Delivery** | | | | |
| 41. Service providers have clarity on the role they play in delivering the customer experience. | 0 | 1 | 2 | 3 |
| 42. Service values are well communicated, understood, and translated to performance standards and in objectives. | 0 | 1 | 2 | 3 |
| 43. You regularly listen to frontline personnel to understand and remove the barriers they face in service delivery. | 0 | 1 | 2 | 3 |
| 44. Customer feedback and skill coaching and development are provided to elevate service. | 0 | 1 | 2 | 3 |
| 45. Service providers are provided with the tools to enable them to have the most efficient and effective interaction with customers. | 0 | 1 | 2 | 3 |
| 46. Customer contact personnel are able to identify high-priority customers during their service interactions. | 0 | 1 | 2 | 3 |
| 47. Customer data connecting all of the customer interactions are provided to customer-facing personnel so they can manage and understand the comprehensive customer relationship. | 0 | 1 | 2 | 3 |
| 48. Service providers participate in the development of the customer experience. | 0 | 1 | 2 | 3 |
| Category Score | | | | |

**EXHIBIT 7.11. Section Seven of the Reality Check Audit**

| | Company Performance | | | |
|---|---|---|---|---|
| | Never | Sometimes | Usually | Always |
| Section 7: Motivation and Recognition | | | | |
| 49. The company practices a well-rounded approach for driving customer focus that includes motivation, encouragement, and incentives. | 0 | 1 | 2 | 3 |
| 50. Customer-driven motivation and recognition are tied to operational performance that people can change. | 0 | 1 | 2 | 3 |
| 51. Customer projects are elevated as a privilege for people to participate in and receive executive exposure. | 0 | 1 | 2 | 3 |
| 52. Company motivation and recognition reinforce and drive behavior to make continuous improvements. | 0 | 1 | 2 | 3 |
| 53. Leaders reinforce the development of innovative customer experiences and recognize ideas from throughout the company. | 0 | 1 | 2 | 3 |

| | 0 | 1 | 2 | 3 |
|---|---|---|---|---|
| 54. The company's performance framework measures those dimensions critical to delivering differentiated value and managing customer profitability. | 0 | 1 | 2 | 3 |
| 55. People receive timely recognition applauding efforts to improve customer experiences. | 0 | 1 | 2 | 3 |
| 56. Leaders reward and celebrate cross-group collaboration and successes. They are actively involved in elevating the importance of customer work through motivation and recognition. | 0 | 1 | 2 | 3 |
| 57. Leaders regularly deliver purposeful and personal informal recognition. | 0 | 1 | 2 | 3 |
| 58. Exposure and presentations to customers are a part of what motivates and encourages company members to stay focused on the customer work. | 0 | 1 | 2 | 3 |
| Category Score | | | | |

## CONCLUSION

The reality check audit takes the concepts and ideas of Chapters One through Six and rolls them up into a concise to-do list that defines the task ahead. It will perform three functions:

- The list of tasks will give the collective management team and organization an understanding of the scope of work and efforts required to lead and manage customer profitability and how customers experience the brand.
- The audit function will allow you to measure what work you have accomplished and the scale of work left to do. It will provide a baseline of performance to measure progress going forward.
- The process of completing the audit should allow you the opportunity to reflect on your organization and its ability to get this work done.

There are seven categories to test yourself and your organization on to determine how far along you are in your customer work and if you have the stamina to proceed:

- Customer leadership
- Customer listening
- Metrics
- Accountability and taking action
- Unified customer experience
- Enabling service delivery
- Motivation and recognition

Taking the leadership audit with your leaders is a good place to begin the work. This defines the scale of the undertaking and demystifies what is necessary to make a commitment to customer management. Reaction will give a great indication if this is something the organization is able and willing to take on.

Administering the audit to the rest of the organization provides an eye-opener to leadership. They identify how well they have clarified and are leading customer focus in the eyes of the organization as compared to their own opinion of their effort.

As a result of conducting the audit, the questions to ask yourself are:

- Are these tasks for customer management getting done?
- Is someone on point to accomplish them? Does this person know and accept this accountability?
- If there is no point person, does the company have the stamina and focus to divide and conquer the list of things to do?
- If the company does decide to move ahead, what will sustain the momentum? And who will be the glue bringing the parts of the organization together?

Chapter Eight will enable you to assess if a CCO or other customer champion is required for advancing the customer agenda inside your organization. In chapters Nine and Ten you'll determine if you have the level of leadership support required and will define the organization structure best suited to assist your company in driving the customer work ahead.

# PART THREE

# IS A CHIEF CUSTOMER OFFICER THE SOLUTION?

# DO YOU NEED A CHIEF CUSTOMER OFFICER?

Throwing head count at the customer challenge is not necessarily the automatic solution. Throughout this book, you've seen that getting this work done is about specific functions and tasks that need to be executed. The reality check audit laid everything out to define the work.

Take the time now to review how your organization is performing in each category based on your responses to the audit in Exhibit 8.1. This will expose for you what you're able to get done and what you're not gaining momentum on and what the root causes might be for inactivity. Knowing the answers to these questions will get you closer to determining if the best approach for your company is to divide and conquer the tasks or create a leadership position to spearhead the work.

## CAN A CCO HELP YOUR CORPORATE MACHINE?

This customer work requires all heads nodding in the same direction. You don't have to go to the extent of a chief customer officer (CCO) if you can drive a company connection at the beginning of the work, have a consistent process to manage throughout the work, and build in metrics to consistently judge the work. Use your Summary of the Reality Check Audit (Exhibit 8.1) and the following assessments to understand if your company is at a standstill in driving customer relationships and profitability and if a CCO can help.

**EXHIBIT 8.1. Summary of the Reality Check Audit**

| Category | Characteristics of Best Performance | Your Company Performance |
|---|---|---|
| Leadership | • Focus and clarity<br>• Leadership consistency<br>• Know what drives value for customers | |
| Customer Listening: Feedback, Voice of the Customer | • Regular process for listening<br>• Push to take action<br>• Customer-first decision making | |
| Strategic Customer Metrics | • Customer metrics top of mind<br>• Accountability for customers<br>• Clarity on customer goals<br>• Regular accountability forums | |

Accountability and Taking Action

- Agile in making changes
- Customer-driven action bias
- Process for measuring change
- Clear forums for accountability

Unified Customer Experience— Managing Silo Dysfunction

- Clarity on brand experience
- Inspired organization
- Risk taking to differentiate
- Clarity of cross-company roles
- Accountability for experience

Enabling Service Delivery

- Constantly removing barriers
- Listening to front line
- Development of front line
- Passion for front line as heroes

Motivation, Recognition

- Clarity in customer metrics
- Team accountability
- Enthusiasm for customer-based recognition
- Built into business priorities

## Do You Need a CCO? Assessment One

To conduct the first CCO assessment, fill out Exhibit 8.2. If "Lack of Focus" was a consistent response, you need to determine if this is a priority with leadership. What's going to make it important if it's not already important to them? Hiring a chief won't do the trick at this stage; that will just frustrate someone.

If "Disjointed Efforts" was a consistent response, bringing in a ringleader in the form of a CCO could work for you. You could also choose to have someone take on that role in addition to his or her regular operational role to drive the process for doing the work and drive the discipline in metrics, reporting, and accountability. Layering this on to an already busy person who has neither the time nor skill set drives you straight to the "Lack of Focus" result, however, and it can send the message that the customer work has not yet made it to the status of top priority.

If "Lack of Clarity" was a consistent response, you could benefit from someone driving consensus for what you want to accomplish. I started referring to myself as a "roll of human duct tape" because so much of my time was spent getting people together to agree on the direction, disbanding the group so they could go work, and then bringing them back intermittently to course-correct. Again, this could be a dual role for an operations executive, but that person needs to have ample time and leadership commitment to make it worthwhile.

## Do You Need a CCO? Assessment Two

To punctuate your assessment of your company's ability to drive this work, consider each of the following statements and determine whether it applies to your company:

*There is someone in our company who clarifies what we are to accomplish with customers.*

☐ Yes there is          ☐ No there is not

*Implementation tip:* These agreements need to be established in partnership with the functional owners across the organization. It is important to make sure that the CCO or executive leadership does not do this in a vacuum and then try to "throw the brick over

**EXHIBIT 8.2. CCO Assessment One**

| Category | Reasons for Less-Than-Great Customer Performance | | |
|---|---|---|---|
| | Lack of Focus Not a Company Priority | Disjointed Efforts Everyone Does Their Own Thing | Lack of Clarity Not Sure What to Do or How or When to Do It |
| Leadership | ☐ | ☐ | ☐ |
| Customer Listening: Feedback, Voice of the Customer | ☐ | ☐ | ☐ |
| Strategic Customer Metrics | ☐ | ☐ | ☐ |
| Accountability and Taking Action | ☐ | ☐ | ☐ |
| Unified Customer Experience—Managing Silo Dysfunction | ☐ | ☐ | ☐ |
| Enabling Service Delivery | ☐ | ☐ | ☐ |
| Motivation, Recognition | ☐ | ☐ | ☐ |

the wall" to the leaders to rubber-stamp. That brick will be tossed back so fast you won't know what hit you. However, just starting a meeting with an open-ended question is not going to work either. I've found that creating a straw man of the options for defining the priorities for the work can be a good way to go. This works especially well when there's a struggle to figure this out. Don't do this as an annual series of activities. Rather, drive quarterly consensus for what will be accomplished. You don't need a CCO to do this. If you are tracking customer complaints and comments; this can be as simple as picking off the top three items to resolve each quarter. The main thing here is that the customer conversation is happening.

*There is a clear process to drive alignment for what will be accomplished.*

☐ Yes there is    ☐ No there is not

*Implementation tip:* Alignment is tricky. I've seen people stay silent in a meeting, which becomes interpreted as implied consent. The top leadership has got to be rather strong here. The best leaders I've worked with drive people into discussion by going around the table and asking each to state his or her commitment or dissent. These leaders make it okay to disagree if someone is not comfortable with what's being proposed. In fact, they seek it out. Getting dissent out in the open is critical in this work. It is the dissenters who spread more dissent after the meetings that tear the work apart. Unless you have an environment that encourages people to step up and say that they don't agree, you won't make progress here. Think of alignment as requiring three steps:

1. Propose. Put the idea out there for what will be accomplished.
2. Don't suppose. Seek out dissenters and their reasons.
3. Close. Work out the solution and alternatives, and then ask for consensus again.

*We have a roadmap for the customer work and know where progress will be measured.*

☐ Yes we do    ☐ No we do not

*Implementation tip:* To achieve success, this needs to be a group effort. Bring together a team of people with at least one person from every operational area. This group needs to get into the ramifications and work involved in getting the priorities done. They must be ensconced enough in the operation to understand the implications and complexities of getting the work done so they can stage it realistically. They may also need some positive prodding to ensure that they don't talk themselves out of every proposed idea. Someone needs to check in with this team regularly to encourage them of the possible and to (gently) squash the "we've never done it that way" syndrome. This team needs to think through when pauses should be scheduled in to track progress and understand how things are going. Finally, give this group the limelight to roll this out to the organization. Make sure you follow the alignment process to ensure that key players are signed on.

*Clear metrics exist for measuring progress that everyone agrees to use.*

    ☐ Yes they do      ☐ No they do not

*Implementation tip:* Start with the guerrilla metrics. Remember that simple is good and repetition works. Start here. Get everyone counting customer metrics consistently throughout the organization. Getting started with the guerrilla metrics is going to take a huge amount of effort. Focus on these, and then add more when you're ready.

*There is real clarity of everyone's roles and responsibilities.*

    ☐ Yes there is      ☐ No there is not

*Implementation tip:* This is about the handoffs between the silos. Make sure that there is a task list that clearly states which parts of the organization must come together to get the priorities accomplished. Too often these goals are kept lofty and high, and people aren't made accountable for their completion. Reward individuals only when the group has accomplished the entire task. Be firm about time lines and task and responsibilities, and ask the pointed questions in reviews that uncover specifics for how the tasks are being accomplished.

*People really participate and care about the customer work.*

    ☐ Yes they do      ☐ No they do not

*Implementation tip:* You need to get a commitment from each operational area leader on the number of staff and the amount of staff time they will contribute. The best way I've found to do this is to create a formalized team where 25 to 50 percent of people's time from areas throughout the company is dedicated to the customer work. When these companywide contributors are doing customer work, they have a reporting relationship with the assigned leader for that project. To make participation stick, however, requires the commitment of the senior leadership to whom these people report and to create a partnership with them. Form an alliance with the vice presidents of each operating area and agree to what will be done with them. Let the marching orders to your virtual team come from their direct supervisors. Have the supervisors make it clear that they sanction and praise the new role they are having in the customer work. Finally, make the participation in the customer work a privilege.

When I was at Allstate, one of the members of our virtual team was a well-respected director within the sales organization. When he was redirected over to my area, his initial thought was that he had taken a misstep and was being exiled to "customer land." Our president quickly corrected him, pointing out that the new assignment was recognition for good performance; he was not being sent to Siberia. In fact, he benefited from an increase in direct time with executives in his stint with me. We followed the same path with the directors who came over to our group from both the underwriting and claims organizations. But this could not have happened without the commitment of our president and that of the leaders of sales, underwriting, and claims.

*Appropriate resources are allocated to make a real difference to customers.*

☐ Yes they are     ☐ No they are not

*Implementation tip:* Hand waving without investment won't get you anywhere. The key here is to have an organized annual planning approach that dedicates time to the customer objectives and customer investment. The chief executive needs to be personally involved. To achieve success, specific actions with defined parameters of what needs to be accomplished must be identified. For example, at one company, we dedicated ourselves to fixing the top ten cracks in the foundation: operational execution breakdowns that were preventing customers from having reliability in basic interactions, such as receiving appropriate service documents. There needs to be oversight on reviewing the annual plans as they come in to make sure that the investments for the customer effort add up to the achievement of complete efforts in resolving customer issues and advancing the delivery of the customer experience. This is uncomfortable and unpleasant, but at least in the first few years of doing this work, this needs to happen. Otherwise you'll continue to have cobbled-together investments that drive partial improvements in each area but don't connect in a real and meaningful way at the customer contact point.

For example, someone's plan might be to invest in programming time to fix the customer user interface on the Web site. But another group not connected to that objective has not allocated the resources to ensure that there are fast, responsive answers on the new space where customers can post questions and give feedback. A black hole in the customer experience has been inadvertently created. The company is spending money, seemingly investing in a better customer experience. But it goes to waste and may end up annoying customers because the back-end investment is not connected to the front-end investment for that year.

*There is an understandable process for people to work together.*

☐ Yes there is     ☐ No there is not

*Implementation tip:* This work is as clear as mud. It starts with a high-level frenzy that in the blink of an eye has people going back to business as usual. The process for how the work will be defined, reviewed, executed, and rewarded has got to be laid out clearly.

*The work is considered attainable.*

☐ Yes it is     ☐ No it is not

*Implementation tip:* There's a term that people used a lot at Microsoft: *boiling the ocean.* And this is something that can easily happen in this work. Our frenzied enthusiasm gets away from us, and we talk about the end "nirvana" state rather than the steps to get there. I've been called a lot of things in my career, and "blue-sky girl" and "ocean boiler" were definitely in there. What I learned is not to abandon strategy but to dole it out in bite-size pieces. You need to know the end game. But then you need to bridge the gap between strategy and execution so people can work it into budgets, priorities, and planning.

*A process exists for marketing achievements to customers and internally.*

☐ Yes it does      ☐ No it does not

*Implementation tip:* What I've come to refer to as "marketing back" is often overlooked. *Marketing back* means telling your customers and the company what action you have taken as proof of your commitment to the customer. This is a frequently missed opportunity because when you don't tell people internally what's going on with the customer, it's all white noise to them. No report equals no action. Do some visual things inside your company to catch people's attention. A large corporate client put a ticker-tape board in several highly visible places around the company and had the screen rolling with the improvements being made. One was also posted behind the front reception desk so customers and visitors could see it. Now that caught people's attention!

Don't forget to purposefully market back to customers. When you don't tell your customers what you've done, you leave it to chance whether they will notice and appreciate the changes you've made. Some will; some won't. But if you make a point of marketing back, you will get credit for taking action, and that counts with customers. One powerful tool in client service companies is to send an annual letter to top customers. The content states what customers have asked for and what's been done and why (or not been done and why) along with other company-initiated actions. It's sent by and personally signed by the president.

*Recognition and reward are wired to motivate customer work.*

☐ Yes they are      ☐ No they are not

*Implementation tip:* The customer work is not going to seem important until people start to be publicly commended and rewarded for it. Make every company gathering an opportunity to call out customer achievements and reward people for them. One company I worked with created a customer loyalty tote board. They flipped the numbers to show the number of active customers versus lost customers at each company meeting. Everyone was rewarded when the numbers climbed.

You may be one of the many companies wanting to tie customer successes to compensation. If this is the case, make the targets be actual operational achievements versus customer feedback or survey results. I've seen way too many companies arbitrate survey results to meaningless metrics when people who just missed the performance bar plead their case. Attach recognition and performance to process improvements achieved, positive customer recommendations or service performance achievement, such as never being out of stock of critical customer items or on-time airline arrival. Know what customers value most from you, and make the achievement and recognition tied to the performance of those specific things. You'll get people acting differently because they'll know and understand the targets and what they need to do to achieve them.

## BASED ON YOUR ASSESSMENT, DECIDE WHAT'S RIGHT FOR YOUR COMPANY

Now the question now comes back to you: Is anyone doing this stuff? Is anyone even thinking about it? Does anyone have the time to? Is it realistic in your organization to divide and conquer these tasks? If you can, your organization is well adjusted. Having the operational areas own the responsibility and having them share the administrative parts of this work would be heaven. But I haven't seen many evolved companies that are ready for this. It's the pushing and prodding part of the work that most companies need someone to spearhead.

Think hard about your appetite and aptitude for the work. Temper this with the fact that this is at minimum a five-year journey. Pace yourself.

### ENGAGE BEFORE YOU LEAP

Finally, engage before you leap. There needs to be an active and highly involved debate among your company leadership on the need for a chief customer officer. Your top leadership and your board need to agree to make this commitment to push and prod the company in this direction. Use the next chapter, which describes a straw man for the role of a chief customer officer, to get the conversation started. Executives need to commit in advance to the resource and focus drag this will seem to have (at first) on their operations. Most important, this team needs to be the one that picks who this person will be. The role and impact of this role will be greatly diminished if these steps aren't taken first. Take the time to think through this decision and getting everyone involved who needs to have a voice in the matter. I've seen too many customer crusaders brought into companies that didn't have their eyes open to what they just hired. It's in no one's best interest to feel this pain. But if you know what you're signing up for and you do it, this can be a great boon to the organization for making some headway where you've been standing still in the past.

When the teams are ready to proceed, the proposal should be presented with the partners to executives. I also like to include people below the vice presidents for these presentations. It gives people the ownership and exposure to executives that they might not get and strengthens their understanding of the work. They also get the chance to see their direct boss advocating and selling the work, which will do wonders to strengthen their buy-in. The CCO wants to get to a point down the road where he or she doesn't always need the blessing of the vice president to go to their people to get committed participation. But this is just a fact of life of what's necessary in the beginning. That's why I like planting them in the room at these pitch meetings.

## IF THEY WON'T ENGAGE, MAKE THEM LISTEN

I can't tell you the number of times I've met with executives who had never listened in on a customer call. The CCO must bring the voice of the customer into the company! There is no way any progress will be made if executives and company members don't get to know the customers as people. They need to hear their voices and listen to their stories and understand that they are real, with families and concerns and issues that they have to deal with because of the decisions the company made.

The easiest way to make them listen is to bring taped conversations of customer calls (don't forget to get customers' permission) to senior management meetings. When you do this, organize the calls by the areas that are broken in the relationship so it's not a random series of calls about a lot of different things. The goal is to focus people in your meeting on the content of the call. Get the conversation to be around how the customer responded to the not-so-customer-friendly policies or decisions that prodded them to call in the first place. Then make that conversation about why the company made the decisions it did in that instance. Another key is to keep doing this. Every month, the CCO should be on the agenda of an officers' meeting with tapes of customers.

One last thing about listening to customers: doing a gigantic customer satisfaction survey with the twenty-pound report does not qualify as making leadership listen to customers. Yes, I know that there are plenty of customer verbatim comments in these reports. But it's a toss-up how many people take the time to really read them thoroughly. And those who do have so much information swimming in their heads from the volume of comments, it's difficult to piece it all together to know what to do with the information. I know many people believe these reports are great and they help, but they can't take the place of live customer voices and contact.

### Hope in a Case Study: SAS Data Mining Product Institute Takes Customer Listening Seriously

SAS is a world leader in business analytics software. It provides software to ninety-six of the top one hundred companies on the Fortune Global 500 and to 90 percent of all five hundred.

Helping to fuel this market position is the way that its leaders listen to customers. SAS gathers, compiles, and acts on complaints and suggestions that come in from customers every day over the Web and by phone. And then they mine the gold of this information to make improvements. They prioritize complaints and route them to people to work on them. And they don't just shoot these into the atmosphere. They are logged and tracked with answers and resolutions expected. Once a year, they ask, "What more do you need?" through a SASware ballot executed on their Web site. They've take action on about 80 percent of all the requests fielded. SAS also hosts an annual users' conference through its robust SAS Users Group International, where they get more feedback. This is like a pep rally and a hugely energetic forum for SAS software users throughout the world to meet and mingle with people from SAS. The focus of the event is to improve and innovate. More than thirty-three hundred people attended the thirtieth annual convention in 2005 (Florida and Goodnight, 2005).

## CONCLUSION

CEOs no longer have to be convinced of the importance of retaining customers and developing relationships with profitable customers. What's on their mind is how to accomplish this feat inside their organizations.

- With achievement in customer work remaining elusive, organizations are now considering the creation of a high-level position to drive the action. This should not be an automatic or easy decision. Because many organizations are now on their third or even fourth gasp of focusing on the customer, missteps here would make the customer work sink lower and lower as something not to be taken seriously.
- The key to making that decision lies in first understanding what the work encompasses. By reviewing and taking the customer experience audit, you can get a sense of the road ahead if you are really to commit to driving a customer agenda. You'll want to ask whether the parts of the work outlined by the audit are identified as priorities and if there is clear accountability for getting it done. If the answer to this question is yes, you are way ahead of most other companies. You may not need a chief customer officer because your organization is working together to get the job done. But if the answer is no, a chief customer officer may be a potential solution.
- Before you rush out and hire a CCO, take stock of where the company is culturally and decide if the time is right to bring someone in to make the big customer push. If you have lack of focus, disjointed efforts, or lack of clarity, the answer may be different.
- If you decide to proceed with a CCO exploration, make sure that you have consensus to go ahead with the role. The people whose sandbox the CCO will be in frequently had better agree up front to the company and to the discomfort that's to come as a result of the work.

# CHAPTER NINE

# THE CEO AND CCO PARTNERSHIP
## The Tom Sawyer Formula

So who is this elusive person, the CCO? The chief customer officer (CCO) has to be a pied piper, strategist, and illusionist. The CCO must be able to paint the future with customers, lead people to it, be realistic about what can be accomplished, and then actually get something done. The CCO has got to get people to *want* to paint their fence. I call this ability the "Tom Sawyer formula." And it works when the CCO is in lockstep partnership with the CEO.

Tom Sawyer's ability to get his friend to paint his fence was because of his relationship with Aunt Polly and the power she wielded with the kids in the neighborhood. You might not remember this slick piece of cat herding, so I'll nudge your memory and recount the story. This is based on Mark Twain's masterful creation where Tom convinces his buddy Ben Sherman to whitewash his fence.

It turns out that Tom's Aunt Polly had been hounding him to whitewash a fence for her. Aunt Polly wielded great power, and people didn't want to get on her bad side. Getting on her good side was very good. So it's a warm, sunny day, and Tom is begrudgingly whitewashing the fence. When his friend (and sometimes nemesis) Ben Sherman appears on the scene and begins to taunt Tom that he can't go swimming because he has to do the awful work of whitewashing the fence. Tom has a flash of genius that day: he would deflect Ben's harassment by presuming to like the chore that he in fact didn't like one bit. I'll let Tom jump in here with his response to Ben's taunting that he had to work and could not go swimming:

> Tom contemplated the boy a bit, and said: "What do you call work?" "Why, ain't that work?" Tom resumed his whitewashing, and answered carelessly: "Well, maybe it is, and maybe it ain't. All I know it suits Tom Sawyer." "Oh, come now, you don't mean to let on that you like it?" The brush continued to move. "Like it? Well, I don't see why I oughtn't to like it. Does a boy get a chance to whitewash a fence every day?"

It's in that last line where Tom found his genius: "Does a boy get a chance to whitewash a fence every day?" That put the work into a totally different light. Tom Sawyer moved whitewashing Aunt Polly's fence from being a chore to being a privilege. He did it so well that Ben Sherman went from thumping Tom for having to paint the fence to being jealous of Tom because he could. The way that Tom accomplished this was by presenting the work as highly elevated because he was doing it at the behest of Aunt Polly. And because of the esteem that everyone had for her, he let it be inferred to his buddy Ben that he who does something for Aunt Polly stands in very good stead indeed. Ben was taunting one of the chosen ones. Ben ended up begging Tom for the joy of whitewashing that fence and even threw in an apple for good measure. Tom sat and watched while he munched his apple with the sun streaming across his face.

So let me connect this story to the role of the CCO and the CEO relationship. That little flip that Tom did when he turned whitewashing from work to something to aspire to: that's the magic. That's what I want to bottle for every person out there who has to push the customer rock up the hill. It's the magic of "Tom Sawyerism": the ability to have people *want* to come and paint your fence of the customer work.

The linchpin for Tom is Aunt Polly. Everyone reveres Aunt Polly. She holds the key to many good things if people deliver for her. Tom's got it made because he's painting her fence, and that brings reward if he does it right, as he cunningly convinced his friend Ben.

A well-positioned CCO is even better off. If the effort the CCO is leading is truly critical to the organization, he or she must have access to the senior leadership and even the board. As Tom might put it, "It's not every day you get to change the company." To do this work, the CCO must be able to huddle regularly with leadership to keep the action moving. The CCO becomes a partner and adviser with company executives, giving the CCO a unique and admired position in the company. They are seen to be leading an effort of great importance for the company. The CCO's "Aunt Polly" is the combination of importance of mission and proximity to the top of the organization. It gives the CCO momentum and the ability to draw people to the work. People will want to do the work if it is truly taken seriously, and they will be drawn to the political upside to being a key participant in bringing the solution to the table. The bottom line is that the success of the CCO is largely dependent on the commitment of the CEO. And the message I send to you, CEOs, is this: you've got to have skin in this game. The customer work must be a shared mission between yourself and the leader of the customer work.

In the early days of my career as a customer zealot, what I had mostly going for me was a lot of vim and vinegar. I got so whipped up about doing things it seemed that people came to my meetings just to watch the show. It didn't take long for me to figure out that the way to be successful with this work was to let others steal the show.

There was a particular person at Lands' End whom I needed with almost every project to make it a reality. He was the vice president of operations. He was a seasoned operations guy and had brought huge success to the company through automating the warehouse functions and driving efficiency into the business. We came up with some pretty crazy ideas for the marketplace back then, and almost every one of them played havoc with his world. For example, the packaging for outgoing shipments was all over the board. We proposed new boxes and inserts into shipments targeted by customer, which increased packing time. That played with production rates for pieces packed per hour. We also wanted to offer a guarantee to customers who ordered by a certain date that their orders would get there by Christmas. That played with his sensibility for overpromising during the height of the season. The fact that we offered to give customers the order free if it didn't get there in time really drove him a little nutty. We saw lots of spreadsheets on the potential loss we'd experience on that one (by the way, there were hardly any). When we pitched the idea that high-end products should be packed in boxes instead of plastic bags, I thought smoke might come out of his ears.

After doing what came naturally for me initially (the vim and vinegar bit), I learned about "Tom Sawyerism." Instead of pushing a list of warehouse-oriented customer problems in front of Phil, we discussed the customer objective and opportunities together and then with his leaders. These guys became more creative than any other operations folks I'd ever seen. Big burly guys were coming up with ideas for wrapping blouses in tissue. When the ideas were put together and finally pitched to the president, they were the ones doing the talking. It was their show. And that paid off. By the time the next year rolled around and I suggested that we begin offering gift wrapping, they still looked at me like I was nuts, but it didn't faze them. Even the bit about having to take the items out of the automated system, have people remove items from the plastic, and wrap them in tissue and place them in a box with a bow didn't make them flinch. Not even the notion that we had to rig up a shipping box that wouldn't crush the bow got in their way. They had become believers and partners in the mission. And they were convinced of its importance to our president. They had tasted the glory of the pitch and the bravos that followed. It had become apparent that this focus was here to stay, and they wanted to remain a part of it. That gift boxing service became the first of its kind in the catalogue business. I'm proud to say that we made it up in a cornfield in the middle of Wisconsin—my warehouse buddies and me.

# What to Look For in a CCO: The CCO Attributes

CCOs worth their salt have to be wired a certain way. The job's an energy-fest. There is so much personal energy you've got to build up inside yourself. And so much of the job is about pumping up other people to hang in there. And then there's the rebuilding that needs to happen when hiccups occur. If you're thinking about a

CCO for your company, look for these attributes and listen for these approaches in your candidates. If you've already got the job, dig deep inside to make sure you've got these covered.

## Passion and Persistence

When you are considering a candidate for the CCO position, first listen for passion. Then probe for persistence. Ask CCO candidates how they do with resistance. Do they thrive on it or just survive? These should be the times that really get a potential CCO's adrenaline flowing. I can't tell you how many times I was running on fumes doing this work. This is when the person in the CCO job has to remain stronger and more committed than ever. I know there were some folks who hoped I would just burn out finally and go away. No chance. This is when stamina for the long journey is most important.

Fundamental to CCO passion and persistence is the ability to stay motivated for the long haul of the work. The CCO needs to be close enough to the end game to stay  motivated even when it's off into the future. CCO's must harness that passion regularly to sell the virtues of the work and the journey to believers and non-believers. They've got to believe in it enough to stake their reputation on making it happen. This is not one of those jobs you can rotate people into. There's no faking passion. You either thrive in driving change or you don't. Make sure you hire someone with these attributes, and make sure you've got them yourself if it's your job to drive the action.

## Ability to Give the Power Away

Paradoxically, one of the greatest lessons I learned is to check my ego at the door. Astute CCOs understand that this unique power they possess cannot be abused; in fact, it must be given away. With a strong CEO and CCO partnership, people are going to want to jump on this bandwagon, and one of the greatest tools a CCO has to continue motivating participation is having people present their own actions, and putting them front and center to take the credit. The greatest measure of success for the CCO is when the work is adopted by people as their own, when the prodding starts to taper off, and when it becomes a part of the DNA of the organization. That will never happen if the CCO is a credit hog.

## REVENUE = ATTENTION

Let's not delude ourselves. The work's about building the business through the growth of customer profitability and company revenue. The CCO has got to be able to make and prove this case to gain executive and board support. Know that this is job number one. In order to begin to make this case, I suggest that CCOs first spend the time to understand the different accounting methods throughout the company to learn how and if customers are valued, tracked, and accounted for. This will likely be disjointed and will take real effort to tease out the information from throughout the organization. Establish a partnership with finance to cobble together the customer accounting approaches and establish a system for tracking customers and the cost to serve them.

The company has to move past the classic quarterly sales goals or production goals or operational objectives as the only metric to define how the business is doing. The answer to this one isn't, "Okay we'll put that in our scorecard." Those things are sometimes fifteen pages long.

This is why I created guerrilla metrics. These cut through the clutter and force accountability on the state of the company's relationship with customers. These are likely metrics that someone might be collecting somewhere, but they're not front and center like quarterly sales goals. They're certainly not debated and challenged in the same way, but they should be—for example:

- Do you know the volume and value of your incoming customers?
- Do you know the top five reasons that your customers left this quarter?
- Do you know how many complaints are occurring by category?

The job of the CCO is to facilitate the definition of what these are. CCOs have to use their passion and persistence to get people to believe these are important. And they've got to convince senior leaders to commit the time to making these a part of how they ask questions and define the business.

## Action—Not Banners and Coffee Mugs

The company will need to see substantive change to believe that the commitment is true and real and understand what it means in terms of things they should do. The CCO's job is to keep it real. There have likely been efforts that have come before this most recent proclamation to the customer. The corporate memory keepers have little patience for empty commitment to the customer. The CCO has got to get real change going. People will respond a lot better and will be pleased and relieved that they finally have some actions to take their cue from in terms of what they should do.

I'd like to have a big tote board for all the money that's been spent in corporations on banners, coffee mugs, and various other trinkets that have been created to make the customer top of mind. One company I worked with had one of the oddest solutions I've seen. Draped over employees' chairs were fuzzy blue blankets with "CUSTOMER" printed on them in big block letters. "What are these for?" I inquired. The answer: "To make sure that the customer is at every meeting. We pull up a chair for the customer and put this blanket over it so people remember the customer."

This is *not* the answer. It's action that people want. It's action that they'll remember. It's clear action that will finally signal to them that this is the real thing.

## Survival of the Chameleon

There's nothing that will take the place of knowing the business to build accountability. The CCO can't be seen as an outsider, even if he or she is brought in from the outside. A new CCO should understand the functions of the organization to move as quickly as possible from being labeled an outsider to being considered "one of us." Most important, CCOs need to know the players and what their hot buttons are. The CCO will use this knowledge to thrive as a chameleon, modifying approaches as necessary to connect with each part of the organization. Talking with the sales vice president and sales force to understand their priorities requires a different approach from understanding and working with marketing from that perspective. Operations may need another and human resources yet another. Driving change at times is like throwing pasta against a wall: the message and commitment will stick for one part of the organization but not for another. Persistence and ingenuity need to kick in frequently for CCOs as they will find it necessary to provide a multitude of approaches and deliver multitudes of messages for driving the work.

### Hope in a Case Study: Chameleon 101

A colleague has the customer defender job in a large member services organization. She works in a culture that's on its way to figuring out what it means to be customer focused, but it loses its way frequently. Nonetheless, she is charging ahead. She has found that engaging each part of the organization a little differently is the key. The front line understands what she is doing and wants to collaborate on ideas to make the customer experience better. So the work with them is focused on developing a discipline for tapping their incoming customer feedback and improving skills. The strategy group is pushing for a return on investment. Rather than allowing that monkey on her back, she has thrown it back to them to partner with her on defining the customer groups and the return on investment on building up the profitability of each. The more work that's done, the more that others in the company are joining her ranks as advocate rather than as adversary. Now the president who was on board in theory but not necessarily in spirit has just personally made the customer effort the platform for her presidency. By bringing together the president's team to discuss their views on customer experiences, the obvious became apparent: the company is currently fractured and ineffective in how it approaches customers. The president has just publicly made a personal commitment to drive the customer agenda. Bravo!

## MARKETING HOPE

In this CCO job, you're nothing if you can't understand what customers and the company needs, deliver it to them, and remind them that you gave it to them. Marketing back is the promised land to helping customers believe that the company is listening and acting on their words. It jolts the naysayer out of thinking things can't or won't get done. It's absolutely essential to getting the future momentum you need by feeding the organization hope one morsel at a time. All CCOs need to have a little bravado in them to do this marketing back. They've got to be unabashedly proud to toot the horn of the company's accomplishments. And they've got to have the guts and gusto to stump throughout all levels of the organization to get people out of their ruts and into taking action. Shrinking violets need not apply.

# WHAT THE CEO NEEDS TO DO TO ENSURE CCO SUCCESS

The leadership of the company must be behind the CCO. In addition to building partnerships across the company, this person needs a partner at the highest level possible in the organization—a strongly supportive Aunt Polly. The executive advocate has to be personally tied to this work in both passion and day-to-day support. In the real world of multiple agendas and quarterly goals, this person must provide the air cover to get the organization to understand what it means to do this right and to do the right thing.

There is great relief at the prospect of hiring a CCO. It signals that something is being done. It gets precariously close to letting the president make a check next to "customer" on his or her list of things to do because it's now being "handled." This couldn't be further from the truth. Senior executives should know that before they commit to a CCO, this will require a lot of their time. Especially if the CCO comes from outside the business, he or she will need these executives to cut a swath through the politics of the organization. Here we look at the major things the executive sponsor needs to do to ensure CCO success.

## TAKE PERSONAL OWNERSHIP

Position the work as your agenda. Don't make it the sole mission of the CCO. You must become the Aunt Polly to your CCO by putting this at the top of your agenda for the corporation. People must understand that they will be delivering directly to you through working with the CCO. Make people aware that you grasp the importance of the mission, and give examples of what will be accomplished if you reach the goals and what's at risk if you don't. Let them know that this will change the questions that are asked about the business, accountability, and the way people are recognized. Stress that you are in this for the long haul and that to drive these changes, you've named a lieutenant to facilitate this across the organization. Be clear that part of the natural organization of the corporation has precluded the organization in working as cohesively as is necessary to drive a better customer environment. But let people know that participating is not an option; it's your will to take the organization to where it must reside in the marketplace.

## MAKE THE CCO AN OFFICER OF THE COMPANY

It's illogical to think that your leaders will want to collaborate on strategy with a CCO not considered a peer. Ensure that the CCO has a role in the critical planning meetings to ensure that the customer agenda is wired in. Incorporate part of your staff meetings to be facilitated by the CCO to drive the agenda. Especially in the early stages (that is, the entire first year), make suggestions for meetings and events where the CCO should present at, participate in, or be invited to.

I can't stress this point enough. If the CCO is not an officer, the customer effort will be greatly compromised. It's just plain human nature that peers won't be as anxious to be led by someone at a lower level. Don't put changing the course of human nature on the back of the CCO. The CCO will have enough to handle in working with you to change the course of how the company thinks about customers.

## ACCELERATE CCO VALUE-ADDED RIGHT AWAY

Put the CCO in the position of doing specific and tangible work within the first month of beginning the job. Make the first order of business driving the metrics of customer loyalty and customer profitability—what I call the customer math for your company. You can use the guerrilla metrics for this purpose. Define your company's customer math components, the players necessary to comprise them, and how leaders will work with the CCO to incorporate the metrics into the running of the business. Do this during the first quarter that you have the CCO position in place. This tactical set of actions will accelerate understanding of the CCO role. People will be able to observe the cross-company action required to identify and connect metrics across the organization. The point can be made that almost all customer issues require this level of synchronization and that it why the CCO position exists. Another potent first-quarter action for a new CCO is to understand how the company collects and uses incoming customer information. This pushes past the concept of the CCO job, moving involvement into the tactical work of the operation. Start a trend line on the issues if you don't have this going in your organization already. The CCO can begin working in partnership with the operating areas to identify the issues. From there, the CCO can publicly present the top ten issues. Create reliability to the leadership team that this is one of the things they can count on in the future from the CCO. But it doesn't end there. The CCO should continue to partner with the operating areas to get down to the bottom of the issues that are escalating and growing in number. Have the CCO go to the operational areas where the issues exist and understand them. The CCO has to get dirt under his or her fingernails at this point to be able to talk about the business issues. I've seen people come back and talk on these issues in strategist-speak, and this just doesn't fly. If done well, this will further remove people's questions about the validity and need for the CCO and will move the company early on from talk to action. It's this type of kickstart that will help you gain the momentum you need for the long-term success of the CCO.

## Establish Acceptance and Role Clarity

The functional vice presidents who will be working with the CCO must be part of the interview loop and decide if this is the right person. I personally experienced the power of this approach. During the interview process for one of my positions, the CEO required every vice president to conduct an interview. Beyond that, he required consensus on the hiring decision. Because of that, these officers took ownership that I was *their* hire and also took ownership in ensuring that the position was a success. The job I took required consensus to make sure that no one later could come back and say that hiring me wasn't a good idea. It gave me a great start with that group, and it worked. They took ownership that I was their hire, and they had to take responsibility for the decision they made collectively to bring me in.

After initiating the CCO job, it's also important to establish the working relationship between the company leadership and the CCO. Define the process the two of you will use for driving change throughout the organization. Then agree with the other leaders how their organizations will participate with you. It is a good idea to define how each operational area contributes to the mission and what the metrics are that they will be accountable for. In addition, have each operational area commit to assigning at least one person inside the organization who will be the point person for driving the work. Get consensus from these leaders that the CCO has the authority to have a working relationship with these participants. In this way, the CCO is facilitating real change at the operational level rather than pontificating constantly into the air and hoping that something happens. To make this stick, you'll need to think through recognition for these newly developed ad hoc teams. Since they do not follow the regular organizational structure, it will be important to determine what the team reward should be cross-functionally for making progress.

## DRIVE REGULAR ACCOUNTABILITY

Demand regular accountability sessions for the sole purpose of identifying and tracking progress with the customer agenda. Resist the temptation to tack it on to some other meeting. What often happens is that the customer topic moves from the top of the agenda to the bottom of the agenda and then is erased off the agenda completely as other priorities prevail and the meeting time runs out.

Don't make your CCO expend energy and cycles lobbying to get a place on the corporate agenda. That's the irony to this work that I've never quite understood. Why bring someone into the job and then make it nearly impossible that he or she be heard? Instead, establish a set of meetings with the specific agenda of discussing and advancing the customer agenda. Create continued clarity by having the CCO drive these meetings and steer the process. The CCO can create a flow and meeting focus by topic area and can facilitate the meetings. However, the executive sponsor will need to step in as the person asking for and expecting the performance.

## PROVIDE POLITICAL AIR COVER

Whoever takes on the CCO role must believe in his or her personal strength and ability to be successful. That will make this person by nature an independent thinker, someone who will take the ball and run with it. But even the most clearly focused CCO will need to huddle regularly to work through the people and politics of this work. What the CCO needs most is someone at the highest levels to collaborate with who is willing to step in and course-correct to drive the action when it stalls. And it will stall; that's a built-in component to any work that challenges the status quo, which is what this position is meant to do.

This partnership will become the cornerstone for achieving the optimum benefit from your investment in a CCO. When this partnership is optimized, you will be able to create a nimble and realistic approach to changing the organization. The organization will see that this is not a program that will fade away like the others they've seen.

This partnership is also critical to feed the CCO's vigor for driving this action. It will boost the CCO's perseverance and fortify him or her to keep moving forward. With this strong partnership will come a real understanding and appreciation by the senior executive of what it takes to move the work ahead and the level of effort the CCO is putting forth. This becomes supremely important at review time. However, a CCO who is forced to navigate this work alone will wear out over time as the isolation of the job mounts. An absent executive sponsor who is there just to sign checks and see the pitch meetings isn't going to have the level of understanding to be able to advance or rate the work. It takes such a strong internal push for people in these positions to stay singularly focused on this work. Motivate the motivator by providing this air cover that he or she must have from you to get the job done.

## INSIST ON CORPORATE PATIENCE

This work is not for the mild-hearted or for the quarterly inclined. People are going to need to understand that this is a multiyear endeavor. They can't bail in the first year; that would be a huge waste of human and financial capital. It will be the executive sponsor's job to get everyone to stay the course. In the beginning, it will feel like you're force-feeding your young. But over time as you do the things you say you'll do, people will step up. The momentum will then build, and you'll be on your way. You must set realistic expectations that this is at minimum a five-year path. Later on in this chapter is an overview of the specifics you could expect throughout that time line.

## DEMYSTIFY THE ROADMAP

To create the wholesale shift for an organization to cohesively deliver customer experiences is a huge undertaking. Yet it's quickly agreed to when that charge comes from the president. "We must improve customer relationships and profitability." Who wouldn't salute that flag? But what flag did the company salute? What did they agree to accomplish? Therein lies the problem: the CEO's request for customer commitment contains no direction. So the organization doesn't know what they've agreed to do or how they'll get it done. Here the CCO can provide significant value to the CEO and company leadership by framing the scale of the undertaking and establishing a straw-man roadmap for getting the work accomplished over time. Once the roadmap is created, leaders will have a much better idea of what the work is. And it's then that the president should promote a healthy debate with company leaders and their organizations about how and when the work can happen. They should reach agreement on the stages of the roadmap, the key things to be accomplished in each, and an initial time frame for achievement. After a CEO, CCO and company leaders put this amount of discussion and rigor into framing the work they will have a much clearer case to lay out to the organization.

# THE CEO AND CCO PARTNERSHIP: CAUSING THE SHIFT

Figure 9.1 depicts a roadmap to use to cause the shift in your organization. You'll note that the roadmap is broken into stages. This is a good approach to take for your organization. Break the work up into stages that are agreed on with company leadership and have realistic performance expectations attached to them.

FIGURE 9.1. The Roadmap for the Shift in the Organization

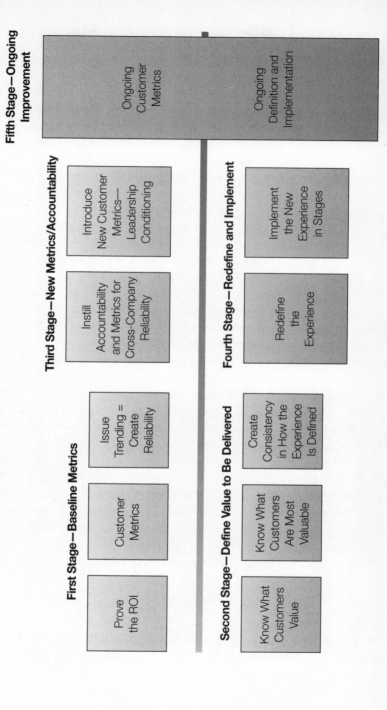

## FIRST STAGE: ESTABLISH THE BASELINE METRICS

To make this happen, the CCO will need to understand how you are defining customers. Every company's customer math calculations are different, and I'll venture to say that you're also likely to find that the silos differ in what how they define a customer and the metrics they use. Establishing a common methodology and way to look at and define customers will require all parts of the organization to share their databases and customer data methodologies. This sets the organization up for creating a unified and strategic way to think about customer data and how you define your success in managing customers as they relate to the profitability of your organization. A good first step is to bring together a group of people to come up with the initial set of guerrilla metrics. Once this is created, they will need to be adopted across the organization.

Tracking and trending of customer issues is a key part of establishing baseline metrics. Next you need to tackle a quantifiable and actionable tally of the issues your customers face on an ongoing basis. Reliability in the execution of the interactions with customers is the first hurdle that you must manage on your way to delivering something differentiated in the marketplace. I agree that it's tempting to dream up really great touches, like sending a customer a personalized calendar with a photo of their family after they've bought twenty sets of prints from you. It's natural for companies to want to leapfrog past the blocking and tackling work to get to the really fun stuff of adding new great features and services. But if the prints aren't delivered when they're promised, if the counter personnel don't give good advice, and if the photo quality is inconsistent, that calendar isn't going to have a positive impact. There's an absolute gold mine of information that you get every day from customers in the form of incoming comments, feedback, and complaints. You need to mine this information, and make your customer listening effort a part of your DNA for moving forward.

## SECOND STAGE: BEGIN DEFINING
## WHAT YOU'LL DELIVER AND TO WHOM

This requires a major partnership with marketing, data, and research. Part of the work here is collapsing existing research and data into a uniform way of looking at the information and filling in the gaps with new research and information. Make sure that this is done in full partnership with marketing. As you move into identifying your most valuable customers, you'll also need to partner with those who run your database work to dig into the data and create a commonality about how you classify, organize, and finally segment your customers. At this stage, it's important to begin to define the customer experience the same everywhere inside the company. This is going to become critical for doing the hard accountability work later. As I work across organizations and I ask if there is a consistent life cycle that everyone can think of to describe the customer experience, I am always surprised to hear that there is not. Do this well here, and it will provide the groundwork for doing the work that comes next.

## THIRD STAGE: ESTABLISH NEW METRICS AND ACCOUNTABILITY

Start holding people's feet to the fire through new metrics and accountability forums. This is when you should begin putting the C-A-T-S system into place. There will need to be a complete partnership with the executive sponsor because he or she will be the key player in the accountability forums that need to be introduced in this stage.

Begin to publicly post performance levels, and hold those stand-up accountability sessions where you go around the room, and leaders must step up and explain why situations exist and what they're doing to resolve them. You will have needed to bring the leadership together along this path up to this point to ensure that they know what's coming and relish the thought of being able to show what they can do.

As the enormity of what needs to be done starts sinking in, there will be questions about how to layer on this work with everything else that has to be done. This will be the test of company commitment, and the CCO will need that air cover as you slide into this part of the work. It will take at least a year and probably longer for this to feel like standard operating procedure. You'll have to build new skill sets across the organization, and the company will have to learn how to understand what to measure, how to identify breakdowns, and how to have people identify how to fix issues. This is the hard work of process change. This is also the hard work of leadership conditioning: bringing in a new set of things for leaders to be passionate about and drive performance toward. It won't be easy, but it will be very worth it.

When you get through this stage, you will be well on your way to being an organization that cares about and commits in a fundamental way to the profitability of its customers.

## FOURTH STAGE: REDEFINE AND IMPLEMENT AT A HIGHER LEVEL

The competencies and understanding that will be created in the third stage will condition the organization to take on the work of redeveloping the experience for greatest marketplace differentiation. For many people, this is the work they thought was going to happen right away. Managing the corporate patience to work through the development of the competencies required to get to this stage will not be easy. But if leadership has the fortitude to move the company through the pragmatic stages of what people will see as endless "getting ready," the payoff in this stage will be worth it. Because the organization will have accomplished the process work and customer-facing metrics, they'll understand how to rethink through the customer experience.

In this stage you'll find it more natural to create cross-company teams for rebuilding aspects of the experience because cross-company metrics will have been introduced and commanded in the third stage. People will be more sensitized to what customers respond to because of the trending of comments and feedback you will have created and managed for. This will build a more intuitive approach to brainstorming new customer experiences. Finally, leaders will have been conditioned to have a greater understanding of the importance of letting go of functional execution and will be more willing to inspire people to think "experience," not operational execution.

## FIFTH STAGE: ONGOING IMPROVEMENT

This is the promised land. It will take at least three years to get here and more likely five to seven. This is the new world where the company is wired to understand and manage customer issues. There are daily, real-time metrics that reduce your dependency on external surveys and put your company in complete touch with customers. The DNA of the organization has become more intuitive and speaks about customers, knows how to classify them, and understands what to deliver to them. Cross-company orchestration of experiences is a natural. You start to wonder if you need a CCO anymore.

# THE CCO JOB DESCRIPTION

This boils down everything covered thus far in this chapter into a shorthand description for the chief customer officer job. You can use this as the starting point for a job description, modifying it as necessary for your organization. The three goals of the CCO are to:

- Engage the organization to purposefully manage customer relationships, revenue, and profit.
- Create a persistent focus on the customer in the actions the company takes.
- Drive the organization to work together to create unified and optimum delivery to customers.

As a change agent inside the company, the CCO performs four specific functions:

1. Establishes metrics for defining the relationship with customers. Partners: Usually finance and marketing for guerrilla metrics; issue trending requires engagement and alignment with all functional vice presidents.
   a. Guerrilla metrics.
   b. Issue trending and tracking.
2. Influences cross-company agreement on what and how to deliver greatest value to customers. Partners: Marketing, finance, and perhaps sales, depending on the organization.
   a. Defines what customers value—how to determine the differentiating experience to be delivered.
   b. Determines what customers to invest in.
   c. Decides where to make investment decisions, that is, the highest-impact contacts and efforts.

     d. Creates a common language set and definitions for the customer experience.

3. In partnership with the chief executive, drives accountability through cross-company data and metrics. Partners: The chief executive and all functional vice presidents.

     a. Facilitates the development of the accountability action chain, establishing the approaches and implementation of research to understand customer loyalty and return on investment (ROI).

     b. Works with leaders to identify baseline metrics for tracking interaction with customers.

     c. Drives tracking and reporting to get to reliability in key interactions.

     d. Leads the accountability forums—when to meet with whom to drive accountability.

     e. Works with leaders on messages, reinforcing, recommendations for recognition, and driving the culture change forward.

4. Clarifies a common approach and process for driving the work across the organization. Partners: All of the functional vice presidents.

     a. Identifies operational accountability cross-functional alliances.

     b. Facilitates working together across the silos instead of separately within them.

     c. Instills the discipline of process change and change management into the organization.

## SHOULD THE CHIEF CUSTOMER OFFICER OWN A FUNCTIONAL AREA?

Whenever we work on defining these roles, the question comes up, "Should this person also run a functional area?" This frequently arises in the context of running some part of the customer service organization in addition to driving the wholesale change across the corporation. The answer depends on the maturity of the service organization and where it is in performance. If it is a well-oiled machine and knows how to manage and continuously improve the customers' experience for the company, there might be an advantage for the CCO to have an operating area to get something done that is under his or her control.

These are the things I define as "well oiled" in terms of performance in the service area: (1) the service personnel have good listening skills and can relationally build conversations with customers; (2) the company excels at using the customer data it receives to drive real-time operational change; (3) the service area has moved past a cost center to an R&D center and a dynamic source of information for the company to improve relationships with customers; and (4) the service organization leaders know how to inspire and develop the skills of the service staff to ensure that they believe that their role is far above that of "phone person." That's a tall order. But if these are covered, the leader who accomplished all of that may be the one to lead the company to greater things.

It's a real question as to just where this CCO leadership position should reside. It's been tried a number of places. We're going to drive through the pros and cons of the options in the next chapter.

## CONCLUSION

• Every chief customer officer must have an "Aunt Polly" CEO: an executive who will back up the customer effort and the work that the CCO is trying to drive ahead inside the organization.

• A CCO should possess the following characteristics and approaches to the work in order to thrive, survive, and drive the customer agenda ahead:

- Passion and persistence
- Ability to give the power away
- Revenue = Attention
- Action—not banners and coffee mugs
- Survival of the chameleon
- Marketing hope

• Executives need to make sure that they do everything they can to ensure the success of the CCO. They need to take personal ownership of the work, not just check it off their list and pass the whole thing over to the CCO. They should elevate the CCO role to officer of the company, since this is the level where he or she will be working to drive the action. CCO value should be accelerated as quickly as possible by putting the role at the head of an important project. This will clarify what the CCO does and how people work with the new role. They need to provide political air cover to help with the pushback that will occur when the CCO starts asking people to change how they do work. They need a plan for how the work will proceed that's not out of sync with the organization. If executives are willing to commit to these actions, then the new CCO will have a good chance for success.

• For a CCO to make progress inside an organization, they need to constantly earn the right to have the role. The shift inside the organization must be a clear process that people can follow. They need to move the corporate machine from the initial customer metrics that the company must adopt to getting inside the operational work and changing business processes. To do this, they need to understand the business, not just stand on the sidelines.

• Defining the role of the job of CCO is still in progress in many corporations. Once established inside an organization, the role will continue to change and adapt as the company evolves in its ability to work together on complex customer issues.

• The three goals of the chief customer officer are to:

- Engage the organization to purposefully manage customer relationships and customer profitability.
- Create a persistent focus on the customer in the actions the company takes.
- Drive the organization to work together to create unified and optimum delivery of experiences to customers.

For more information on the life of a chief customer officer, see Chapter Eleven. Six chief customer officers currently in this role explain how it's going and tell their story on the experience of driving the customer agenda inside their organization.

# CHAPTER TEN

# STRUCTURES FOR DRIVING CHANGE

We're finally down to the nitty-gritty of organization. When I'm asked about the CCO role, the frequent questions are, "What does a CCO do?" and "Where does the CCO report?" The answer to both of those questions is, "It depends." The capacity or the role, structure, and organization depend on your commitment and how large you scale the work. It depends on the age and stage of your organization. It depends on how much backing the organization has for the role, and at what level it resides. These are the things you need to consider before you drop someone into this role. So we begin this chapter with a probe to help you think through the right structure for your organization.

Consider these things when trying to determine which area of your organization should command the customer leadership role. Is there an emerging customer zealot who seems a natural to take on this role? This should be someone with the capability to bring the organization together and facilitate conversations toward actions and accountability. I equate this work to being "human duct tape"; the job is to get people to come together, then work together, then accept accountability together.

## THE CUSTOMER FOCUS SMORGASBORD

Zealots try everything and anything to get the momentum going. I have seen the customer effort initiated in each way noted here. They have been met with varied levels of success based on the

maturity level of the organization regarding leadership, understanding the mission, and ability to work cross-functionally. (Table
10.1 provides a summary of these possibilities.)

## Grassroots Uproar

DEFINITION: Valiant and passionate effort started from within the
ranks.

This often has an infectious ability to get people fired up, although
the effort can flame out quickly without the right exposure and
senior-level commitment. If it creates enough of a bandwagon
effect, the senior folks have got to take notice to understand what's
going on. But this approach to trying to light a fire in the organization is not for the faint of heart. It's not what I recommend to
get things going. But if nothing else is working, it's worth a try. To

### TABLE 10.1. The Customer Focus Smorgasbord

| | |
|---|---|
| **Office of the president** | If the commitment is there, this is ideal. Ensures cross-company cooperation and provides air cover for clearing roadblocks and gnarly issues. |
| **Marketing** | Often becomes the initiator because of metrics. Burden of process work and change management can be challenging when led from here. Success is dependent on the leader. Sometimes leading from marketing breeds turf issues. |
| Customer service | Focused group of people want to elevate and fix the issues they hear about day after day. Great place to initiate efforts. Highly respected leaders can lead the change from here, although there are challenges. |
| *Companywide hoopla* | High-level edict followed with a lot of early energy, tchotchkes, and meetings. Initial hoopla is often followed by unclear accountability and outcomes. |
| **Grassroots uproar** | Valiant and passionate effort started from within the ranks. Often has infectious ability to get people fired up. Effort can flame out quickly without the right exposure and senior-level commitment. |

make this turn into something, the uproar ultimately has to get the attention and passion of someone with power who can make something happen. Look at this only as a way to get attention. It would be difficult to lead the change from here.

## Companywide Hoopla

DEFINITION: High-level edict followed with a lot of early energy, tchotchkes, and meetings. Initial hoopla is often followed by unclear accountability and outcomes.

Most of us have lived through various companywide hooplas on the customer stuff. I can't tell you how many crystal balls, notepads, and coffee cups are rattling around companies with labels like "Customer First," "We're here for our customers," "Customer Satisfaction Is Number 1," or something similar. These are usually more energy than plan, rather like a pep rally. Everyone gets into a frenzied state. Then it's deemed that some task forces should be formed. Depending on how much forethought has been put into the work, the task forces may have a very lofty mission to work on, like "customer loyalty." What exactly does that mean? Now you've got multiple groups within the company working on a vague concept, and they are all basically spinning their wheels.

My advice is to skip the coffee mugs, the kickoff meetings, and the banners. In fact, skip this stage entirely. This is what has made a lot of this work look like the flavor of the month. There's not a lot of credibility or interest left for another big customer kickoff.

## Customer Service

DEFINITION: Focused group of people dedicated to serving customers who want to elevate and fix the issues they hear about day after day.

This can be a great place to initiate the customer effort from. Highly respected leaders *can* lead the change from here, although there are challenges. This is the area that feels the customer pain most acutely because of their personal interaction with customers. The issues to be fixed are very clear to them, yet they often continue without resolution. A requirement for a leader expecting to lead the overall customer effort from customer service is that the operation must be running at the top of its game. Service has to be run like a tight ship to earn the right to lead the broader scale of the work across the company. People have to see what is being done there and want to emulate it in their organization. The following conditions should exist to ensure a successful customer crusade is led across the company from here:

- The scope of work expands beyond service issues to strategic customer management.
- Rigorous strategic customer metrics can be applied across the organization.
- The leader has the company respect and ability to bring the different factions together.

## Marketing

DEFINITION: Vision to take marketing beyond customer campaigns, data management, and traditional advertising. Expand the brand focus across the enterprise to deliver a differentiated customer experience.

The marketing area can often emerge as the lead on the customer work because marketing is frequently the keeper of the customer data. The familiarity that marketers come to have with customer data can cause the "aha!" light to go on before others in the organization. With the emerging knowledge that comes from the data, marketing evangelizes the importance of customer management. This can quickly morph into managing the overall customer experience for brand continuity.

In some ways, marketing is more prepared than other areas to try to take on this challenge. In a matrix organization, the marketing department is already seasoned at the work of facilitating across the silos and has become used to the work of bringing disparate organizations together to make a comprehensive marketing plan. However, even with this wider net thrown, many marketing departments underestimate the amount of process work and cultural change management work required to make this shift. Because these aren't natural core competencies for most marketing organizations, the burden of digging into the operational side of the business can be challenging and tax its time and capabilities. The customer work is a lot about numbers, data, and metrics but is just as heavy on process and operations. It may be difficult for marketing to take on the hard cross-company facilitation role that is required.

To drive the comprehensive customer work, marketing needs to gain the acceptance of the organization to move into an expanded role. Marketers are seen in the organization as possessing a defined set of skills, and because they frequently wield a lot of power, sometimes people resist what looks like scope and power creep if they also begin to lead the customer work. Success is dependent on the leader. This can be assuaged through thoroughly working the inclusion principle in the planning and roll-out of the customer work. Marketing should position itself as the facilitator, not the kingpin. However, as human nature has it, this does not always happen. So know ahead of time if this is bred where you are. Then manage it offensively.

## Office of the President or CEO

DEFINITION: This is the ideal location to lead the customer effort from. Ensures cross-company cooperation and provides air cover for clearing roadblocks and gnarly issues.

If the commitment is there, you should grab it. However, reporting to the president requires a number of conditions that he or she must agree to in order to give the traction needed. You're going to have to test the commitment of the president frequently to get the alignment needed throughout the company. Therefore, it's vital to make sure that this backing can be counted on. In addition, test the president on his or her personal view of where the work should be taken. There should be a committed point of view of who needs to participate and the level of participation expected, as well as an understanding of time and resource commitments. Finally, run through a number of scenarios to see what the reflex reaction will be when the mettle of the commitment is tested. Here are some examples:

- What if one organization is strongly of the opinion that the customer work doesn't apply to it?

- How will the president get the attention of leaders to make the time to do this work?
- What will happen in compensation if customer performance is a metric and the goal is not met?
- What is the amount of time the president will devote to this monthly?

## Making Your Leadership Choice

Determining where the customer leadership position will report is something to think hard about. The strength of an operating area's ability to be an influencer in the company should drive this decision. And determining how much executive backup is required depends on how far along the company is in driving the customer agenda.

## Variables to Critique

There are three variables to critique where the customer leadership role can successfully reside and to whom it should report: leader commitment, understanding the mission, and ability to work cross-functionally. Review the variables to determine which stage your organization is in. As a general rule, if you rate yourself as "early" in most of the variables that follow, the more executive firepower you'll need to gain and maintain momentum:

- *Leader commitment.* How serious are your leaders about the time commitment, people commitment, and work involved in managing customers and customer relationships? Is your most senior leader personally engaged? Does he or she own the mission and have a strong viewpoint about where to take this? Has your company board committed to the effort, and do they understand that the time trade-off for making progress here? (See Figure 10.1.)
- *Understanding the mission.* Think here about the level of clarity and consistency in your organization. Is there across-company buy-in? Are people collectively weaving customer metrics into the standard business metrics they are comfortable with to define their operation? How much leadership backup is still necessary to move the agenda ahead? Are all leaders in agreement, or do some disagree or question the mission? (See Figure 10.2.)

**FIGURE 10.1.  Leader Commitment**

| | Early | Developing | | Evolved |
|---|---|---|---|---|
| **Leader Commitment** | Hand-wave | Focus on a few projects. Still reactive. Metrics don't change accountability. | Personally engaged and willing to drive change. Falls back to traditional silo and sale priorities, but reengages when possible. | Fully engaged and has engaged leadership team. Drives accountability hard, changing metrics and priorities. New definitions of company success. |

**FIGURE 10.2.  Understanding the Mission**

| | Early | Developing | | Evolved |
|---|---|---|---|---|
| **Understanding the Mission** | Reactive problem solving. No customer value metrics | Some zealots get it. Some metrics exist as one off efforts. | CEO/president is engaged. Beginning to bring the company around. Automated a few metrics. | Customer metrics are defining conversations more now. Less time taken explaining why than how. |

- *Ability to work cross-functionally.* Do you regularly initiate projects with the determination of cross-company dependencies and accountabilities? Have the traditional silo ownership powers been put aside when necessary for collaborative projects? Is there a real understanding of the need to define outcomes, metrics, and priorities with cross-functional teams for customer deliverables? How far along are you on that path? Are you willing but still feeling the pain? Are people mostly unwilling? Or are you the rare evolved organization that has this nailed? (See Figure 10.3.)

### FIGURE 10.3. Ability to Work Cross-Functionally

| | Early | Developing | | Evolved |
|---|---|---|---|---|
| **Ability to Work Cross-Functionally** | Silos rule. Little connection between shared metrics and recognition. | Some funky task forces—with not great results. Trying but not sustainable. Silos compete. | Have executed a few cross-company efforts. Metrics are bringing silos together. More combined projects than prior twelve months. | We present together and key metrics are tied to outcomes. Accountability is clear and managed. |

The more evolved the organization is in each of the attributes, the better your chances are of achieving success in a divide-and-conquer approach to spreading out the work. The more evolved you are, the more willing the organization will be to see the customer effort led from somewhere within the organization besides the president's office. If you assess that you are at the early stages in more than one of these areas, your company likely needs the backing that comes from reporting as high up as you can go.

## THE EXECUTION CHASM

When the president doesn't make the customer work a focused position directly reporting to him or her, the customer effort is frequently added to the responsibilities of customer service or marketing. While the work can be led from these two operational areas, it's important to go into this with your eyes open. For both marketing and customer service, layering the customer work on top of existing responsibilities should not be considered a no-brainer. There are skills required to do the job that don't exist automatically in either organization. Each will excel in its area and will have natural gaps in its skill sets that are necessary to lead the customer work. This is natural. An execution chasm will exist with either choice. This is not insurmountable. You just have to be aware of this and plan for how to fill in the missing leadership skills.

## Leading from Customer Service

Customer service sees the issues that prevent reliability. They repeatedly hear the things that get in the craw of the customer. Resolving these issues will greatly advance the chasm in your relationships with customers. In fact, in some industries, just getting good at reliability is an advancement. For example, in a complicated industry like insurance, the companies that are advancing do so because they've demystified the mechanics of getting a quote. For example, Progressive Insurance has opened up the black box of insurance rates. When a potential client asks for a quote, Progressive provides it and a number of competitors' rates so the customer can make an informed decision.

When you lead from customer service, the most natural order of business will be to take away the customer pain. Your customers will tell you this. It is relatively straightforward and easy to understand. It takes commitment and pressure and the force of a real zealot to make the company make changes to take away the pain. By aggregating the issues that most greatly ail customers, customer service can drive change to fix the company. If you can excel in driving the company to eliminate those baseline issues, customer service can earn the right to expand the role over time.

## Leading from Marketing

The core competencies that marketing will drive are the metrics side of the business as they relate to customer segmentation metrics and response to campaigns and offers. Some marketers are now digging in deeply into the life cycle management side of the business, which forces their toe in the water on the process side of the work. But I've found here that the life cycle work frequently is cordoned off to be limited to defining contact points for marketing touch points. Driving the customer work for the organization would require an expanded mind-set and ability to drive the work into the operating areas of the company. Again, the main issue here is if the operation has the bandwidth of time and resources to layer the work on to existing responsibilities and if the passionate desire exists to drive this type of gnarly cross-company work.

## THE CHASM FOR BOTH CUSTOMER SERVICE AND MARKETING

There are skill sets specific to driving customer change that need to be present for doing this work. They are not obvious or natural skills considered necessary to the running of an operating area. The lack of these skills comprises the execution chasm (Figure 10.4). This is the hard work of driving a new set of metrics and accountability around customers. It is in leading work that may seem vague and with a longer time line. It is the work of engaging an organization. It is the work of motivating and driving accountability. And it is the hard process work of breaking the operating areas up so that accountability can be identified and managed. Especially when the CCO duties are layered on, there is a heightened vulnerability that these skills aren't identified and purposefully developed.

When you're making a decision about where the customer work should be led from, don't just layer it on to the existing mission. And make sure that you provide the people and skills to get the job done effectively. Which customer structure you choose will have a bearing on how difficult it is to add in these new skills:

- *Accountability metrics.* This is the work of translating and adapting the variety of metrics we have worked through in this book. This

### FIGURE 10.4. The Execution Chasm

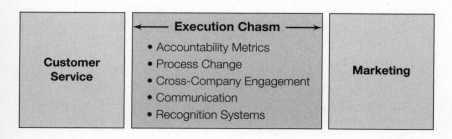

also includes close collaboration with executives to determine how and when they will hold people accountable. Someone has to be able to work this into some sort of system and event that people can count on and perform to.

- *Process change.* This is driving the organization to make changes in how it does its work to improve interactions with customers. This is a specific skill that people either love or hate doing, and it takes great discipline to herd the cats of an organization. You need this skill set in the group that leads the customer work. This will also ultimately include the work of facilitating the organization to moving beyond fixing the broken issues to redesigning and mapping a new customer experience. You may not be ready for this now, but you'll want to get to this stage. While this skill set may exist in some pockets in marketing, it's important to determine if anyone has the background and ability to do the complex mapping that occurs when you map the experience across multiple silos. This may be a skill set that you bring in from outside the organization as a consultant, but someone from within the organization will be required to manage the process.

- *Cross-company engagement.* This is the work of herding cats and one of those skills that someone really loves doing or avoids like the plague. It's the work of bringing people together to agree on where you're headed. It's the fun times of facilitating the meetings, workshops, and accountability forums.

- *Communication.* This is the most often forgotten yet one of the most critical aspects of this work. Leaders need to communicate the when, the why, and the how of the work. The company needs to receive constant updates, encouragement, and feedback on how the effort is going. And most important, customers need to be told and retold how the company is listening to them and making improvements on their behalf. The perception of this work and its success is strapped to the back of the communication plan, which is often completely void from this work.

- *Recognition systems.* The work here is tying the priority to action—putting the corporation's money where its mouth is, so to speak. This won't happen naturally. If people are left to their own devices, they'll come up with all sorts of things that will send completely different messages by the organization. The point here is not to make everything a corporate program. But there does need to be some overriding objectives and performance standards that people will be rewarded for customer performance.

# HOW TO ORGANIZE FOR CAT HERDING

Once you've determined where the effort should report, determine what structure will work best in your organization based on commitment and resources. Organize for cat herding the silos together based on your culture and how far along you are in working together. The structure you select should enable you to influence change and drive action (Figure 10.5).

Based on whether you are creating a staff position reporting to the president or a line position taking on the additional duties of CCO, there are four ways you can go with organizational structure, with two versions for staff leadership and two versions for line leadership:

- Staff leader with dedicated team
- Staff leader with dispersed team
- Line leader with dedicated team
- Line leader with dispersed team

### FIGURE 10.5.  Choosing the CCO Structure

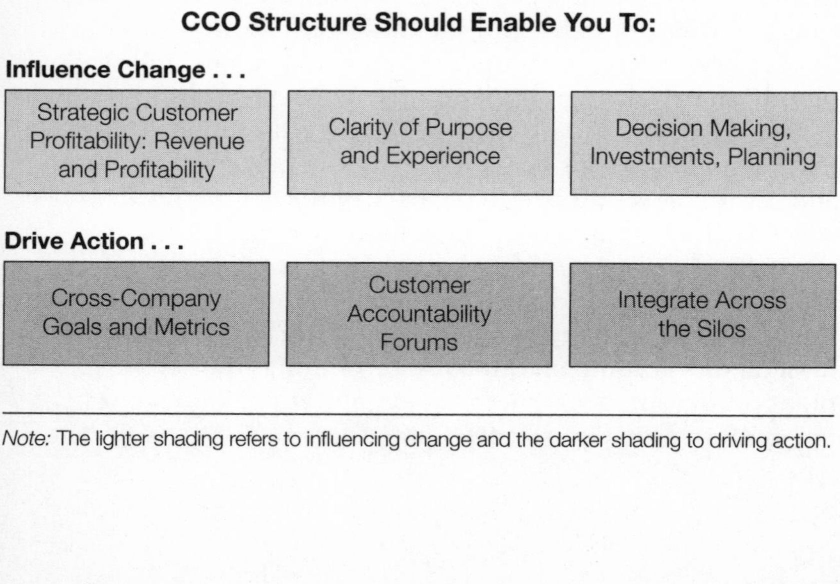

#### CCO Structure Should Enable You To:

**Influence Change . . .**

| Strategic Customer Profitability: Revenue and Profitability | Clarity of Purpose and Experience | Decision Making, Investments, Planning |
|---|---|---|

**Drive Action . . .**

| Cross-Company Goals and Metrics | Customer Accountability Forums | Integrate Across the Silos |
|---|---|---|

*Note:* The lighter shading refers to influencing change and the darker shading to driving action.

You'll notice that two options include a dedicated team and two options a dispersed team. You're going to have to push to get a dedicated team and make a strong case for this level of resources. A dedicated team is what I call a hard-wired engagement. With a dedicated team, you secure a commitment up front by having a person from each operating area become a part of the change team. They can be a direct report to the team or a dotted-line member. A direct report participant suspends his or her official duties in the operating area to be a part of the customer team. A dotted-line participant retains what's supposed to be a paired-down version of his or her duties with a commitment to devote half-time to the customer effort. When working on the customer effort, this participant has a dotted-line reporting relationship to the leader of the customer effort and takes marching orders from that person for that work.

You might also consider having a dispersed team. The principle here is that you need practitioners who know the inner workings of the operating areas to be able to dig in and help redefine the experience. In having them be part of the team, you develop the new skill sets the company needs to drive the change and integrate the customer work into the operating areas. It makes sense that a direct report from each operating area residing on the customer team is the ideal formula. But it just can't work that way in many companies.

## STRUCTURE OPTION 1: STAFF LEADER WITH A DEDICATED TEAM

The advantage with a staff leadership CCO role is that the customer work is not layered on an already bubbling over plate of line responsibilities (Figure 10.6). This means that someone is tapped to give focus and discipline to the customer effort. Reporting should be as high up inside the organization as required, based on the level of change needed inside the organization. When companies commit to these staff positions, it is frequently at the behest of the president or chief executive. For the many reasons laid out already, this is an optimum solution. Most important, a staff position does not call a silo home. This enables the CCO to cut a swath through the organization in the name of the chief executive.

**FIGURE 10.6.  Staff Leader with a Dedicated Team Structure**

This structure has the best of both worlds. The position commands the attention of the senior executives, and it's staffed to get something accomplished. The top row of boxes in the figure represents the disciplines that should exist as staff positions on the team. These skills should either reside in staff or be acquired from the outside. In any event, the staff needs to be able to facilitate the organization in developing these skills. You do not necessarily need a staff member for each of the disciplines. This will depend on the size of your organization and the scale of the effort you are undertaking.

The bottom row of boxes noted as "functional expert" denotes the team of people you should assemble from within the silos to drive the work cross-functionally across the organization. For example, in the insurance business work, we had functional experts from the organizations of claims, marketing, operations, underwriting, and sales on our team. The goal is to rotate these team members into the customer team at six- to twelve-month intervals. This structure of rotating the functional experts through the customer organization is based on the "teach them to fish" theory. By bringing functional practitioners onto the customer team, they learn firsthand what the company is trying to accomplish. And they get a taste of the skills required to think and act differently. Their role as a member of the customer team is to represent their operating area in the development of solutions. The thought is that as a continued active member of their functional area, when they rejoin their home base in meetings and in doing work, they bring the new learning about the customer work to bear. As people rotate through the customer group, more and more functional experts begin to understand what needs to be done where they live, well beyond the conceptual hocus-pocus that the work sometimes seems to be. This works well to create lasting change as the functional experts adopt the approaches over time in the way they do work.

*Pros for This Option*

- Most overall control in managing the moving parts of companywide change
- Requires great leadership commitment ahead of time to yield better results once work begins
- Rotating staff into the customer group breeds home-grown talent for driving customer-centered change once they go back to their operating area

*Cons for This Option*

- Large resource commitment
- A tough sell if leadership is not ready
- Possibly viewed by some areas of the operation as too controlling or powerful

## Structure Option 2: Staff Leader with Dispersed Team

In this option (Figure 10.7), the team retains development of the skill sets to drive change (metrics, process, engagement, communication, recognition). However, the team of functional experts does not report to this group. They are earmarked by their leadership for participation in the customer work. In other words, they do it when they have time. This may be the only option for many organizations. Be aware that you need to compensate for the lack of direct control over people's time by spending a lot more time engaging the leaders of the functional areas. If they don't completely buy in, the time they advocate having their folks spend on the customer stuff will be negligible and frequently hard won.

FIGURE 10.7.  Staff Leader with a Dispersed Team Structure

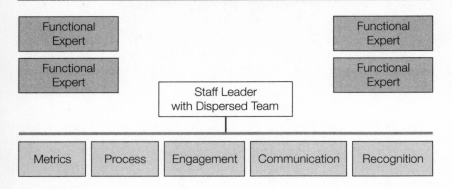

## Pros for This Option

- Quite effective if dispersed team members are generally sanctioned by their leaders
- Balances the resource-pull question

## Cons for This Option

- Significant amount of "plate spinning" required here to balance schedules and time commitments
- A longer time line

## STRUCTURE OPTION 3: LINE FUNCTION LEADER WITH A DEDICATED TEAM

This can be done, but it takes someone with an extreme amount of energy and very robust pull in the organization. What you're signing up for here is to take someone running an operating area (such as customer service) and layering the cross-functional customer work on top of that (Figure 10.8).

In this option, the leader has proven optimum effectiveness in running his or her operating area. This is usually either the leader of customer service or marketing. In addition to running the operation, this person now layers on three more dimensions of work:

- Creating the company discipline and skill sets for customer management (metrics, process, engagement, communication, recognition)

## FIGURE 10.8.  Line Function Leader
## with a Dedicated Team Structure

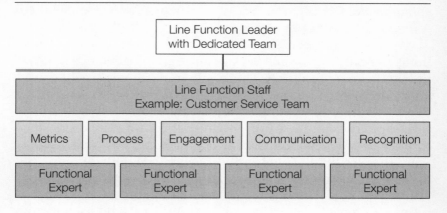

- Bringing together a team of people from throughout the organization to craft and drive the change
- Emerging as the company spokesman, leader, and communicator on the customer work. Ideally, this is shared with the highest company executive who also delivers these messages. Even if this leader is not the communicator, he or she will have a large function in crafting the messages and timing to internal company and customers about the progress being made. This is a significant new amount of work that needs to be considered and planned for.

Many leaders accept this additional role without really knowing what they're accepting. That's why it's critical that their operation is a well-oiled machine before layering this on. It's also important that the leading operating area has proven to the organization it already practices optimum customer practices that others want to emulate. If the area taking this on is known for totally annoying, disregarding, or insulting customers, this won't work.

This option then flows pretty much the same as the staff leader with a dedicated team. Work must be done extensively in the beginning to define what will and will not be done. Clear timing and requirements for the dedicated team must be outlined. The parameters for running operating area members into the customer work must be defined, and it must be clearly communicated that being tapped for this work is an honor. Then the team must be assembled and developed. Finally, the process for working must be established. After that, the work can accelerate.

As you can see from the explanation of this work, it's not something you can strap on the back of an already loaded-down operation and expect to thrive. There will be staffing issues here and most definitely commitment issues. The person who takes this on also better have some straight conversations about how he or she will be rated in this new work because there won't necessarily be tangible by-products immediately. There needs to be explicit agreement that credit will be given for moving the company along the difficult path to acknowledging and aligning for change besides just measuring the change itself. Here is a simple path to rate performance against in the first year when the work and its outcomes may appear the vaguest (Figure 10.9):

1. Acknowledgment that there's a problem (this in itself can take months)
2. Agreement on the issues
3. Alignment on how to proceed
4. Commitment to resources
5. Beginning the process and driving company participation
6. Installation of accountability process
7. Guerrilla metrics in place
8. First results accomplished and reported

Getting this agreement is critical to ensuring that there is a real understanding of what can be accomplished in the first year, with all its "get-ready" and alignment issues. Once that first year is over and you've gained momentum, it will be much simpler to define success metrics.

### Pros for This Option

- Usually a seasoned, well-respected leader is the one to take on this role.
- Since there's a decent amount of selling to make this happen, good consensus is in place by the time the structure is adopted.

**FIGURE 10.9. What to Assess and Measure in the First Year**

| | |
|---|---|
| 1. Acknowledgment that there's a problem | Agree to do the work. |
| 2. Agreement on the issues | |
| 3. Alignment on how to proceed | Define the work. |
| 4. Commitment to resources | Drive the first stage. |
| 5. Initiate the process; begin to drive company participation | |
| 6. Installation of accountability process | Begin accountability. |
| 7. Guerrilla metrics | Begin measurement. |
| 8. First results | |

### Cons for This Option

- Significant new work is layered on top of an already full workload.
- Unless silo competition is kept at bay, it could compromise the operation's ability to lead.
- The burden rests on the lead operating area to develop new skill sets to lead the customer work.

## STRUCTURE OPTION 4: LINE FUNCTION LEADER WITH DISPERSED TEAM

This is the most challenging structure (Figure 10.10). A strong functional leader must take on the development of a new focus area for the company. New skill sets must be developed to drive the significant change required throughout the organization. Functional experts throughout the company will need to be corralled continually for work to be done and advanced.

This is not insurmountable. In fact, this is the default approach that most companies do end up taking for all the reasons that are probably rattling around in your head right now. This leads us to a rather simple reason that these efforts fail so frequently: the weight

### FIGURE 10.10.  Line Function Leader with a Dispersed Team Structure

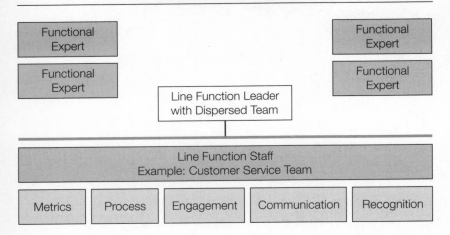

cripples the valiant efforts of the brave soldiers trying to take it on. They simply don't know or aren't prepared in advance for what the work entails, how to define and stage it, what resources are required, and the unrelenting heavy lifting to get the job done.

### Pros for This Option

- Usually a seasoned, well-respected leader is the one to take on this role.
- Since there's a decent amount of selling to make this happen, good consensus is hugely in place by the time the structure is adopted.

### Cons for This Option

- Extensive cat herding is required to manage commitment for work to keep proceeding.
- Significant new work is layered on top of an already full workload.
- Unless silo competition is kept at bay, it could compromise the operation's ability to lead.

- The burden rests on the lead operating area to develop new skill sets to lead the customer work.

## WHERE DO YOU GO FROM HERE?

Where the customer work originates, is led from, and structured all play a part in determining how you do with this work. Now that you know what you know, take some time to consider where you've been and where you'll go.

Use Exhibit 10.1 to determine which area of your company will have most impact and is best suited to lead the charge. Then review the four most commonly used structures in Figure 10.11 to determine which will work best within your organization and culture.

---

**EXHIBIT 10.1.  Who Is Best Suited to Lead the Customer Effort?**

### Who Is Best Suited to Lead the Charge?

1. Check where the customer charge has been led from.
2. State the reasons for success or challenges.
3. Identify where the change should originate from and the reasons why.

| | |
|---|---|
| ☐ Office of the president | |
| ☐ Marketing | |
| ☐ Customer service | |
| ☐ Companywide hoopla | |
| ☐ Grassroots uproar | |

## FIGURE 10.11.  Summary of Potential CCO Structures

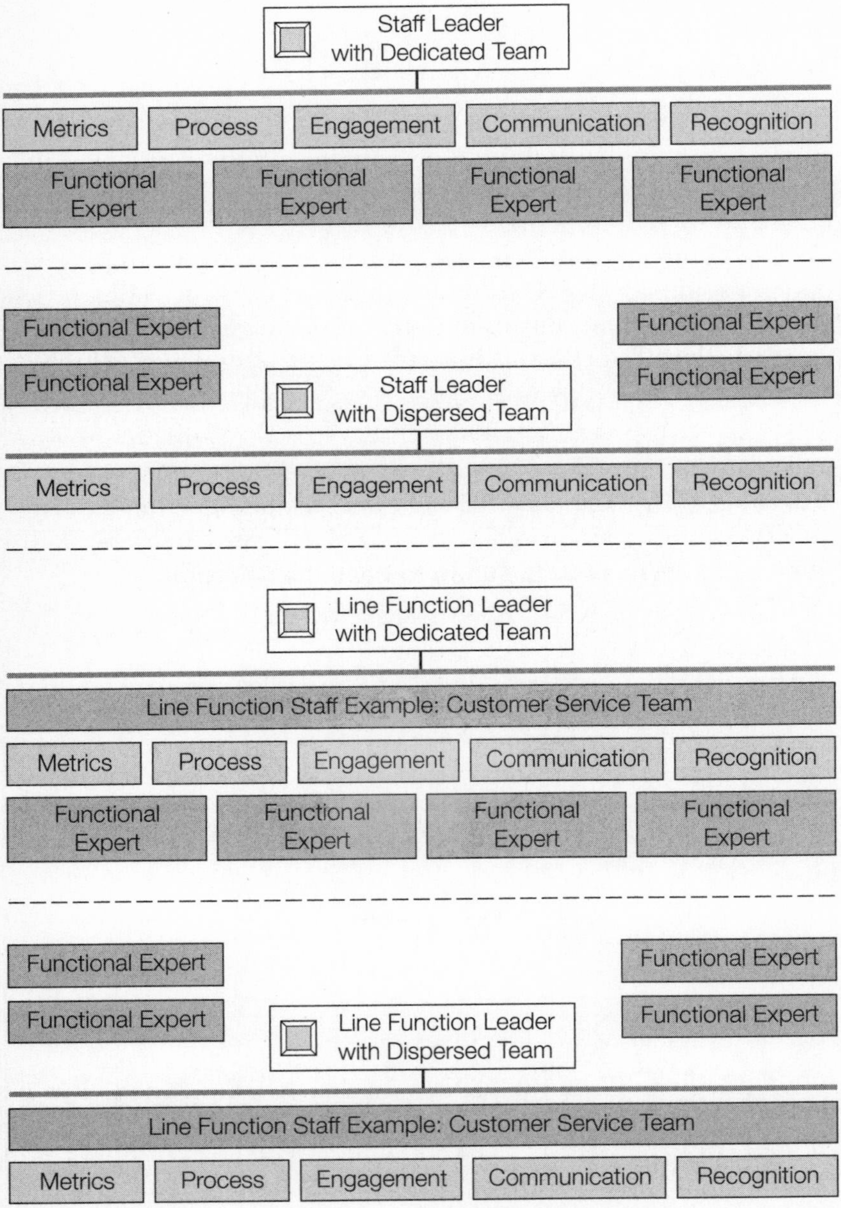

# CONCLUSION

- The CCO reporting relationship and function should be established after careful consideration of the organization, its culture and leaders, and how work gets done across the company.
- Determine how the new effort to initiate the CCO role and company involvement will be received.
- Understand the level of fatigue the organization has had with repeated tried and failed efforts on customer focus. Does your company have indigestion from having eaten from the customer smorgasbord way too many times?
- Make the customer mission report at the highest possible level in the organization to provide the firepower required to get the job done. Lobby hard to get the support you need.
- Ensure that you have consensus with key leaders on the CCO role and its impact and responsibilities before you initiate it. Introduce the CCO only into an environment that's ready for this change. In the interview process, a seasoned change agent will be able to sniff out if the commitment is less than real, so don't waste time bringing anyone in until you've got this commitment.
- Be aware of the skill sets required to drive the customer work and ensure that they exist in the leader and staff to whom you assign this responsibility.
- Determine which of the four potential CCO organization structures suits your organization. Weigh the pros and cons of line or staff position. A line position works best if you've got the gusto of senior leadership behind it. If you layer the work onto a line position leader, make sure that this person's operation is in top working condition and has the respect of the organization to lead the change.
- Establish clear goals and performance targets for the first year of a new customer leadership position to manage expectations on what can be done and how long the entire journey will take. Without these, the effort is at risk for being misunderstood, short-lived, and abandoned by those with differing expectations of the process and outcomes.

# PART FOUR

# JUST IN FROM THE FRONT

CHAPTER ELEVEN

# TRUE LIFE STORIES OF CHIEF CUSTOMER OFFICERS

The intention of this book has never been to rubber-stamp the insertion of a chief customer officer into your organization as the automatic answer. Rather, it has been to walk through the activities required to drive the management of customer relationships, profitability, and revenue. The audit, diagnostics, and questions were meant to push the issues that you may be grappling with to the surface. Finally, this book is meant to offer you a way to frame the organizational challenge to this work and offer food for thought on how you might begin to integrate a solution that's right for your company.

A variety of factors will determine how your organization should approach the customer work. The tenure of your organization is a factor. Companies that wire in customer management from the beginning knit the discipline into the organizational DNA. Retrofitting it is always a challenge, especially when strong disciplines of functional excellence exist. Perhaps there has been a market disruption that has the company rededicating itself to customers. A new market entrant that has changed the rules and is distracting your loyal customers away from you may be the forcing function for a renewed focus on customer loyalty. You may have seen a progression of sliding sales over the past few years. Or there may be a consortium of leaders who want to drive the customer agenda. No matter what your motivation, it's inevitable that as a part determining the solution for your company, someone will ask you, "What are chief customer officers in the marketplace doing today?"

This chapter does just that. It provides a glimpse into how six corporations of different sizes and disciplines have organized to drive the customer agenda. These are the companies and the people I spoke to at each:

Nautilus, Inc.: Chief customer officer and chief marketing officer

The Evercare Company: Chief customer officer

Cisco Systems: Senior vice president of customer advocacy

The Colorado Rockies: Chief customer officer and vice president of ballpark operations

Monster.com: Senior vice president of customer experience and service

Unica Corporation: Vice president of customer success

This is a snapshot in time, because even as I am writing this, people are changing from one job to the next and positions are shifting. That's why this is purposefully the last chapter; it will always require updating as we all get better at figuring out how to accomplish customer management in our organizations.

Here you'll see why the customer efforts were initiated and what the forcing function was that got the action moving. You'll read about how these companies are organizing, what positions are named, and to whom they report. Importantly, I think you'll be able to recognize glimpses of your own company in these stories and in them will recognize that you can drive similar achievements. This is meant to be one full chapter of hope that you can do this! You'll note that not all of these people are called "chief customer officer." Since the point of this book was never to mandate that position as the global answer, that's okay. Companies don't have to have a position with a specific title to drive the focus. They just need to figure out the best way to do it inside their corporate machine. These six companies that kindly let us peer into their operation represent both business-to-business and business-to-consumer companies, as well as an Internet-based organization. These companies run the gamut in size. What they all have in common is a focus on the customer and the passion to do something about it. Here are their stories.

# NAUTILUS, INC.: FLEXING THE "AHA!" MUSCLE FOR CORPORATE ALIGNMENT

Nautilus is an ideal chief customer officer's playground. Formed in 1970 as Nautilus, it has a strong foothold in its marketplace categories of health and fitness equipment and solutions. The company is growing and profitable. In July 2005, Nautilus posted second-quarter net income growth of 70 percent and net sales growth of 29 percent. The chairman and CEO, Gregg Hammann, is a "customer guy." And he has the history and context for understanding the role. Hammann was chief customer officer for Levi Strauss and Company from 2001 to 2003, where he also served as president of the Americas. Tim Hawkins, who is also accomplished in customer work, most notably at Coca-Cola and at Levi's, is Nautilus's chief customer officer and chief marketing officer. If any company can figure out how to crack the nut on this job, it should be these guys.

In September 2005 I spent some time with Tim Hawkins to find out how things are moving along. Here's Tim's rendition of the state of the customer effort at Nautilus today.

## WHEN WAS THE CCO POSITION CREATED FOR NAUTILUS, AND WHY?

The chief customer officer job at Nautilus was created about one and a half years ago. The main forcing function was that Nautilus as it stood at that time was like a big spaghetti bowl to our customers. We showed up as a holding company and four separate divisions with firewalls between them. The four companies are Nautilus, Schwinn, Bowflex, and StairMaster. You'd never know we were all part of one company. The structure had each division fighting for the same consumer (the people who sell you the equipment) and the same customer (you and me sweating at home on our machine). The phenomenon we were living was not unlike my experience at Coca Cola with Minute Maid and us competing for the same market space. We were carnivores of each other's market resources, which meant we were all basically harming the collective hand that fed us.

When Gregg and the rest of the new leadership team came in, the first "aha!" light went off. They said, "This just doesn't make sense. We are the power of four. We need to become the power of one." And so that's what we decided to do. This was greatly validated by our customers, who thought we were a little bit nuts for operating the way that we were. For example The Sports Authority is our largest retailer customer. Their buyer actually had to introduce our Bowflex sales rep to our Nautilus sales rep at The Sports Authority's headquarters! They not only didn't know each other, they were in effect competing for this one guy's time, open to buy, attention, and marketing dollars! They were competing with each other for the role of category captain. Needless to say, like many other customers, the buyer was flummoxed as to why we'd randomize him that way. We didn't do it on purpose. It was just how we'd always done things. Remember, we were four companies that just happened to have the same corporate roof over our head. That was as far as the blood line took us. Customers, of course, had the issues and frustrations with us that you'd expect. They just couldn't get why we didn't keep track of them from one product line to the other or why we made them give name, rank, and serial number as if we'd never heard of them just because they crossed the product lines. The nerve they had! Expecting us to know who they were when they went to buy a Schwinn just because they'd bought a Bowflex®!

And so my role was created to bring the pieces together, to help us bring all the parts together, and to make us aware of all of those "ahas!" we weren't seeing ourselves, but which our customers painfully experienced on an ongoing basis.

## HOW WAS THE ROLE DEFINED INITIALLY? DID IT CHANGE OVER TIME?

The chief customer officer role was established at a high level to ensure the end-to-end management of customer relationships. In the beginning, functionally this meant that my role oversaw sales but not marketing or customer service. The role was revised, so now I do have the benefit of having oversight over the four functions that have an impact on the customer relationship: sales, service, marketing, and product development. Not included in the CCO role are the other functional areas of the organization: operations, human resources, information technology, general counsel, corporate strategy, and communications.

## WHAT IS THE ORGANIZATION STRUCTURE? WHY?

I report to the chairman and CEO. In my perspective, it's the only possible place where this could report. The scope is too vast and the impact too great to report anywhere else. The chief customer officer is also a member of the executive leadership team along with the leaders of the functional areas noted above. As a group, we work to ensure that we make this transition.

## WHAT DO YOU THINK MAKES SOMEONE SUCCESSFUL IN THIS SORT OF JOB?

Customer perspective, for one thing. The fact that I was once a customer helps me. I was a retail marketing director for Famous Footwear, so know how it is to be a customer of a manufacturer and how it is to be a marketer for a retailer. The empathy factor is important because you really need to suspend how things have got to run from a business perspective to move them from how things have got to go from a consumer or customer perspective. Sometimes it's hard to see that.

In terms of the kind of attributes a person should have in this kind of role, I'd say it comes down to three big things. First, you've got to have thick skin. Things are coming at you so fast and furious and the push back to ideas will be enormous at times. The person wearing this hat has got to have the ability to act rationally without emotion. You've just got to be able to laugh at yourself and see the humor in these situations because the work can seem downright comical at times. Next, whoever's got this kind of job must be able to articulate a strategy. People aren't going to follow just because. They need to follow some kind of beacon, and it's up to this role to either establish it or work with the CEO to get it crystal clear so everyone knows where this work is taking them because there's some pain involved and people are going to want to know (a) why they should care and (b) what it will do for them. I have found that internal selling, which is what this job is, is much harder than external selling.

And that leads to the final attribute, which is persistence. This is supercritical if you're going to last in this job. You've got to believe in it so much that you'll keep going back for more.

## WHAT HAVE BEEN THE CHALLENGES?

I'd say that *the internal selling part of the job* was harder than I'd anticipated. It's a snap to get customer feedback. Once you're equipped with that knowledge, moving the organization from box A to box B through using that information is much harder. So *the next challenge I'd call out is execution.* For example, an order management issue showed up as an obvious thing we needed to fix. It was pretty simple. A large customer of ours told us they wanted an advanced ship notice. Turned out so did most everybody else. That was so much harder to do than expected. It wasn't a cognition problem. People are smart and understood what the customer was saying. But it was getting past how we'd always done things that was the logjam. That takes more work than I'd expected.

The third thing, and this is a big one, is *staffing for this kind of job.* We need people who can work inter-functionally. That means that they can traverse across the organization. I can't just fit one of the functional guys, for example, from Coca-Cola, who go deep in one area, to our business model. We just aren't big enough or structured in a way where that deep and singular skill set would fly. Beyond staffing in terms of selection, the challenge continues in helping them to *establish a balance.* It's hard because we put these folks in the customer role, but they have to be able to toggle between the company and the consumer to establish solutions that have a mutual payoff. Once we assign someone a customer role, we see a tendency to go AWOL on the company perspective. The stance shifts to, "I'm a customer person and all about the customer. Whatever the customer thinks is right is what we need to do." Our position with fitness dealers is to sell the highest-end home fitness equipment. We have worked hard and are fortunate that Nautilus enjoys being seen as having the highest value. This is not the same as selling the most at the lowest prices. But there may be a rogue fitness retailer out there who we have as a customer who has positioned themselves that way. So now we have a salesperson, marketing staff, and inordinate resources working to support that customer's platform. And at the same time, we are eroding our own. We need to continue to work at the blurring of that line and helping those teams that are so close to the customer to establish a partnership where success is defined for both of us to be profitable.

## What Are Some Accomplishments?

We now have one voice to the customer. That means that Nautilus has one selling team and one marketing team. If you're one of our reps calling on The Sports Authority, you're representing Nautilus Inc., not just one of our brands. The spaghetti bowl is gone.

We're getting better at connecting all the pieces for how we show up in the marketplace. It didn't make sense to customers that they could call us direct to buy a product but that we couldn't help them find a retailer to buy it from instead. Well, we just completed our first ever direct channel promotion where we directed customers to The Sports Authority customer to receive two hundred dollars off the price of their equipment. Before that, inside our own minds we considered it heresy to promote a retail customer through our direct channel. It made sense to everyone else but us.

We've become clearer about the purpose and value of each of our products. There is now a very clear delineation throughout our messaging that the Bowflex product caters to the home user and Nautilus to the commercial club.

Because we've gotten our act together internally, we've been able to put together comprehensive materials and marketing so retailers can present our products under our one banner. We've helped them to promote something called "Make room for fitness." You can now see a ten by ten pad in retailer sites with branded point-of-sale information to assist their customers on how to build a fitness room.

If you call us now, you'll be able to speak to only one service rep who can answer all of your questions about all products versus only our home gym. And we have a central collection of all of the information we know about you. Most important, if you call service, you will reach someone whose entire job is to serve you until you don't need help anymore. We actually had done the number before of having the same bank of phone reps fielding both the service and sales calls. But they were paid totally on commission.

So how do you think those service calls went? As they saw the queue backing up, you can bet that the unfortunate service customers were pushed off the calls as quickly as possible for the greener monetary pasture of a sales call. We split those groups up a year and a half ago. They are now compensated and trained and managed differently, as they should be. They are completely different types of people with different types of motivations. Mixing them was just something we'd always done. It was one of the harder-won "aha!" moments that I've had.

### WHAT ADVICE CAN YOU OFFER OTHERS IN THE ROLE OR TO LEADERS CONTEMPLATING INITIATING THE ROLE?

- First and foremost, you've got to trust your instincts. Do what you think is right versus what is easy. Become comfortable swimming against the tide. Pick a couple of streams especially right away to swim up, and either stand there and fight the current or walk up the current. I can't stress this enough: you're gonna step into this rushing river, and you're the only rock in that river. Many times you're going to feel as if you're the lone person on this mission. If you're not prepared to do this or act this way, don't jump into this type of job.
- Determine who your allies and partners will be for the work. I sought these people out early on, and we determined how we would work together to hash things out. Know who these thought leaders are, and establish a healthy give-and-take relationship with them. It's in these informal sessions that you'll find that you do a lot of your best work figuring out how to unscramble things.

## THE EVERCARE COMPANY: BRUSHING UP ON CUSTOMER PARTNERSHIPS

The Evercare Company began in 1956, a business born out of the necessity to get the lint out of a tuxedo. As urban company legend now has it, Nick McKay Sr. and his wife, Helen, were on their way to a dance when they realized that his tux was full of lint. The young engineer wrapped masking tape around a toilet paper tube and stuck in a wire coat hanger, thus fashioning the first ever lint roller. A business was borne. They patented the invention as "The Lint Pic-Up," and started a fledging company proffering the single product for sale. The company was christened Helmac products for his wife, Helen McKay.

Steady business growth followed largely because of The Lint Pic-Up. When son Nick Jr. got out of Harvard Business School and joined the business, his goal was expansion. He wanted to fly with the strong relationships that had been developed through that that one core product with giant retailers K-Mart and Wal-Mart. His plan worked. He added over fifty new products in the first three years after he joined in 1993. An article in *Forbes* (Gordon, 2003) indicates a ten-year upward sales spread of $60 million in sales. Under Nick Jr.'s helm, sales grew from $15 million in 1993 to $75 million in 2003. In 1998 the company became the Evercare Company. This decision was made for two reasons: (1) to reflect the expanded product line presence and (2) to have a handle to compete with a new lint roller competitor that entered the marketing in 1998: 3M.

You may be wondering why a company whose biggest product is a lint remover needs a chief customer officer. Consider this. If your customers are Wal-Mart and Target and PETsMART, how do you differentiate? Do you sell them the way everybody else does: down the product category line? Or do you build a collaborative partnership with them, extending the assets they receive from you to be far greater than a lint remover shipment?

The answer: you talk to customers constantly and with fervor. You take the relationship out of the ordinary and back to the time when a handshake sealed a deal—back to when it was a personal thing between companies to help each other. And you hire yourself a chief customer officer to make it happen. Judging from the results, it was worth the head count. Target awarded this relatively small private company its Bulls-Eye Award for Department 02 (Cleaning) in 2004. Target awarded Evercare for its collaborative mode of operating with the buying organization and also for its reliability and consistency in logistics and supply measure performance. For 2005, it has been named a Category Advisor for the closet category for Wal-Mart. As a Category Advisor at Wal-Mart, Evercare has developed a relationship far beyond a traditional selling relationship. It works within a relationship built on trust that says Evercare will focus on the building of Wal-Mart's category business first and foremost. Gaining trust at Wal-Mart and other larger retailers is earned over time, but once accomplished, it's a bit like reaching a pot of gold at the end of the rainbow. The relationship is about working together to build long-term mutual businesses. And in that process, many of the day-to-day tactical issues that you might otherwise see in a typical sales relationship tend to disappear. And unless you've been living under a rock somewhere, you know the power of a strong relationship within the Wal-Mart system. That's a lot of lint rollers!

I interviewed Jeff Neppl, chief customer officer for Evercare, in August 2005.

## When Was the Chief Customer Officer Position Created and Why?

The role was created in November 2003 by the then CEO of the company Nick McKay Jr. It replaced the senior vice president of sales position. Nick knew that being a small company, we had better deeply understand our customers and have an advocate in the company for those customers. We wanted to be much more than a supplier; we really had the goal to be a partner in providing our customers' needs, which are the buyers at approximately sixty thousand concerns where our products are sold. If we were going to win over the next decade, we had to make a commitment to becoming very intimate to the needs of our customers. And we wanted to make our smaller size an asset to drive a competitive advantage of being nimble and rapidly responsive to them.

## How Was the Role Defined?

The sales community typically takes the company to the customer, but we also wanted to set up a reverse flow of an open relationship between the customer and the company. The chief customer officer role was defined to drive planning to ensure that we understood customer needs and delivered on them. It was to make sure that we had those open lines of communication. It was created to foster two-way relationships of trust, and it was established to move mountains to get things done. My job is just to get out of the way when necessary to respect the sanctity of the relationship between the Evercare company rep and the buyer customer he or she is serving. A big part of what I do is get out and be with the customers and the buyers. I want to understand what's important. We want to know what it says that they must accomplish on their scorecard. Then we want to figure out how to be the people they count on to help them achieve those goals. This is not about schmoozing. These are professional progressive relationships. We were Vendor of the Year last year in our largest department at our largest customer because of our collaborative process in new product development and implementation. And these meetings and conversations lead us to those achievements.

## How Are You Organized?

Everything that has to do with revenue reports to me, so I ensure the complete relationship with customers and the outcome of those relationships. I'm responsible for new business development, sales, the leaders for key customer relationships, and the leaders building relationships and sales in our vertical markets: food, drug, mass merchandise, pet, and commercial.

## What Have Been the Accomplishments?

We were awarded the Bull's Eye award at Target for 2004 in the Home Décor Cleaning Department and became Category Advisor for Wal-Mart for 2005. This is a large part of how we define our success: based on customer reviews and feedback of our contribution to their business growth. The buyer at Wal-Mart looks at us as kind of the "out-of-house" assistant. They are talking to my organization as consultants to help her build her business.

The organization from the top down is very willing to listen and progress to a different way of doing business. The work gets the highest level of support required and access to the board and chairman, which is critical for us to move where we need to go. I talk to our board and our chairman at least every week. And they become personally involved. The chairman of the board just last week was trying to help me and another guy design a presentation for a customer. Now you don't see that at most companies. It makes a real difference here.

## WHAT ARE THE CHALLENGES?

Every customer is different, and they should be. They all come with different challenges. It's been an evolution moving to personalized individual relationships to deliver based on their changing goals and priorities. You can't manage these customers as a group. We need to get to know them one by one. So the work is to get my people to look at each customer separately and to go deep with them. Let them know that we can customize and do things for them that work well for them and work well for us. And have them stay the course with customers until that relationship of trust clicks. Because we're smaller and in some space of some big players, gaining that credibility just doesn't happen over night.

## HOW ARE YOU MEASURING PERFORMANCE AND MANAGING ACCOUNTABILITY?

The major accountability is to the customer annual plan document. We make sure that each plan puts us in a position to drive specific actions with measurable progression that connects to customer goals and objectives. Planning effectively to deliver on customer needs is a critical element defining how well we are performing. It establishes how well we end up meeting customer needs and strengthening our relationship and differentiating position with them. For every one of our top twenty customers, we have a very detailed customer plan where we look at the three or four things that are the strategic choices of that customer. We make sure we establish with complete certainty what they are trying to get done, what we are trying to get done, and where the common ground is for us to deliver on to meet the customers' needs. We manage accountability on how well this phase is performed and expect alignment in this approach.

For execution accountability and performance measurement, customer validations are the highest honor. We rigorously review and dig deep with customers to find out how we're doing and where we need to improve. We did a third-party audit and went deep with customers and found common themes to work on.

## WHAT ADVICE WOULD YOU GIVE TO OTHER COMPANIES CONTEMPLATING THE CCO ROLE?

- You absolutely have to have the buy-in from the top of the organization. If you have only lukewarm support, don't do it. You need CEO support and board support that the company will do something about what your customers say. The last thing you want to do is pretend you're listening to them and then not follow through.
- Be prepared, because when you listen intently to your customers, you're not going to hear things you want to hear.
- Enjoy the work. It's great to have a position like this that spans the organization. And it's great to be in a company that wants to make this happen.

# CISCO SYSTEMS: HARD-WIRING CUSTOMER LISTENING

Cisco was founded in 1984. Since its inception, the role of customer advocacy has been a key part of its culture and its support system for its customers. Today, customer advocacy is a large organization within Cisco, with fifty-five hundred employees accounting for 16 percent of Cisco's total revenue.

I spoke with Wim Elfrink, the senior vice president of customer advocacy, in August 2005 to find out more about the role and the attitude of customer advocacy inside Cisco.

## WHY WAS THE ROLE OF CUSTOMER ADVOCACY CREATED?

For us at Cisco, we have been fortunate because the focus on the customer is an idea planted in the company from the beginning by one of our founders, Sandy Lerner. She felt strongly that there had to be a counterweight between the strong research and development and sales organizations that would take care of the customer. So that's how the role began. This is something very deep in the culture of Cisco—almost mystical.

## HOW IS THE ROLE DEFINED?

It starts with the listening function. We created a way to understand what the customer issues are so we can use that information to improve our products, and we also have people who directly support our customers. These people comprise our technical services function. Their job is to have but one process to conduct their business, which is to have no process. That means that they do what it takes to fix what ails the customer first. And this is absolute. They have the power to stop the line to resolve a customer issue without being disputed. It can't be a trade-off. If there's a problem that needs a programmer, they get a programmer. These customer issues they face can reveal quality issues. We take those customer data and turn them into action by sharing this information with our business units and manufacturing to drive continuous improvement. Our job is to drive the understanding and use of this critical data across Cisco worldwide.

## WHAT IS THE ORGANIZATION STRUCTURE?

I report to our CEO, John Chambers. The customer advocacy role needs that level of empowerment. For some customers, we're the last resort they have to getting their problem solved. We need to have John's attention, and I need to have the ability to drive actions directly to him when needed. Every day he gets communication from me on our critical accounts and what is happening with them.

## WHAT HAVE BEEN THE ACCOMPLISHMENTS?

Last year we received over ninety thousand replies from customers when we asked for feedback. That equates to over twenty-seven thousand hours customers spent because they knew we would do something with the information. Over the last twenty years, we have been able to make the customer listening function more of an art form than a task inside Cisco. We have a mechanism for capturing survey data that gives us high-level trends. Every five out of ten transactions are balloted to determine what happened with the customer, which gives us real-time information. These are trended to prioritize issues that we can take proactive action on.

We also measure customer loyalty now at four levels to understand those who are truly loyal, those who are high-risk "trapped loyal" customers, and those in between. And we use that information to manage those relationships. The information captured from listening is embedded into the way we design our products and services. We have achieved that elusive closed-loop process. When we tracked the issues we received on one of our voice-over-IP products and provided that to the product development team, they made five critical changes to that product that our customers needed; our number of support calls went down by 17 percent and sales increased, demonstrating product improvement. Self-service is also an important factor to our customers. Now almost 79 percent of our engagements with customers are over the Web. When a customer calls in, we have a rule that they can be transferred only once; then that person owns the customer and the issue. There is no customer hot potato at Cisco.

## WHAT ARE THE CHALLENGES?

Maintaining the level of innovation required. The cost of raising the bar to reach the increasing expectations and needs of customers is a challenge. We need to continue to learn reactively and then drive that into how we do work to be proactive. Of course, the human element of people interacting with customers is always a challenge. Our employees need to take personal responsibility for knowing when to follow the process or when to make an exception for the customer. We need to keep them motivated by exposing them to the leading edge of technology and keeping them engaged. And it's a constant job to ensure that after we compile the data from our customers, the data become information so that marketing, research and development, and the sales teams can make the improvements and adjustments needed to better serve our customers. Just recently in our executive staff meeting with our forty leading vice presidents, we spent over an hour reviewing the trends of our customer information and what we see happening. We need to make sure that we continue to use this information to understand what's happening today and to assist in predicting what will happen in the future. We have to be relentless about this because the moment you stop listening to customers is the moment you lose.

## WHAT MAKES A SUCCESSFUL CUSTOMER ADVOCATE OR CHIEF CUSTOMER OFFICER?

This type of role requires an all-around business perspective. Since this is not a function but rather a role that traverses the organization, it requires a seasoned executive. In a multinational organization like Cisco, the ability to understand different cultures is critical. The person requires empathy to understand how business takes place and how the customer needs fit into that. It requires the skills of a diplomat to know how to get things done inside an organization. Then they must be persistent to get the work done. A sense of balance is required to know when to make the call and when to say, "Stop. Let's not take this any further." It is critical to understand process and how it enables or inhibits interactions with customers. You need clarity about what is an improvement to the process. And you need to know when it's right to make an exception. Exceptions are required to keep in touch with customers and their needs. People in customer-facing positions can sometimes hide behind the process or a specific rule or regulation. And operational organizations can use process to list a litany of reasons that a change can't be made. This adherence to process gets in the way of moving past the way things have always been done to forge a better approach. It's the job of this role to figure this out and to work it out.

## WHAT ADVICE WOULD YOU GIVE COMPANIES CONTEMPLATING THE CHIEF CUSTOMER OFFICER ROLE?

- This work is not a single function. It's part of the culture.
- You need the support of the chief executive to make the improvement process an end-to-end effort across the organization. Make sure that you have the empowerment to drive the change. Don't begin the role without it.
- Make sure that the organization understands clearly that the role is to provide perspective and tools and support, but it is not there to do all the work or "own" the customer. Accountability has to be driven across the organization in real time with metrics that people care about. Everyone at Cisco has their compensation tied to how customers are saying we per-

form. That's a critical part of the cultural commitment made in 1984 that we carry on today.

# The Colorado Rockies: Making the Experience Rock the Ballpark

I was intrigued to discover that the Colorado Rockies' vice president of ballpark operations also bears the title chief customer officer. Think about it. The product at the ballpark is completely the experience, and it is dependent on a wide array of constantly changing frontline folks. It seemed that their story could benefit a great many leaders running sporting venues, amusement parks, and other businesses where the experience *is* the product.

In August 2005, I interviewed Kevin Kahn, the chief customer officer for the Colorado Rockies.

## When Was the CCO (or Similar) Position Created and Why?

Our owners and president created the chief customer officer position in 2003. The title was actually the formalization of how we had been operating since the Rockies began in 1992. They felt it was time to put a formal title with our commitment to customers. It was an addition to my existing title of vice president of ballpark operations.

## How Is the Role Defined?

Since the inception of our franchise, customer service has been the number one priority. My role is to coordinate what is currently being done on a department basis to ensure we are maximizing our opportunities on an organization basis. There are several departments that are directly responsible for the customer experience at the ballpark. My responsibilities are to ensure that in addition to our guests' enjoying their ballpark experience, our employees value their experiences, as well as our sponsors and media constituencies. The purpose of this role is to give a holistic view of the customer experience and facilitate the end-to-end conversations. It's also gives an opportunity to discuss more ideas from the frontline staff.

## WHAT IS THE ORGANIZATION STRUCTURE?

Our organization structure includes a chairman/CEO, vice chairman, president, and officers who are responsible for directing the operations of the ball club. I am the officer who oversees the ballpark operations department.

## WHAT ARE SOME OF THE ACCOMPLISHMENTS?

A broad array of service programs have been put into place as a result of our all-encompassing approach. The biggest accomplishment we have is when we can suspend thinking about whether the team wins or loses and make the experience be about going to the ballpark. We created Autograph Sundays where every Sunday, the players are out signing autographs. We looked at our in-game entertainment to make sure our video features, including sponsor features, are entertaining for our guests. We have strived to reach out more to our Spanish-speaking community and make the ballpark more inviting. To that end, we have provided Spanish lessons to key ballpark staff as well as installed Spanish-language signs on our rest rooms. Our outside gate messages are in both English and Spanish. We have created a customer service database that sits on each department's computers as well as our service partners. This captures and shares customer calls, e-mails, and issues that we trend and use to make improvements. As a result, our staff takes ownership of guests' issues and ensures they are handled to create satisfaction and positive feelings towards the organization.

## HOW DID YOU GAIN ORGANIZATIONAL ALIGNMENT FOR THE WORK?

We have so many entities that touch people through the course of their ballpark experience. My job is to bring them all together to understand the experience we want to deliver and to make sure that they're all committed to delivering that experience with us. For example, some of the different functions involved in the operation are outsourced contractors like Central Parking, Aramark for our concessions and janitorial, and Staff Pro for our site security. Off-duty Denver police officers provide our security services. Our event services employees provide the services of ticketing, ushering, guest relations, and security. These are in addition to all of our Rockies departments.

We have established a Coors Field Customer Service Committee that I chair to ensure that we all work together to deliver one unified and optimum ballpark experience. This is not just something that people attend as a mandatory meeting. Upper- and midlevel management participate, as well as the general managers of our service partners. The leaders of the other operational areas within the Rockies, such as the vice president of ticketing, are involved to ensure that their functional area is connected to what we are delivering. And we regularly bring the ideas and feedback from our frontline people into these discussions. I give a CCO report at all of our department head, officers, and organization meetings to communicate our initiatives, programs, and feedback throughout the organization. The bottom line is that service is what drives our organization, and everyone must keep that in focus.

## WHAT ARE THE CHALLENGES?

We are very sensitive to trying not to get in the way of departments' service programs. Different departments have been implementing different service programs from day one. We do not want to step on any toes. Having representation from all departments on our customer service committee has gone a long way toward helping coordinate all the existing programs with newly developed programs. Any early fears of my or our committee taking over all the service programs quickly dissolved shortly after we started the committee. The biggest challenge is managing the emotions that come with sports. Trying to balance the highs and lows is hard. When you're a winning team, guests feel you can do no wrong. But when the lows are low, it's a challenge trying to make people feel good and that they're having a positive experience just coming to the game. We have on average about eight hundred part-time people working any game. A challenge we work at constantly is getting the message down from top to bottom about what we want to mean to guests in their experiences with us—and then, of course, how that translates to their own personal demeanor and how they interact with them. We are always reinforcing that we are expected to provide the same high level of service whether we are in first place or last place.

## HOW DO YOU INSTILL ACCOUNTABILITY AT THE CORPORATE LEVEL AND AT THE FRONT LINE?

Shared accountability exists among those of us who make up the Coors Field Customer Service Committee. We have created smaller subcommittees to work on specific measures and allow for additional brainstorming and discussion. We have also had our marketing partners come in and share their customer service philosophies and strategies with our group. Executives from Federal Express, Frontier Airlines, King Soopers, and the Broadmoor Resort shared their approaches. This has really helped our group broaden their perspective.

We find that keeping people accountable starts with communication. We require our entire staff to participate in a customer service seminar. During these sessions, we discuss our organization's service philosophy as well as the service expectations we have for everyone, not just the employees who directly touch our customers. This sets the tone for everyone that service to our guests, marketing sponsors, media, as well as fellow employees, is what drives our organization. One way that we communicate and create accountability is that we have our owner, president, manager, and players talk with our frontline guest services staff to offer their perspective and answer questions. This helps to keep our staff plugged into the organization and feel a sense of ownership and responsibility to our process. We stay tuned in and focused through feedback from our various constituencies. We've implemented formal guest communications through comment cards, surveys as well as review of letters and e-mails. Through formally monitoring the guest experience, we stay focused and accountable to our service philosophy.

## WHAT ADVICE WOULD YOU GIVE OTHER COMPANIES CONTEMPLATING THE CCO ROLE?

There has to be a genuine commitment from the top. Otherwise you will not have the ability to empower people and reach service goals. Include the entire organization in some way from top to bottom in the service process. You must create an understanding that every single person in the organization is responsible for providing service. We have our department heads, officers, and owners outside the entrance gates welcoming our guests to the ballpark. Our owners and officers regularly meet season ticket holders for breakfast or lunch to talk about the ballpark experience and team direction and answer questions. It is important to keep in touch with our guests so that can make sure we understand their needs and to ensure we are exceeding expectations. I would also recommend that as many staff members as possible be empowered to solve problems. It works much better if someone with an issue or question is not handed off and that all it takes is one call or letter to get issues handled. If everything works right, all employees will strive to do whatever it takes to provide value and long-term customer loyalty.

## MONSTER.COM: SEARCHING TO RETAIN MARKET DOMINANCE

Monster.com is the fourteenth most visited Web site in the world. It has over 58 million job seeker members worldwide, more than 49 million resumés in its database, and over 200,000 member companies. Monster was founded in 1994 as The Monster Board—the 454th commercial Web site in the world. Monster is the flagship brand of Monster Worldwide Inc. During the second quarter of 2005, Monster's revenues were $198.1 million (a 40 percent increase over 2004 first-quarter level of $141.9 million). *Fortune* magazine named it one of America's Most Admired Companies in 2003.

In 2001, Monster.com created the new position of chief customer officer. The press release announcing the role said it was created "to enhance customer experience with sales and customer services." These days, Ed Benack has that responsibility for Monster. I interviewed Ed in August 2005 to discuss what's going on at Monster.com to continue that work.

### WHAT ROLE WAS ESTABLISHED FOR DRIVING CUSTOMER FOCUS AND PROFITABILITY?

My role is senior vice president of customer experience and service.

## WHEN WAS THE ROLE CREATED AND WHY?

I joined Monster in February 2005 in this new role. This is a very competitive industry. The barriers to market entry are not that high. There's a real need to ensure that we're a major marketplace differentiator. Steve Pogorzelski, group president, international, of Monster Worldwide and Bill Pastor, COO of Monster Worldwide, made this commitment together. They have vowed to make Monster one of the truly great customer companies.

Monster North America, as with all other companies, has had some fits and starts. Monster has performed very well as a sales and marketing company. Deep investments were made in those areas. We had a record of incredible incentives for the sales force to bring in new accounts: spiffs, achiever trips, and sales and marketing conferences. We practiced motivating the sales and marketing force very well. We needed to become better at bringing the customer experience onto the radar screen of what we tracked and monitored. Prior to this, there was insufficient time carved out at operational or strategic reviews on how we were performing as a customer-focused company. Steve saw that as a piece of the equation. He was thinking long term: "Yeah, we're doing fine now. But when the economy turns down and things get soft, we want Monster to be the one that stays strong because of the loyalty created through our customer experience." Our goal is to make that transition from being a sales and marketing company to becoming a great customer experience company.

## HOW IS THE ROLE DEFINED?

My job is to bring everyone together so we can make this commitment happen for Monster. This role is to give the customer and customer issues a seat at that table. I am responsible for the overall customer experience across all segments and functions. The function of the role is to evangelize the value of the work, define the return on investment, and then drive change by motivating and collaborating across the disciplines of the organization. Our approach is not to have the customer experience work trump everything else or to have complete authority. We want people to own and be accountable for the customer experience, which will define and drive what they do. A big part of what I do is to identify how the customer is affected in the decisions we make. And there is the work to bring people to work together and collaborate for the creation and delivery of a solution. This is not something that came naturally to businesses.

We need a framework to build in competencies that we just haven't had the time to build because of our rapid growth. Those are consistent execution of processes. And seeing the big picture and translating it into a shared operational plan across the functional areas. We will also bring discipline to how we identify and solve problems, such as the use of a quality management framework.

Our responsibility is to create a common point of reference for the company of the customer experience. We are completing life cycle framing now to make sure that there's that consistency. Then we will translate that to operations and ultimately accountability.

Functionally, I am responsible for the management of all of the frontline service for Monster.com North America. This is a real boon to this position as I have the opportunity to practice what I preach and have impact and personal accountability for an operating area of the company.

## What Is the Organization Structure?

I report to the president of Monster North America. Reporting to me are our directors of service delivery, our director of quality, our director of operations, and our Voice of the Customer managers.

## What Have Been the Challenges?

We're a relatively small company experiencing rapid growth. Because of this, we've grown through the survival method of everyone doing everything to get the job done. There has been so much created very rapidly, and there hasn't been the ability to connect the pieces. So for the customer, there are inconsistent customer touch points. The two biggest are in sales and service. Because of our rapid growth and the fact that service was not a core competency from the beginning, we have had some inconsistencies occur which translated to poor service from the customer perspective. We spend an inordinate amount of time tracking down problems and fixing them individually. Larger companies that are more evolved are more seasoned in knowing and recognizing the signals when there are customer issues. We're still getting there, but the focus is tight and commitment resounding.

In terms of how this translates to my job, we work hard to drive home how the decisions we've made are showing up to our customers. For example, we have policies for things that people stick to hard and fast. One example is the way we put in ads for our customers who are the employers seeking candidates. Our job has always been the execution of the ad into the site. Then they're on their own. If an employer's ad was not responding, we didn't necessarily take accountability for the customer's success. We've changed that now. Our pledge now is that we will work with you until you're successful. If the ad's not working, we'll work with you until it gets the responses you want. In a company growing rapidly, we're filled with all kinds of guidelines like that which let us execute. Our challenge is creating a common understanding for what we're trying to accomplish beyond the execution of putting an ad on the Web site. And we have to then quickly turn the high-level definition into actions that people can understand and drive.

## WHAT ARE SOME ACCOMPLISHMENTS?

Job seekers and corporate clients use our site after hours. About 30 percent of our total volume is completed during the time after 5:00 P.M. Yet our service was available during the regular business day. We've now switched to 24/7 availability. That's just one example of the shift we're working to make execution be on the customers' terms, not on ours. We will be pledging to our customers, both businesses and job seekers, that we will guarantee them availability of the right tools and the right people to make them successful. So in June 2005, we rolled out a newly created Monster.com Web site supported by Monster Central, our 24/7 live online and phone customer service center. We wanted the redesign to address the changing culture of job seekers and companies. These features go hand-in-hand with our pledge to make them a success. The key features of the new Web site include a streamlined resumé builder, greater customization to improve each individual's job search, refined job search as to location and job category, and expert-driven career content.

Monster is learning to become a much improved culture of accountability for customers. For example, our mantra in Monster Customer Central for people working with customers is, "You own it until you absolutely own it." Transferring a customer and their situation away is not tolerated. In fact we measure the number of transfers through our phone switch. We're moving from an environment of, "It's not my job," to, "I own this issue until the end."

We are learning to eliminate the boundaries that got in the way. For example, whose job is it to help a customer rewrite a low-performing ad or extend post dates to get more responses? At this stage, we're making it crystal clear by providing our people a "make it right" tool kit that allows them to make our customers successful. Later this will become clearer, but this is very helpful at this stage and is creating that clarity needed to translate the high-level pledge into a reality people can grow into.

## HOW ARE YOU ESTABLISHING ALIGNMENT AND ACCOUNTABILITY FOR THE CUSTOMER?

To drive accountability, we are establishing a disciplined process for the competency of bringing the voice of the customer into the business. There's now a companywide listening system to collect the voice of the customer information in a unified way. You now don't have to beg, borrow, and steal to get resources and a voice to fix customer issues. I recently presented this to our board of directors meeting to show the correlation and what's broken and the connections to long-term customer loyalty and ultimately profitability. They've made the commitment financially and stand behind it.

We are the fourteenth most visited Web site in the world! Yet the huge amounts of customer feedback we received went into disparate places with highly varying levels of follow-up. Everyone was concerned about customer feedback when it hit the right desks, but it was very tough to get accountability without a real-time tracking and trending of the issues. Because of this, we weren't always able to see the operational glitches that hurt us with customers. The

Monster Customer Listening System is now addressing this. It was rolled out first to customer service. It then goes to the e-commerce group and product and to sales. This lets us aggregate, prioritize, and analyze the issues to mitigate customer pain. Accountability for the operational issues that are uncovered is assigned to the applicable senior vice president. That is connected to actions and dates. And a robust follow-up is connected to that. Operational metrics are then finishing the loop to ensure that the change is sustainable.

The tool to drive the accountability is a dashboard that tracks and trends the feedback and issues. We diligently watch for the reduction of complaints around issues to ensure that the operational areas are taking accountability for the fix. For example, one of our Achilles' heels was that it was taking us longer than our competition to post a job. That's not world class and just not acceptable for a Monster commitment to customers. It's causing credibility issues with salespeople and our brand. We have changed our process, and now turnaround time is the fastest in the industry. This occurred directly from the voice of the customer.

## WHAT ADVICE WOULD YOU GIVE OTHER COMPANIES CONTEMPLATING THE CCO ROLE?

- Make sure that the move has the absolute backing of the board and key leadership. I interviewed with the head of sales, chief marketing, and product officers for Monster Worldwide, as well as Monster North America, to make sure that the commitment was consistent and would be backed financially. The team I interviewed with was committed to excellence.
- Gain agreement on the lengths to which the organization is willing to go to achieve the vision. Know down to the operational level what you aspire to be and what you are willing to do to reinforce it.
- Make sure that you can quantify that you are winning customers and customer loyalty. Translate that into profitability for your shareholders.
- Commit to driving a culture of customer intimacy through customer listening and accountability. Every leader needs to have this translated to his or her objectives in a real operational way.

- Create a way to identify issues and take action that the organization understands and will step up to. We have created the CEEP—Customer Experience Enhancement Program—which is a vibrant program that aggregates customer feedback, suggestions, requirements, and internal ideas. From those data, we design programs, products, and strategies mapping the customer needs.

## Unica Corporation: Customer Success = Their Success

Unica is a provider of enterprise marketing management software that assists companies in building better relationships with customers. So its leaders ought to know what they speak of when it comes to building strong relationships with their own customers. I wanted to know: Were they practicing what they were preaching, or "eating their own dog food"? (as is often asked in the software biz). I caught up with Laurie Long, Unica's vice president of customer success, in August 2005 to hear the answer to the question.

### Why Did Unica Decide to Invest in a Customer Success Organization?

In July 2000, Unica's executive team made a strategic decision to invest in an organization solely focused on and representing the customer. They knew that in order to be successful as a company, customers needed to be successful. Other companies relied on salespeople to "farm accounts"—in other words, call in when the customer was ready to buy again. But Unica wanted to partner with customers in a much more strategic, ongoing fashion. Customer success means that both Unica and our customers will be successful when we establish a partnership geared toward meeting common goals.

### How Was the Role Defined Initially? Did It Change over Time?

It was pretty high level at the beginning. The founders and the management team knew that they needed to put some focus on the customers, and they knew that success was the end game. They were willing to take the leap that we would figure it out when we made the commitment. And that clarity about the tactics and process would show themselves once we got out of the conceptual and into the day-to-day reality of working with customers.

## WHAT ARE THE RESPONSIBILITIES OF YOUR ROLE? WHAT ARE YOU SCORED ON?

I am responsible for ensuring that our customers are running in production with the software they purchased from Unica. In other words, we make sure they are successfully using the products to run their business. This is another thing that makes us unique. Many software vendors are content to sell the software, and if the customer actually ends up using it, that's a bonus. That's not the case at Unica. I am also measured on whether customers would recommend us. We value our customers as our best salespeople. Finally, I am measured on the number of customers renewing their annual maintenance agreement. Maintenance renewals are an indicator of the customers' commitment to continue to invest in the partnership.

## WHAT DO YOU THINK MAKES A SUCCESSFUL CUSTOMER ADVOCATE?

There are four core competencies that I believe are necessary:

- Have the ability to balance the objectives of the company with doing the right thing for the customer.
- Be someone who knows how to really understand the impact of company decisions that are having an impact on the customer.
- Be able to get people's attention and mobilize the troops.
- Give the power away. I want the operating areas within Unica such as product development, technical support, and consulting to be the hero, and they know they have a vested interest in customer success. The most successful efforts are when the operating areas take ownership for the problem and get credit for the solution. People who are customer advocates can't be a praise hog.

## What Is the Organization Structure? Why?

The reporting structure has evolved during the past several years as the company has grown and we have learned what the true internal dependencies are at Unica for customer success. I initially reported to an executive vice president who had responsibility for sales, marketing, business development, and customer success. Then I reported to the CEO for a couple of years, and he continues to be personally updated by me a couple of times a month. Now the position reports to our VP of consulting. Being part of the consulting group works well because we are the most consistent customer-facing team at Unica. We are the group that is most intimately familiar with the business and organizational challenges our customers deal with each day. Many of the resources I need to respond and anticipate customer needs reside within the consulting group, so being closely aligned with that group has delivered huge benefits.

## How Does the Organization Gain Alignment Around the Work?

I am on a daily call with the CEO and his direct reports. We call this the 11:48 "daily huddle." It's a twelve-minute call to discuss "what's up" and "what's stuck" and to make sure that every issue is being driven for resolution at the highest level. This is important because if we can keep customers top-of-mind, we can cap any issue that might arise early on. We also create a companywide, more holistic approach to problem solving in this huddle approach. It's amazing what can be achieved if you're communicating every day. I also have a regular one-on-one with the CEO to give him an update on what's happening with the install base of customers. Finally, I provide an ongoing report to our board of directors. In these meetings, we review the metrics necessary for ensuring that we will achieve recurring customer revenue. And I make the link for the board to tie the customer work directly to the metrics of the business.

In our operation, every single person has skin in the game. The goal is that our customers' application is running, that the customers will stand up as our references any day of the week, and that they are renewing maintenance. So that's what people are scored on. There's a clear line of sight that people have for the actions they take that will have an impact on these resulting behaviors from our customers. Marketing needs happy customers who will speak to analysts and the media. Sales can't sell if we don't have references. We can't sell into the install base if they haven't had a good experience the first time around. Finance is in because when customers don't renew, the money stops rolling in. The people managing the relationships with customers here are not a quota-carrying group. We've taken the quotas out of the sales formula, and it's worked. Instead, our people are motivated by the value that they deliver.

## WHAT ARE THE CHALLENGES?

I'd say it's about establishing balance. The balancing act is about delivering what's best for the customer without breaking the bank and about determining where to push on the organization. Some people are more analytical than others and need more of a return on investment, and I need to know when that's more necessary as part of the sell of an idea. Balance is also key to knowing which customers most require what level of attention at different times of their relationship with us. By creating an order to this flow, we are then in a better position to allocate resources accordingly. This also gives us perspective on what is really an emergency situation requiring a full-court press of people and attention.

## WHAT HAVE BEEN THE ACCOMPLISHMENTS?

Our stride as of today is at a 93 percent maintenance renewal rate. This is pretty great achievement in software and, from what we have heard, considerably higher than our closest competitor. This affects all sides of our business, because it's really a domino effect. For example, we can absolutely meet all of our sales requests for references. There is just never a loss of customers who want to step up and vouch for us. I can't recall losing a deal because of a lack of references. And that puts us in a very admirable position.

Because we've built a partnership-based relationship with our customers, we've built up a trust that between us we'll always find a way to make things right. Even though we might hit a bump in the road, they know that we'll work with them. This gives us a pass for receiving the benefit of the doubt. And that translates to how customers vote financially on whether to continue to renew their relationship with us. For example, one customer had a major initiative that they thought would require a multimillion-dollar investment in third-party software and services. By maintaining an ongoing dialogue with them and understanding their challenges, we saw that 90 percent of what they were trying to do could be achieved with the Unica software they'd already purchased; they just needed to use the software in a different way. As a result, our key sponsor looked like a hero because she saved her company a significant investment, and we strengthened our relationship with the customer. We also uncovered an opportunity to sell them a new product that would allow them to meet 100 percent of the project requirements at a fraction of what they had thought they would need to spend.

## What Advice Can You Offer Others in the Role or to Leaders Contemplating Initiating the Role?

- Know going in what the scale and state of your customer relationships are in. Are you stepping into a mess or laying the foundation?
- Get clear about boundaries. Define your top three priorities—things you will accomplish.
- Just as important as knowing the priorities is being able to define what are *not* your priorities. These jobs tend to expand in people's eyes to include everything that has the word *customer* in it, and it's really important to rope off what you will and will not be doing.

The people on my team are extremely talented and capable of many things. The challenge is to ensure our efforts support Unica's biggest opportunities and rely on other areas of the organization to help as needed. I have the best job at Unica because I work for a company that from the top down is committed to and takes pride in our customers' success. Make sure that the commitment is there from the start, because without that commitment, this is a much different, more difficult role.

# EPILOGUE: CONNECTING THE DOTS

It is my great desire that you have clarity now that you didn't have before you cracked the cover of this book about how to drive the customer agenda inside your organization. Figure E.1 presents a visual summary of the book's contents, meant to connect the dots on the multiple moving parts on making the customer leadership decision that is right for your business. Take a minute to consider these dimensions by answering the questions shown below. They should illuminate a clear picture on the state of your organization, its likelihood to engage in the changes required and what potential there is today in successfully deploying a CCO-type position. Should you like to discuss any of this, I'm only a few keystrokes away at http://www.customerbliss.com. I am humbled that you took the time to get to know these ideas and methodologies. I wish you all the best in your effort.

## STEP ONE: KNOW WHERE YOUR POWER CORE LIES

This should be one of the first examinations undertaken to determine the scale and appetite for driving the customer work.

1. What is your company power core? You may have a primary and secondary power core. List them both if this is the case.

   _____

   _____

2. How closely aligned are your company's power core competencies with the customer focus competencies?

   _____

   _____

## FIGURE E.1.  Connecting the Dots to Find the Right Answer for Your Company

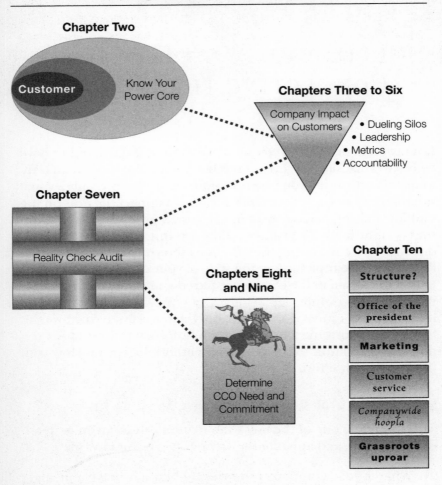

**Chapter Two**

Customer — Know Your Power Core

**Chapters Three to Six**

Company Impact on Customers
- Dueling Silos
- Leadership
- Metrics
- Accountability

**Chapter Seven**

Reality Check Audit

**Chapters Eight and Nine**

Determine CCO Need and Commitment

**Chapter Ten**

- Structure?
- Office of the president
- Marketing
- Customer service
- Companywide hoopla
- Grassroots uproar

3. How difficult will it be to incorporate the customer focus competencies in the organization?

_____

_____

4. How would you say your chances are of partnering with the power core to drive the customer agenda?

☐ Poor    ☐ Okay    ☐ Good    ☐ Great

## STEP TWO: EVALUATE THE QUICKSAND INSIDE YOUR ORGANIZATION

This lets you know how well the silos will work together to get the job done. Think about where you are on each of the following:

5. How coordinated is your customer experience? Do dueling silos exist?

_____

_____

6. Motivation: Do leaders currently motivate the organization toward customer competencies and profitability management. Will people want to do the work?

_____

_____

7. Metrics: Do the customer metrics across the organization connect? Can they? How far along are you with guerrilla metrics?

_____

_____

8. Mechanics: Are people going to want to do the work together? Can they?

_____

_____

## STEP THREE: SUMMARIZE YOUR REALITY CHECK AUDIT RESULTS

9. How many of the actions outlined in the Reality Check Audit is your company currently executing?

☐ None      ☐ Some      ☐ Most

10. Does the organization have the tenacity to engage in this comprehensive level of customer work?

_____

_____

11. What priorities have you identified that the company should begin doing or improve as a result of completing the audit?

_____

_____


## STEP FOUR: CONSIDER THE RIGHT SOLUTION FOR YOUR COMPANY

Give thoughtful consideration to your leadership commitment, organizational capacity, how you would engage the organization, and what structure would work best inside your corporate machine. Coming up with a realistic approach with the commitment of leaders and clear role clarity and accountability is the linchpin for success in driving your effort forward.

12. Is your leadership committed to and engaged in the benefit of driving a customer agenda?

_____

_____

13. Is your leadership willing to personally stand behind the commitment and drive people to action?

_____

_____

14. How is the customer agenda being driven today? Who is driving it, and from what part of the organization?

_____

_____

15. What is working and not working with your customer agenda?

_____

_____

16. Is a chief customer officer the solution?

_____

_____

17. Will your CEO and executive team sponsor the engagement of a CCO-type position?

_____

_____

18. Can the company commit to a focused full-time CCO position reporting to the CEO?

_____

_____

19. Is a more realistic solution to add the CCO-type role to existing responsibilities of one of your leaders?

_____

_____

20. How would you define the CCO role?

_____

_____

21. Where should the position report?

_____

_____

22. Which organizational approach would work best inside your company?

_____

_____

23. What process do you plan on using to have the company work together to drive the customer agenda between the silos and with the help of the CCO?

_____

_____

24. How will leaders drive accountability for the action?

_____

_____

# Afterword

*Jill Griffin*

Consider this. Having the information in this book and not acting on it is a lot like sitting on a winning lottery ticket and not cashing it in. In both cases, the only way to get the reward is to take action. *Chief Customer Officer* does not belong on your bookshelf! It belongs on your desk. Think of it as the indispensable coaching tool that will help get you from point A to point B countless times throughout your customer journey. Here are a few of the ways to put this book to work for you every day.

- *Leadership strategy guide.* In this resource, you now possess a planning guide to help you determine the scope and strategy for your organization's drive for customer profitability. Use it to gain alignment in your organization on why you haven't gained the traction you had perhaps thought you might have reached by now. And refer to it to determine what your leadership role should be.

  Through the years, I've observed that the day-to-day grind can often leave customer leaders feeling rudderless and without a sense of "due north." This book's Reality Check Audit is the perfect panacea to such a condition. Think of the audit as your reassuring to-do list of strategic customer initiatives that, one by one, will move you ever closer to your destination. Refer to the audit often to gauge where you are today and where you need to go tomorrow in your customer profitability journey.

- *Accountability blueprint.* From corporate boardrooms to every office in the C-suite, leaders are being held more accountable for

---

Jill Griffin is the best-selling author of *Customer Loyalty: How to Earn It, How to Keep It.*

results. Heed this call by adopting this book as your accountability blueprint. Its metrics and processes provide a clear-cut method for accountability that until now has been elusive or missing in most customer strategies.

If you're the CEO, your role is mission critical. It's up to you to support and oversee the installation of an accountability process whereby the alignment of measurement dashboards ensures consistency across functions and business units. Be sure to walk your talk by holding your leaders accountable to these metrics and processes. It's how you drive outstanding results.

- *Weekly guide for discussions and meetings.* Use this book to prompt discussion at strategy meetings and weekly or monthly leadership meetings. In advance, request attendees to prepare for the meeting by reading a section or chapter from the book and then pinpointing the ideas they'd most like to pursue. Then use the meeting to agree on one or two ideas and their implementation requirements.

- *Turf wars intervention.* Every customer leader knows only too well how friction and tension between departments can haunt customer work and stymie its progress. Use this book as your first line of defense in defusing these turf wars. Simply circulate copies of the book with the "dueling silos" commentary highlighted, and let it serve as an objective voice in educating turf players about the real reasons behind the tension and friction they feel. The key message to communicate is that the turf battles at hand are less the fault of departments and people and more a by-product of a misaligned corporate machine. Making this point early can help you massage bruised egos, calm rising tempers, and earn the cooperation so necessary to moving your customer work forward.

- *Burnout prevention.* Experience has taught me that many customer leaders are by nature overachievers. The work attracts can-do, passionate, ambitious people who have successfully charged the hill throughout their lives and succeeded. They naturally bring this same Herculean commitment to this demanding work. But as Jeanne demonstrates throughout her book, the corporate machine is a daunting opponent. It is little wonder that customer leaders can be especially vulnerable to professional burnout. Perhaps this book's greatest gift is its acknowledgment of the complexity, challenge, and just plain hard work associated with the day-to-day responsibilities of customer leadership.

I suggest that you identify the sections and passages in the book that inspire you the most. Then when you are feeling low and in need of a recharge, take a break with this book in hand. Reread those passages for inspiration and perspective. As the old saying goes, "Rome wasn't built in a day." Remind yourself that your customer work too can happen only one day at a time.

I feel genuine excitement for you and your future as a customer leader knowing you are equipped with these *Chief Customer Officer* tools. So start today to cash in on this book's wisdom. Weave its lessons into your daily customer work plan. And then work that plan diligently. It's your surest way to galvanize your company around your customer.

# REFERENCES

American Marketing Association Research. *AMA 2003 Survey on Leadership Challenges.* New York: American Marketing Association Research, 2003. http://www.amanet.org/research/pdfs/Leadership Challenges_03.pdf.

Association of National Advertisers. "Marketing Department Priorities Often Differ from CEO's Agenda ANA/Booz Allen Hamilton Study Finds." Association of National Advertisers." Oct. 2004. http:// ana.net/news/2004/10_11_04.cfm.

Barrington, L., and Tortorici, F. *CEO Challenge 2006: Top Ten Challenges.* New York: Conference Board, Oct. 2005.

Brenneman, G. "Right Away and All at Once: How We Saved Continental." *Harvard Business Review OnPoint,* 2000, p. 8.

Carlzon, J. *Moments of Truth.* New York: HarperCollins, 1986.

Conlon, G. "Customers Really Matter." *DestinationCRM.com. From CRM Magazine,* Aug. 2002, pp. 1–3. http://www.destinationcrm.com/articles/ default.asp?ArticleID=2455.

"Continental Airlines Reports August 2005 Operational Performance." Sept. 2005. http://www.forbes.com/prnewswire/feeds/prnewswire/ 2005/09/01/prnewswire200509011853PR_NEWS_B_SWT_DA_DA TH085.html.

Court, D., Crawford, B., and Quelch, J. A. "Bringing Customers into the Boardroom." *Harvard Business Review,* Nov. 2004, p. 2.

Datamonitor. *Wegman's Food Markets, Inc.* June 16, 2005, 1–17.

Day, G. S. "Winning the Competition for Customer Relationships." Wharton School University of Pennsylvania, Archived Webcast, Nov. 2002, pp. 16–19. www.bettermanagement.com/seminars/seminar.aspx?1 =4781.

Dell, D., and Kramer, R. J. *Forging Strategic Business Alignment.* New York: Conference Board, Sept. 2003.

Edwards, J. "What's Your Problem?" *CIO Online,* Sept. 2000.

Florida, R., and Goodnight, J. "Managing for Creativity." *Harvard Business Review,* 2005, p. 6.

Gulati, R., and Oldroyd, J. B. "The Quest for Customer Focus." *Harvard Business Review OnPoint,* Apr. 2005, pp. 1–10.

"Harrah's." Aug. 2005. http://www.bluemartini.com/customers/customer_case_study.jsp?CONTENT%3C%3Ecnt_id=174929&FOLDER%3C%3Efolder_id=88289&bmUID=1126051613438.

Haughton, L. "The Rising Tide of Customer Defection." *Small Business Trends,* Aug. 2005.

McGregor, J. "Leading Listener: Trader Joe's." *Fast Company,* Oct. 2004, no. 87, 82.

Powers, K. "How We Got Started: Enterprise Rent-a-Car." *Fortune Small Business,* Sept. 2004. http://www.fortune.com/fortune/smallbusiness/articles/0,15114,681503,00.html.

Prospero, M. "Employee Innovator: Wegman's." *Fast Company,* 2004, no. 8.

Ready, D. A. "How to Grow Great Leaders." *Harvard Business Review OnPoint,* Dec. 2004a, pp. 3–5.

Ready, D. A. "Leading at the Enterprise Level." *MIT Sloan Management Review,* 2004b, *45*(3), 87–89.

Regan, K. "AOL Settles Claims It Wouldn't Let Customers Leave." Aug. 2005. http://ecommercetimes.com/story/45726.html.

Reichheld, F. *The Loyalty Effect. The Hidden Force Behind Growth, Profits and Lasting Value.* Boston: Harvard Business School Press, 1996.

Reichheld, F. "The One Number You Need to Grow." *Harvard Business Review OnPoint,* 2003.

SAS Institute Website. Aug. 2005. http://www.sas.com.

Sawhney, M. "Is Your Company in Synch?" *Harvard Business School Working Knowledge,* Oct. 15, 2001, pp. 2–4.

Schmitt, B. *"Customer Experience Management: A Revolutionary Approach to Connecting with Your Customers.* Hoboken, N.J.: Wiley, 2003.

Smith, S., and Wheeler, J. *Managing the Customer Experience: Turning Customers into Advocates.* Upper Saddle River, N.J.: Prentice Hall, 2002.

SprintUsers.com. www.Sprintusers.com/forum/showthreadphp?/=66352.

Tepe, J. "Understanding the Customer: The Issues, Strategies and Solutions." Cincom Systems, June 2003.

Ulfelder, S. "Catering to the Wealthy." Computerworld.com, Oct. 2003. http://www.computerworld.com.au/index.php?id=839350793

Vandermerwe, S. "Achieving Deep Customer Focus." *MIT Sloan Management Review,* 2004, *45*(3), 27, 29, 30.

Wegmans.com. *About Us.* Newsroom, 2006. "Wegman's Again Ranks High on Fortune 'Best Company to Work For' List."

WorldofQuotes.com. http:www.worldofquotes.com/author/Gary-Comer/1/.

# ACKNOWLEDGMENTS

Trying to get all of this out of my brain and onto paper has been a great and also wild journey. It wouldn't have begun if it hadn't been for the prodding and endless support of my friend, colleague, and cheerleader, Jill Griffin.

The twenty-five years of experiences driving the customer agenda across multiple industries and organizations take center stage in this book. And so I'm grateful for the great experiences where the commitment was real and true. But I'm also grateful where the rigor of driving the customer agenda skinned my knees and pushed me to be persistent and creative in working across diverse organizations and cultures. I learned immensely from each experience.

Neal Maillet, my editor at Jossey-Bass, is a prince. Little did he know what he was jumping into with me! I already thanked my husband, Bill, in the dedication, and he doesn't need me to write his name in a book to know that he's the cornerstone of my world. The passionate customer zealots who agreed to be interviewed are heroes in my book. I thank Tim Hawkins, Jeff Neppl, Wim Elfrink and Christina Olmsted, Kevin Kahn, Ed Benack, and Laurie Long for the hope they inject into this book with the tales of their accomplishments. Bravo!

In the end, I must thank you, gentle reader. Thank you for traveling into this wild and woolly world of customer focus and commitment. And especially thank you for your own persistence and passion in traversing your corporations in pursuit of customer relationships and profitability. I hope that you find this book a wise investment of your time and that it contributes to your mission.

# The Author

**Jeanne Bliss** began her customer zealotry career at Lands' End, reporting to founder Gary Comer and his executive committee as leaders of the Lands' End customer experience. She was Microsoft Corporation's general manager of worldwide customer and partner loyalty, served Allstate Corporation as officer for customer satisfaction and retention, was vice president of Franchise Services for Coldwell Banker Corporation, and at Mazda Motor of America initiated the brands' retention effort as senior manager, customer satisfaction. Today she is managing partner of Customer Bliss (www.customerbliss.com), where she is a coach and worldwide speaker prodding and prompting leaders and organizations to stay focused on customers and customer profitability.

For twenty-five years, Bliss has had the job of "just do it" strapped to her back by corporate presidents who engage her to make their companies focused on customer profitability and loyalty. She has had the opportunity to work with enlightened leaders and organizations, and through these experiences, her understanding of the different approaches required to get the job done have been honed. She has led the achievement of 95 percent loyalty rates, changed customer experiences across fifty-thousand-person organizations, and convinced even the staunchest curmudgeons to focus on the customer.

# INDEX